All Made Up

Janice Galloway

GRANTA

Granta Publications, 12 Addison Avenue, London W11 4QR

First published in Great Britain by Granta Books, 2011

This paperback edition published by Granta Books, 2012

A CIP catalogue record for this book is available from the British Library.

3 5 7 9 10 8 6 4 2

ISBN 978 1 84708 327 2

Typeset in Palatino by M Rules

Printed and bound by CPI Group (UK) Ltd, Croydon, CR0 4YY

This book is for my son with love and gratitude.
You were what was missing.

0

This is my family.

We are standing on the back green, behind two furrows of raked earth where, if we're lucky, potatoes will flourish later in the year. From the flagrant blueness of the sky, it's summer and we, each in our own way, are trying to look up to its charm. My mother is wearing a housecoat in several shades of fuchsia and slacks more akin to tights than trousers: clingy, elastic-waisted, navy blue. These are her first slacks and she is conscious of her behind, aware some might think them unseemly on a woman of her age, so the housecoat is knee-length. That its cherry, magenta and citrus-blossom print maintains her femininity without betraying her fear of ridicule is a kind of genius: a touch of dazzle conceals apprehension like nothing else. Behind stylish cat's eye frames and a subtle slick of lipstick, she is smiling fit to beat the band. Whatever her mood, the camera made my mother Ginger Rogers, ready to roll.

Next, and half a head taller, is me. Without artifice, we are exactly the same height but I am wearing platform shoes: four-inch heels in stripes of shiny peanut butter and brown. Brown is a big deal, all shades. Orange, purples, beiges and florals are *in.* My crocodile-effect leatherette mini with a hip belt is kind of last year but it shows my legs go all the way up and that tights have finally taken over from stockings. My eyelids are slathered with purple sparkles and my lashes are blue. Rimmel makes everything possible. My mother's make-up is two dabs of powder and a modest blot of an old Estée Lauder number called Egyptian Coffee she's had for years. At fifty-six, she will not venture beyond her own front door without lipstick: at sixteen, mascara is how to face the world. Mum's hair is short, dark and wavy: mine is bronze from a bottle and squirrels almost to my waist. After brushing, its ends fray out like burning rope but so do everyone else's. Conditioner will not exist for years. Mum's glasses have clip-on wing-tops in a different colour, 1950s glamour paid for by the NHS. I don't have glasses because my vision is 20-20. My motorcycle instructor told me and he is not a relative so would not lie. Nonetheless it's mum who looks out, whose gaze transcends the paper boundaries. My eyes, as always, are shut.

Mother and daughter. We stand in the sun waiting for the shutter release to set us free, our self-consciousness rising through the gloss finish paper. And we are not alone. Hidden, or so she thinks, is a sliver of another woman: a partial tumble of black, black hair, one cheek, the corner of an eye on the extreme right of the snap. Lower, there's a wrist with a hand attached, its sepia fingers clutching a box of what can only be fags says it for sure. It's my sister, Cora, keeping clear. *As nature intended* is a face she shows to none if she can help it and today, *sans* make-up, heels and hairspray, she avoids the lens. She's thirty-three today and celebrating, after a night on the tiles, in her own way. Birthdays are particular to my sister: they signify. On her twentieth, she caught the fast train away from Glasgow and turned up at our door with a vanity case and a box of matches, consigning husband, toddler and any notion of conventional decorum to the past. She has never looked back. Now, thirteen years on and issuing vetoes like a general from her vantage point off-stage, she shows every sign of staying for ever. The roll-call of boyfriends, fancy dress dirndl frocks and regular turns beneath the glitter-balls of Ayrshire's best dance floors have doubtless helped. She's as handy with her fists as she is with a lipstick barrel, yet my mother claims Cora is *calming down*. She says it every year. By now it seems as likely as snowballs on fire but I keep my fingers crossed. I do not sneer. Hoping Cora will calm down enough to take the train to somewhere else has been my guilty secret for ages and it's not the only one, but today no one is admitting their dark side. The sun is up, the sky is blue and somebody, by being here and holding a camera, is helping to ensure we pull out the stops. I can't remember who he is for sure, but the quality of the photo says someone with a chuckaway Kodak and his shadow is male. It's most probably Phillip, my boyfriend because the shade he casts is tall and thin and alluring. Then shadows are deceptive. It could be Duncan, my mother's friend, a fireman near enough retirement, or even Sandy, Daft Sandy, with his back to the light, stretched to sci-fi dimensions with his quiff not giving him away. Sandy was Cora's on–off affair since as far back as I remembered, a man who cried in my mother's arms every time she ditched him then came back for another shot on the waltzer every time she changed her mind. In the end, who it is doesn't matter. It's someone and, without him, the evidence we were here together on this day would not exist, even if it's partial. The shade he casts is huge and touches each of us in turn. It fills most of the frame and makes us one: the ghosts and the present-but-barely-correct, those doing our best not to be. Our stories mesh despite the gaps and the radio that is always by my sister's side plays tinny Frank Sinatra hits on Radio 2. *You can't have one without the other.* Just another sunny afternoon at home.

1

The year my dad died, Yuri Gagarin became the first man in space. He flew beyond the clouds in a computer-powered capsule; alone but whistling a Russian tune to keep his spirits bright. Suspended in a place none had been before, he must have stared past his own reflection in the dead-eyed glass of the cockpit window and seen the world as a thing apart, turning perfectly well without him. It was blue, he said, and beautiful. Then, done with the unknown, he let the programme reel him back. It was this that took my breath away: how much the man himself seemed to matter. The planning, the investment, the goodwill of the world in general that one of us, against the odds, might be safely brought back home.

Seven years later, Gagarin crashed into the flat plains of Kirzhach near Vladimir, a little over 100 miles east of Moscow on a routine training flight not far from familiar ground. Nobody knew for sure what happened but conspiracy theorists had a field day: the KGB, the FBI, evil scientists, mind-controllers or even the occult must have been involved. They weren't. Hero or no hero, his end was a cock-up, not a plot. Either he made a simple miscalculation, or the crash was the result of bird-strike, snow-geese doing merely what snow-geese do, getting somehow sucked into the turbines in poor visibility over the cloudy marsh-land. It happened in April 1968 and I was twelve. I'd been writing an essay called *My Future* in front of the fire when the announcement came on the TV and I tilted my head to see. The face I had cut from a magazine and placed alongside Elvis on the bedroom wall was looking back: the space-suit snap, grave and long-lashed as Rudolph Valentino, skin white behind the visor, the letters CCCP above his head like stars. The first man in space, on a mission where his safety had not been in doubt, and dropped from the sky like Icarus, in all probability leaving nothing much behind. I tried to imagine torn metal and snow-goose feathers, failed. Good-looking, in the peak of health and thirty-three, Gagarin had seemed as far beyond mortality as a Thunderbird puppet. Now only pictures – Gagarin in a greatcoat showered with flowers, Gagarin under a weight of medals, Gagarin his mother's blue-eyed son, the made-good carpenter's boy – said he'd been here at all. The man, like dad, was atoms.

Apart from that, dad was nothing like Yuri Gagarin. Eddie Galloway was not the offspring of collective farm workers but the son of a van driver and a glove-maker who had been variously a bus driver, a lorry driver invalided out of the war on account of flat feet, and the most unsuccessful insurance salesman in history. His last job was running a tiny corner shop next to the pub at Saltcoats station where, drunk on duty, he left a fag in a stock room full of fireworks and the whole lot went up like a

Roman Candle. Nothing was insured. He died of a heart attack at the age of fifty-one not long after of furry arteries, lousy lungs, liver disease and loneliness. It was, as my mother remarked, no bloody surprise. Whether he was buried or cremated remained untold. Gagarin had been sewn together and buried inside the Kremlin wall. Thousands mourned. Valentina Tereshkova, the first woman in space, was still breathing but it didn't make up. That women last longer and counted for less I already took for granted. I had known neither grandfather and already had missing uncles as well as my father. All the women, whether I liked it or not, were still there. That was what women did: they hashed on. It was their nature.

My mother couldn't imagine why I cared about men in space, never mind women. It wasn't that she lacked vision, but she disliked Russians on the grounds they'd been rotten to the Poles after the war. Everyone was rotten to the Poles after the war, but the march into Prague mere months after Gagarin died confirmed her worst suspicions: you couldn't trust the Russians any more than you could trust the French. Revolutionaries were treacherous. She had no time for Cromwell, William Wallace, Owen Glendower, or the entire landmass of Ireland either. A descendant of umpteen generations of navvies, hewers and labourers, a one-time scullery maid and cotton worker with bleeding knuckles, my mother, though she hated the inflexible backbones of the class system, was a royalist. The Queen embodied duty, service and steadfastness; things, like a virtuous woman, that might be valued above rubies. Mum put a postcard of Prince Charles being invested as the Prince of Wales in the cupboard where we kept the hoover and the ironing board, and one of the Queen alone because Philip got on her nerves. Her biggest hero was Gandhi but Gandhi had died before I was born and postcards of him were not so easy to come by. Every time Gandhi came on TV, his twig-thin legs poking from some kind of blanket in some grainy old footage, mum told me to sit up, watch and learn something.

That's a great man you're seeing there. He hadn't a bad bone in his body. All he did was fight for justice and some evil bugger shot him.

She shook her head at the folly of human beings. Evil buggers were everywhere. When Martin Luther King was shot, she slumped in her chair like a rag doll and had to use her inhaler to come round. Save for one ancient bottle of Harvey's Bristol Cream English sherry and a half bottle of advocaat for New Year, we had no drink, not even for emergencies. My mother had a long memory and booze was never to be allowed in the house again. Frustration at the very existence of alcohol she took out on the furniture; cleaning, scrubbing, dusting, polishing and clattery ironing that demanded strong wrists and the background noise of the TV. TV was a godsend. Switching it off signalled high exasperation or simple despair and seemed reserved for very particular things, among them President Nixon, football, nakedness and the lonely howling noise the TV made after the National Anthem signalled the end of broadcasting for the night. The rest of the time the TV was on. The world in a box, it opened to reveal all sorts the way the window to the real street outside could not.

It was multi-dimensional, chock-a-block with education, laughter, entertainment, history, foreign lands, philosophy and glimpses of the future as well as famine, pestilence and any other Horseman you cared to name. Documentaries, soap operas, talent shows, quizzes, plays and police dramas, the news, comedy turns, variety acts and adverts, we watched and marvelled and felt free to pass remarks on the lot. Mum shouted her opinions sewing the holes out of jumpers, making clear her uncritical devotion to royalty, the Labour Party, British crooners, pop music and the North of England in that order. My sister liked Tom Jones, adverts for aftershave, tennis, modern plays, anything American and satire, but any telly was better than none. It showed us a reality more intense and meaningful than our real lives could hope to possess. It was a jungle out there, full of gorillas and deserts, stock market fluctuations and political debate, captains of industry, captains of ships, bad guys, land wars in Asia, burning monks, good men killed for idiot reasons, Enoch Powell, Lady Isobel Barnett and the Rolling Stones and Princess Margaret's ghastly marriage to snub-nosed Snowdon. And all of it, every last bit, more important than anything that happened round here.

I watched whatever they watched. Two channels left little to bicker over. Most things we watched without complaint, the exception being *The White Heather Club.* I had never met anyone who liked *The White Heather Club.* In general, it was endured in much the way *Black and White Minstrel Show* with its feather-crested showgirls and white men as vaudeville coons was endured, which is to say keen for the finale. It was also because

The White Heather Club was somehow Scotland's fault and sticking it out was penance. A show's being awful was never a reason to switch it off: only football, anything sexy and the National Anthem did that. Telly was distraction from ourselves as much as education and entertainment. If things were going badly, and they often did, telly was at least chewing gum and silence. It was perfect for doing homework in front of, belly-down at the fire, and that was how I used it. The rug was a cheerful orange and the floral-patterned carpet a newfangled fitted affair. Cora and mum had armchairs on either side of the fire for an uninterrupted view and meant I had the option of watching the powerful and famous reflected on the lenses of their glasses if I liked. The gap between history unfolding and those of us who seemed merely to watch it was not isolating and queer: it was *normal.* We were in no doubt that those we viewed through the cathode tube mattered: who did not were the unrecorded, unscripted and unlisted on credits. Us.

The last spring before Big School, the spring Gagarin died, the weather forecast promised *mild* for the coming summer. As residents of a seaside holiday town, we paid attention to the weather. Mild was good. We could get the deck chairs out.

Mild nothing, my sister said. It'll piss down. It always pisses down in July.

The *Wednesday Play* came on and my mother appealed for silence. She liked drama. She said it took her out of humdrum surroundings.

I ignored the *Wednesday Play* by and large because it was *contemporary*, which seemed to mean *embarrassing*. People kissed all over these plays and had babies without being married. Keeping my head inside a jotter saved face. This one had lots of arguments and people shoving each other, which was a mood that could spill over into the living room if you weren't careful. But the language drew me in. It was keen and brittle, things you heard in the street sliding out from behind the glass and onto the carpet beside you. When one of the characters roared *up yours* I couldn't leave it alone. *Up yours* sounded like a punch and a joke at the same time, the kind of thing streetwise people would say. Not sure what it meant but enchanted anyway, I whispered it under my breath to see what being cool felt like. *Up yours.* It sounded funny. *Up yours.* I laughed. Beside me, my sister leaned closer.

What did you just say?

Up yours, I beamed. It was on the telly. I smiled and pointed. He said *up yours.*

I remember her hair muffling into my face, a *crack* like a toffee hammer hitting home and the bridge of my nose singing with cold, dense pain. My skull had condensed to a hole in the middle of my face. Through the sparklers popping behind my closed eyelids I heard mum shouting.

Did you head-butt your own sister, you bad bugger? Jesus Christ what did I do to deserve this?

Through a dog-whistle noise and more yelling, a fat slick of warmth was slithering down the back of my throat. When I opened my eyes, mum was advancing with a flannel, full charge and still roaring.

Back, lean back. Just do it.

She sounded near tears. There was a flabby crunch and grind north of my teeth as she foraged with her fingers for damage.

If that sets bent, she hissed, it's no thanks to *you*. What did you hit her for? What did she do?

What happened next is lost, but life would have sorted itself out somehow. I recall my mother saying *It's all right, it's not spilled* so the carpet was fine, which saved complication. I was all right. The nose had always fixed before and it would do it this time too. There was no need to bother a doctor. Mum didn't pursue what had happened for long. There was no point. Stuff just happened: Cora was *handy*. What happened between families was nobody's business, not even to the combatants. Things went up then they came down: that was life. On full-moon nights, tearing away from the Hans Christian Andersen stories that even at twelve I read in bed because they made my blood fizz, I got out of bed to look at the sky and imagined what it must have been like to be up there. Blackness going on for ever, a confusing barrage of stars. I wondered if he had been scared, circling the Earth with only a radio for company, hoping the life-support systems did not break down. I was not religious and had never been in love, but I had a version of both. And it went like this. I pictured Gagarin, alone in orbit, his face smeared by console lights, and tried to let him know I was on his side. I sent brain-waves, vibes and positive karma. All manner of things would be well. His parachute would open, his landing would be soft. And whether the rescue teams found him or not, he'd pick himself up and walk. He'd walk out of the sea and onto the shingle if he had to, stride over water to the driest land. He'd pass through wood and wild and snow, steering by instinct and the patterns of the constellations the way human beings always had. And as he walked, I wanted him to know one thing and know it for sure. I wanted him to know that we all, one day, however cast adrift, would find our way back home.

2

It had four yellow stars on a royal ground. A castle, a ring, an open book and waves to show the shore. The fork dividing the pictures was to represent the Earls of Eglinton, whoever they were, but that didn't matter. Standard issue heraldry was nothing next to the sky, the sea, a chunk of treasure and a book. The heart warmed looking at them, the shield-shape in padded felt resting in the shoplady's open palm.

See? she said. That's your school badge. It's really smart. She pointed at the embroidered symbols, a banner with words sewn black over gold. *Ad Astra*. Know what that means?

I didn't.

Ad Astra, she said. It's Latin for *To the stars*. I went to the Academy as well. She winked, stuffing two pairs of light grey socks in a bag. *Amo amas amat* and all that stuff. I got Dr Nisbet, so I remember my Latin.

I took the badge and looked for myself while she and my mother wandered off to find a double pack of girls' nylon shirts, age 12–13. She's not big for her age, my mother said, vanishing stage left. We're none of us tall.

I knew the badge had been made on a machine, but I conjured a team of women, grey-haired and hawk-eyed, picking out the picture one stitch at a time with silver needles, never thinking of the children who would one day wear them with chest-bursting pride. I imagined the women had crippled feet, their toes broken in childhood to keep them put, and they had sewn by candle-light, speculating as to how lucky the children who received such an elegant badge must be.

You all right? The woman was back at the counter, concerned.

She's fine, my mother said, opening her purse. Just doesny say much. Do you?

I said nothing. The lady didn't seem that bothered. Don't you worry, she said. All that stuff about the big boys and girls putting your head down the toilet first day – it's rubbish. You'll love it. Everybody loves learning things. She made a sign like Superman, flying. *To the stars!*

We went home without the blazer to sew it onto because it was only the start of summer and the new consignment didn't arrive till August. The badge went under my pillow. Every time I looked at it, I wondered what learning Latin would be like, how a whole different language was formulated. The qualifying exam to get to the Academy in the first place added Latin to your timetable as a free gift if you had high marks. It was for those they called *high flyers.* It was important to be a *high flyer* because it led one more seamlessly to what my mother called *a life,* by which she meant a way out of having to be a dinner-lady like her. Certainly, the woman in the shop was doing nicely and that, most probably, was down to her training in Classics. You got the world for an oyster if you knew Latin, my mother said, and a grammar book on free loan from school to learn it by. The Academy was full of books, and what was in books was gold dust. *The Children's Compendia of Knowledge*, ten blue-bound volumes reacquired the day after dad's funeral, had been browsed so much the pages were coming loose. Now secondary school would take over. Knowledge – for that was what the ten volumes purported to contain – made everything clearer. Good books revealed the engine rooms of history and people who had built them; they uncovered Geography and Government, English Kings and Queens, A Carnival of National Dress and Matching National Flags. My favourite things were Ancient Greeks in general, Ancient Greek and Roman Mythology, the acronyms of the Periodic Table, Famous Composers, British Inventors, The Girls' Table of Embroidery Stitches, Monsters of the Deep, the symbols of the Cyrillic alphabet, Morse Code and Fashion through the Centuries. The Principal Trade Exports of France, German Fairy Tales, The Life Cycle of the Common Frog, The Anatomy of the Buttercup and The Iron Age Family at Home came in as runners-up. My sister said if I read out John Masefield's *Cargoes* one more time, with its *cargo of Tyne coal, Road-rails, pig-lead; firewood, iron-ware, and cheap tin trays*, she'd belt me round the head with a cheap tin tray and see how I liked it. If these books existed in our house, it stood to reason secondary school had even more. Books were the Building Blocks of Understanding and there was nothing, nothing on this earth, better than that. Understanding was Power,

Education was the path through the dark, dark wood, and Books were the treasure maps that led to that which was beyond price. People could trick you and lie and set your hair on fire for no reason, but a book had no malice aforethought. Its only option was to give and what it gave was understanding. With enough of that in your pocket, you could dig tunnels, make plans, slip the guards, escape into the woods and hope you had good enough German to pass for someone else to the border guards or at least make a run for it if all else failed. Soon, all this would be mine.

Acquiring the uniform to support the badge was not cheap, but my mother, who believed that appearance counted for a great deal, had applied for school clothing vouchers. The fact that we qualified was *nobody else's business*.

Don't you say a word at the school about that. I'm a widow. Our financial affairs are private. Remember I can pull you from school if you don't behave.

That widows could take children out of school to act as bread-winners was something she'd been saying for years. It had happened to her brothers so it was probably true, but I didn't believe, after years of encouraging me to *stick in*, that she meant it.

You've two years to cut it, she said. Or you're out of there as fast as jack rabbit. I mean it.

Cora, who had gone to the same school sixteen years before, was keen to remind me of the contribution the tax-payer had made to my future.

You better keep that uniform nice, she said. I paid for the bloody thing. One mark on it, Lady, and you'll be sorry.

I had no doubt this was true. Included in the set of things to keep nice were three nylon shirts, one knee-length skirt, one stripy tie, long white socks and matching rubber bands to hold them up. Most of the grant was for the blazer which still hadn't arrived. Cora had knitted two iron-grey sleeveless cardigans and though nobody was sure the buttons were on the correct side, they fit. A fat briefcase had been bought to replace the old satchel with shoulder straps and waiting in the wings was a blue tartan pencil case inside which pencils with scarlet barrels, a bright green sharpener with double-holes and a thick pink eraser waited untouched. The only thing nobody had made a decision about were shoes. Given the elasticity of pre-teen feet, they'd be left till the day before school started and not before. Mum said shoes showed upbringing and on the evidence so far, I had been brought up very well indeed.

I'd had silver bridesmaid sandals, arch-strapped Mary-Janes, little red wellies and tartan slippers with crimson pom-pom trims. I'd had Clark's best anti-scuff flats and canvas plimsolls for gym, while pink jelly sandals in summer protected my toes from broken glass as I ran along the shore. My preference was colourful. Anything orange, purple, emerald or scarlet I zeroed in on from a distance. School shoes, however, were sensible which meant dull black leather with button straps and bulbous toes all perched on a rubber sole as thick as battered cod. Shoes of this kind marked a girl as able, not vain; someone capable of buckling down and striding ahead without complaint. My sister, her feet a bunion-farm with toes that had been trained to a point even with her shoes removed, claimed she wouldn't wear flat shoes for a pension. Flats were bad for your calf muscles – everybody knew that. Even her slippers had heels. Functional footwear showed the wearer as spiritless, morally aloof or lacking in *joie d'esprit*. It annoyed her. Sometimes, she called me *Goody Two-Shoes* to make clear that I annoyed her too. There was no need. I knew already.

The only time I'd been cut much slack on the shoe front was for the very last Jacks Road Primary Church Service, when I'd been loaned my mother's mid-heel sling-backs and a pair of American Tan nylons to look swish. Both stockings laddered with the speed of a cartoon bomb fuse as soon as they touched the edge of a pew, of course, and I walked to my granny's in the resulting strips of shredded denier where my granny told mum off for sending me out *like a tuppenny whooer*. For Ardrossan, where such dramatic first impressions would be unwise, there would be no nylons. Instead she bought me a *trainer girdle* without suspenders (a girl approaching thirteen without a girdle would get slack ideas) and lots of socks. Knee-socks. White. First, however, there was summer. The promise was *mild*. There would be a gentle separation away from classmates of seven years' standing, a certain amount of stiffening up, preparing for the long march that lay ahead under warm and gentle skies. Before we knew it, or so the theory ran, childhood and all it had meant would take its rightful place as done and dusted.

Mild nothing. Cora spoke to the weather-man knowing he couldn't hear. It'll piss down. Wait and see. This is your last stand before the big school, Custer. You hear me? You'll be up to your oxters in exams then work after that. Your easy days are numbered.

And though the weather-man was not famous for dependability, he was more dependable than Cora so there was hope. She was twenty-nine, mum said, and bitter. Since I'd turned ten and my age required two numbers instead of one, I had known what she had for some time already: you lived with double digits till you reached 100 or died trying. Somewhere, whether we liked it or not, nature's clocks ticked on regardless.

Cora was wrong about the weather. It didn't piss down. It didn't even rain though I wished it had. The sky tumbled around a lot as though willing the sun to break through but heavy cloud cover meant July was leaden. No light breezes blew people's hats off, no sunny interludes encouraged gambolling in the waves. Clouds rolled in from Arran and the sea shoved bladderwrack onto the sand where it sprawled, reeking of cabbage, till it withered to brown wafer rags. Veronica's, the paper shop by the station, sported windmills that creaked but did not turn. Ice-cream, melting too fast for the human tongue, fell in slobbery lumps on the pavement and mongrels, demented with pleasure, rolled for days in the remains of a seal that had burst on the far North Shore. Mum suffered migraines or shortness of breath so I did my granny's shopping and took it over. My Granny McBride was all right.

Don't go near the Glasgow folk, she said. They're on their holidays. Anything could happen.

She was eighty-four, four foot ten and one-eyed. The seven children she had raised more or less on her own had children who by now had had children in their turn and she had given up all pretence of knowing our names without reminding. She treated us all the same and doubtless gave us the same warnings, but telling me to steer clear of strangers was wasted advice. Unlike Cora, horse-faced Cousin Alma or Aunty Marie that worked on the buses, I went near no one on purpose. I watched. The Glasgow people sat out on the sand regardless of the weather, sunbathed fully dressed and poked sticks in rock pools only to scream when anything under the water moved. They fed chips to seagulls, left newspaper spilling from bus-stop bins and generally exuded an air of willingness to enjoy life while it lasted. After a fortnight, they went back on the Glasgow train with shells and sticks of neon pink rock. Even if it was only dead crabs or a few box-brownie snaps of an uncle paddling in his vest near the sewage-pipe outflow, they liked a *souvenir*. It wasn't the object *per se* that mattered. Every bird skull or picked-clean crab shell was testimony: their proof that some other place, the other self they had been within it, had existed at all.

The majority came in families unlike my own, which is to say families with men as part of the show. These men moved alongside women and children in socks and sandals, the hair fighting out of the necks of their shirts. City sorts, their manner of walking honed by years of dealing with road systems, rush and traffic, they stood out as faster and more savvy than locals, more certain of what they liked to do. They knew how to get to the head of queues and weren't embarrassed to carry balloons in public. Now and then a set of twins rose out of the mass, dressed in matching hand-knits as if it was Halloween and they'd gone out as each other. Most had two parents and some, lucky rotters, had dogs. I had no pets and never would have: my mother had asthma. I didn't have asthma but I had cramps which Aunty Rose called *growing pains*. *Puberty*, she clarified over a cold ham salad in her kitchen. That's what you call it.

Puberty was not a word I wanted to hear at all, never mind with Uncle Angus within earshot. *Teenager* was bad enough, but *puberty* sounded wormy. That Rose, who called knickers *smalls* and the toilet *the little girls' room* had allowed the word to form on her lips made me scared. The ancient home medical dictionary in the living room confirmed scared as the right thing to be. Puberty was all hair and swellings, sweat glands and something vile called *growth spurts*. It meant biology was on the warpath and nothing could hold it back. Puberty responded to no appeal. It crept through cells, bones and mucous membranes while you slept, turning everything you thought was *you* into someone else. The idea made me clammy. I wanted to stay five foot two. Given a choice, I wanted to stay wholesome. Staunch denial made me button up the pains and pilfer aspirin from the bathroom cupboard, hiding in the coal-shed if the cramps made me wince. Sitting among the cobblers' lasts and paint tins, leftover seed potatoes and dross was better than being a talking point and *Admit Nothing* was our family motto. I was damned if I was going to be the odd one out. School would rescue me. The blazers would arrive at Duncan's any day and my badge sewn on like soldier's stripes. Long socks, grey skirt, tie. After the summer, I could hardly wait.

It was eight in the morning on Saturday, my sister's day for a long lie-in and somebody who didn't know was banging on the front door.

Godsake, Cora roared from her bedroom. Tell whoever that is to bugger off. She kicked her bedroom door with one foot, making a point. I could picture her doing it, turning her face into her pillow to avoid sunlight. My mother sighed and tracked down the hall, dragging on her dressing-gown. People at the door was my mother's job. Nobody else did it. I shifted into the warm bit and the one foam curler she'd left behind, and pulled the quilt up, listening.

Mrs Galloway? It was a man's voice. Elizabeth Clarke Galloway?

I sat up, turned my ear to the door. The man went on talking, my mother making noises so he'd go on, but they spoke too low for me to catch whole sentences. The word *police* came and went, *elderly*. When it stopped, there was a long, electric nothingness, a barely audible crackle of static. Then came the folding sound, like blankets soft-thudding on top of each other in the ironing cupboard. The man – I knew it had to be him from the suddenness of the movement – shifted so his shoe touched the skirting, as if catching something before it hit the floor. It's shock, he was saying. You should maybe sit down. He had come in from the porch, and his voice was louder. He had to be in the hallway, right outside Cora's door. It's a shock, Mrs Galloway. Can I make you a cup of tea?

My mother was saying, No, son, not at all, before he'd even finished. No, son, no. She sounded as if her asthma was coming on. I just need to catch my breath and I'll be fine.

It's no bother, the man said. Young, anxious. I could put the kettle on for you. But she wasn't having any. I imagined a tall, blue-eyed trainee, face hidden under the brim of his hat, trying to hold my mother's arm.

A minute, son, a minute, she kept saying. I'll be fine in a minute. I knew that voice. If he kept insisting, it would become irritable. Kindness made her nervous.

Off you go now, she said. It was good of you to come.

He didn't shift. There was just the breathy silence, a sense he might be waiting for her to fall. It passed.

Don't you worry, son, she said again. Off you go now and I'll be fine. Thank you.

The edge made her sound almost bright. Then the outer door clicked, the lock following. Goodbye, she said, too loud. The clatter of the bolt. Thanks, she said. Thank you. Dear Jesus God, I'm saying thanks.

There was only breathing for a minute, heavy. I imagined she was looking for her inhaler. Then Cora, wild-haired and her face like lemon peel from being up too early, opened my bedroom door.

Your granny's died, she said. She looked at me and pulled a face. Your granny, she said, like I was deaf. I heard it through the wall. She scratched her neck and her breasts jiggled under her nightie. She's died, hen. Snuffed it. Something about the word choice was wrong. This was surely not what you were supposed to say. All burnt up, she said, scratching. Like a match. Pfffff.

Cora didn't take bad news well, but even so. This was all wrong. I could hear mum still muttering in the living room, getting her breath back under control, and wondered if the policeman was still outside. I almost ran to the door to fetch him in the hope he'd take charge, read out a regulation of some kind that let us in on routine procedure for this situation and force Cora to be normal. I wanted to see a uniform, a capable face. But Cora was watching me so I sat tight pretending I wasn't thinking anything at all. My mother appeared then, one hand clutching her dressing-gown at the neck.

Dear God, she said. He was just a wee boy. She looked at Cora, then looked at me. They shouldn't send a boy to do that sort of thing. He had no gloves on.

When neither of us could think of anything to say, she looked at the carpet, her back wilting. Her candlewick collar was skewed but Cora didn't reach to fix it. The gap between their thinly clad bodies stayed stiff.

Are you OK? Cora asked, eventually. It sounded reluctant, uneasy with the personal invitation in the question. She cleared her throat and tried again, but only managed the OK? part. Are you listening? she said after another while, and my mother said Yes. And the Yes was terrible. I felt sure something ought to be happening now, something that normal people did – an arm around a shoulder, maybe, a word suggestive of kinship – but nothing was happening. We were stuck like moths in syrup, not even flailing. Eventually, my mother stretched her neck and sighed.

Away back to bed, she said. You might as well.

Looking at neither of us, she padded towards the kitchen, reliable, letting us off the hook. For one bright moment as she slipped away, the idea of tea popped into my head. That was what they did on television; they made tea with extra sugar and hovered around looking ready to make more. That was something at least. But I stayed put. It might make things worse, after all. Fools rushed in and trod all over everything with their size nines; they bit off more than they could chew. Besides, my tea – I'd been told it often enough – was a waste of hot water. Thinking I could do anything useful here was stupid.

Imagine, Cora whispered. All burnt up.

She was still hovering at my door, dopey from the hour. She looked at me some more then blinked and shuffled off, scratching her thigh, bare feet shushing on the hall carpet. Beside me, the indent of my mother's head was still clear on the pillow, a single curler like a roll of faded flesh clinging to bone.

That's my mother, she was saying in the kitchen, talking to no one. Godsake mother, you've done it now. Oh mother. My mother.

We had five days to give the keys back to the council, so we went to check the place over next morning. From the top of Guthrie Brae, things looked normal enough. Closer was different. The paint round the window had gone from white to kipper and black stuff like soot was seeping round the frame so the white-washed wall looked smeary. She'll be mortified when she sees that, I thought before the verb hit me. At least I hadn't said it out loud. The smell of peat or something like it got nearer as we walked up the side path, blooming when my mother opened the door to an eye-blurring guff. It smelled like day-after bonfire wood, whisky and burnt tobacco, brackish enough to make you brace yourself simply to breathe. I pulled my jumper over my nose, and my mother coughed behind a hanky before we went inside.

First glance was fine. Then you opened your eyes a little wider. The old peach brocade curtains were tinted mahogany on one side and the wall near the TV was smeary with a nicotine-coloured stain. Electrical cord and bakelite plugs, twisted out of shape, clustered like cockroaches at the socket, and the smell grew thicker. Other things, the big wooden table, the fireside seats and the ironing board in the corner, the coal-scuttles and the horse brasses round the fireplace looked not only perfectly all right but freshly polished. The sideboard, nearest us, had its clutter of ornaments pushed aside and some folded pieces of paper, envelopes and books were spread in a neat fan on the runner. My mother stared at them longest, then walked across. She looked but didn't touch.

Go and check in the kitchenette, she said. I looked at her. On you go. She was looking at the papers. See everything's all right in there.

I hesitated, hoping she'd change her mind but she took no notice. The idea my granny might still be in the house somewhere as yet unaware she'd died seemed entirely feasible. And if she was still here, she'd be in the kitchen. I imagined her emerging from a wall saying Boo. It was exactly the kind of thing she would do. On you go, my mother said. I went.

The kitchenette was freezing as usual, the whistle top still missing off the kettle. It stank less of burning in here, just familiar cold concrete, Vim and the backup from the drain. I opened cupboard doors, making them creak so mum would hear, then closed them in case a spider or something worse rushed out from behind the bleach. Far sooner than she might have liked, I hared back into the living room. My mother was holding one of the envelopes in her hand.

It's her marriage lines, she said. She nodded at the sideboard. The rent book and pension book are there as well.

I looked at her.

They're all laid out, she said. Like she did it on purpose.

I tried to look understanding, but had no idea what she was trying to say.

On purpose, she said. She stopped looking at the papers and turned her gaze on me. As if she knew.

The words *as if she knew* made no sense right away. But something in my memory was wriggling, like a glow-worm, through the fog. My granny's hobby was tea-leaves. She poured the tea with no strainer to leave plenty of dregs, then banged the cup on one side to make the sodden leftovers spatter around the white china bowl. Then she read them. Like messages. All I ever saw were tea-leaves. My granny, however, saw faces and numerals; buses and televisions and letters and coffins; dogs, potatoes and babies' dummies. She saw broken legs and broken hearts and broken marriages, money and Acts of God. I was never sure if it was a game. My mother had always laughed and said *O mother, stop telling the wean rubbish.* But today – my eyes widened as the penny dropped – she thought my granny could see the future. Had somehow known that death was on its way and had laid out these papers for whoever came to find her. Maybe she had known it would be *us*.

I watched, skin creeping, as my mother reached slowly for something from the runner and held it out. Look. That's her wedding ring. She never took that off.

Plain as a curtain hoop, thin and small, my granny's ring looked charged. A dead woman's property was bad enough: knowing a dead woman was worse. Mum tried it on her own fourth finger, but it stuck. One look said it wouldn't fit me either and I realised, as if for the first time, how small my Granny McBride had been. Four foot ten, bird-boned. My mother lifted the ring and held it to the light so it all but disappeared.

She'd have been no bother for them to lift, eh?

Firemen. Firemen were who lifted people. I tried to picture my grandmother being carried over a stranger's shoulder like a princess in a story. Your grandmother meant your mother's mother. Which in turn meant Granny McBride had once been the age my mother was now, that my mother had once been as young as me. One day I'd be mum's age, then my granny's then dead. It was suddenly too obvious so I pictured the fireman instead. Tall, strong and dark. An axe and a ladder. But there had been no need. This was the lower flat. He had broken down the door, then lifted her out of the chair and held her against his body as he walked. Nothing was cut down, nothing scaled. Just lifted. Seven stone of skeletal frame and long white hair. That was it. My mother thumped her chest as though her asthma was kicking off, then leaned back against the wall with her eyes closed. One of the sideboard drawers was gaping, its cache of string and fuses, candles, scraps of airmail paper and saved-up stamps on show. Opened further, it would reveal the matchbox, Bryant and May. Inside it, lived the eye. If you lifted the box, you felt the weight inside move gently, the eye rolling off its cotton-wool nest in search of escape. Her top teeth were in there too, a surgical wrist support in sickly ochre-pink tucked out of sight at the back. Abandoned body parts. Nobody else would want them now.

Leave that, my mother said. Kitty will want to see things just the way they were.

Kitty was the eldest, my mother's only sister. Between them were five brothers who would probably come here to look in at the rent book and the rubber bands and ancient Rizla papers, wonder what they were supposed to do with them now. Some things had been sorted for ages: the horse brasses, the nicest ornaments, the grandmother clock and the embroidered table-covers had been assigned to various offspring for years. Everybody knew who was getting what by this time. My grandmother believed only ignorant people fought over things at funerals and was damned if that kind of thing was happening at hers, so everyone had been drilled and drilled again till they knew what was what. The funeral expenses were saved in a Co-op account designed for that purpose, and the savings book was in the airing cupboard under the lagging. Even I knew this stuff. Mum would get the coal-scuttles, the brass ones somebody had made in the trenches from real ammunition shells. They were hammered round with paisley patterns and the miniature shovels were made of bullets. That the maker had never come home and the scuttles had was something she remarked upon to remind you they were precious. And a coat. I hoped it was the new one. The old one looked like a prop from a BBC Dickens adaptation and was more Aunty Kitty's style anyway. The new one wasn't new, but it was newer than the old one, and that was something. Thinking about coats reminded me my blazer was due any day. After that, the ceremonial sewing on of the badge. What if these things slipped my mother's mind?

What if I outgrew the shirts? A lot could happen in ten days. In five alone this house would be once again the property of the council and we'd not be allowed. They'd give it to someone else and it would be none of our business.

I better take a look in the bedroom before we go home, my mother said. You wait here.

I did what I was told. Not even the doctor had been allowed in my granny's bedroom. The only thing I knew about what happened in there was that every night, my grandmother had loosed her hair from its daytime knot, brushed it, then woven it into a plait for sleep. I tried to picture her in a nightgown, brushing. Her hair had been white, long enough to tuck into the waist-band of an apron. She hated being scrutinised, my grandmother, but this wasn't disrespectful. I could think about her all I liked if she wasn't actually there in person. Death gave all sorts of permissions.

The ashes in the fireplace sighed and I turned, afraid. It was just the grate and the wind. Next to it, her armchair radiated empty space. I moved to straighten her cushion when I saw the blotch on the antimacassar that wasn't a blotch at all. It was a scorch mark. The chair was at the other side of the fireplace to the electrical socket, the awful, brown-streaked wall, but it had been close enough for something. My stomach tightened, realising what it was. This was where she had sat as it happened. The chair I'd sat in on my mother's knee to watch TV – this was where she had died.

There's a Bible, my mother said. She was right behind me when

I turned, something dark buried in the crook of her arm. A Bible, she said again, incredulous. And these. She fished two box-shaped lumps from their hiding place and offered them up. Shoes. Like a man's only smaller, made of grey-brown suede with rat-tail little laces and flat, yellow soles. Brand new, she said, labels on the sole. She sniffed. Your size.

I stared, hoping I was reading this wrong.

They're not going to waste. She poked them at my chest, determined. Never worn. Now take them. Her eyes were beginning to brim. Just take them.

Under my nose, the suede stank of hair torched in a hair-dryer, like burning teeth and hair and tree bark; a brackish, searing animal reek like a cow on fire. But I took the shoes. Gingerly and without much grace, maybe, but I rested their weight on the fingertips of one hand and our eyes broke. Mission accomplished, we took one last look around the room: the dun and olive wallpaper, the ruined curtains, the mirror over the fireplace. A brass bell in the shape of Mary Queen of Scots, a rabbit's foot and a Scotty Dog ashtray I had made with plaster of paris and painted black. My mother looked at the chair for a long time, as if trying to see past the nothing it contained, then smoothed the cushion with the flat of her hand.

No priest. She shook her head. Och well. It's what she would have wanted.

My grandmother, a one-eyed miner's widow and mother of six who had been a dynamite worker and a pool attendant who never learned to swim, who weighed nothing at all and whom

I had never known, even from photographs, as anything other than a very old person indeed, was already dissolving, the smell of her split-pea soup surrendered to the shoes in my hands. I was aware I had little control over whether I remembered her.

Oh you, my mother said suddenly. You're too wee for this kind of thing.

Her hands clenched open and shut, exercising control. Only when they stopped did our separate lines of vision lift and meet. We did not touch, but we took this moment. This speechlessness, the space between us, we knew as love.

When the local paper had a photo of the outside of her house with LOCAL WIDOW DIES IN BLAZE on the front page my mother was furious.

Blaze, she hissed. Can you believe that? It says *blaze* and in real life it was nothing of the kind. It was *smoke inhalation*. That's what's on the certificate – *smoke inhalation*. Stupid papers. They make things up. There wasn't a mark on her. That's it. I'm writing a letter, honest to God I will. Who do they think they are, these people? Bloody *blaze*.

After the extravagance of the coffin, the shocking waste of flowers left to wilt on the crumbly earth, her nerves had no focus. Her control of the funeral had been strict. There was to be no talk of passing away or going to a better place or any religious rubbish, she had said. That kind of talk was fairy tales. If there was no comfort, there was no comfort and she wanted to know it. She was annoyed. The present demands of life – cooking, washing up, cleaning the bath – annoyed her. The rickety carpet sweeper, the loose screw on the fireside shovel, and any other domestic object that drew attention to itself annoyed her. I thought about saying my blazer looked nice now it had finally come, then changed my mind.

As though I've not enough to do, she said, thumping the iron onto my school skirt, rattling the board on its skinny metal frame. It's you should be ironing this, not me. You're old enough.

And she banged the iron some more. I sewed the badge and kept quiet, picking it off and repositioning more than once, while she complained about hippies demonstrating on TV. She steamed all my shirts, the extra skirt, the blazer, the socks and even the tie. If the steam was helping, I didn't mind one bit. Blazer apart, the tie was my favourite. While she put away the ironing board, I sneaked it into the bathroom to practise knotting. I could do a plain knot blindfold, swallow-tucking and diving around the separate ends of the cloth from sheer habit, but this time I wanted perfect. It took several goes, but by stuffing all visible edges of the noose-end beneath my nightshirt collar and not minding the choking sensation, I got there in the end. On tiptoe, working backwards from my reflection in the sink mirror, I turned the tie into a fakir's rope that hid all trace of suspension and my shirt buttons at the same time. It looked efficient. I scanned the windowsill behind the mirror for a kirby grip, something to give the impression of a tie-pin, and saw something else. Cora's razor. Nobody else in the house used such a thing. I knew her repertoire of underpinnings – the hooks and eyelets, buckles, suspenders and other filigree bits and pieces that held her together under a night-on-the-town frock. This, however, from the rigor of its plastic handle to the digger-attachment head, was a different piece of machinery altogether. It looked serious and intimate at the same time, left out by accident. I blushed, imagining her in here naked, running this medical-looking thing over her goose-flesh legs. Tiny whisker ends poked out of one of the slits at the top, and there was a thin fur of dried soap on the plastic head. From watching adverts, I knew the man's kind held a blade. You put foam on your face, pulled the head and stick apart, slid the blade inside, then screwed the whole thing back together again to take the foam back off again. It cut hair. That was how a razor worked. You could cut your wrists with it if you knew how; but it made a mess. I turned it over, looking for an edge, something fine enough to slice and couldn't find it. Wherever the cutting part was, it stayed hidden. In the mirror, fleetingly aware of being observed, my face looked back. There was my tie, my neat, white collar. My neck. It was the most natural thing in the world to lift the razor, tilt my head, and draw one long stroke across the pad of my cheek from nose to ear the way men did in adverts, checking my skin to see if it looked better. Apart from a pale pink curve that stung the more I stared at it, it didn't. It looked sore. And stupid. Maybe the blade was in it after all. Ashamed and confused I'd done it at all, I put the razor back exactly where I'd found it and washed my face till it was crimson and my fringe stuck up. I had a big day tomorrow. I had to get this tie off, fold my shirt and skirt, fetch socks. However unlikely it seemed there and then, I had to hope my face went back to rights overnight and get to sleep.

Mum patted my hair as I stood on the top step ready for the off and confused me into blushing. It was not the kind of thing she did very often, and it always meant withdrawal. She got sentimental for seconds, then withdrew quickly, as though she'd breached a line. I pulled back first and waved at the end of the road, but she'd already gone inside. Braced, my back erect, I walked a mile to school in my dead grandmother's shoes till the gardens of the houses at Sorbie Road hove into view. And there were the gates. One teacher spilled from the main doors and crossed the playground, head forward, her gown ravelling like flags in the wind, heels thunking on the tarmac. Behind her, a cell-cluster of girls in royal blue were dividing and multiplying visibly near one rose sandstone alcove, chatting, tossing back their centre-parted hair, arranging their box-pleats and kilt-pins. Some were big-breasted as married women, their hair shampooed and set. Behind them, from the schemes and bungalows, blazers the same as the one I wore were straggling between the cracks of the academy outbuildings in thin blue streams. I looked down at my chest, the badge sitting proud on the flat top pocket, and crossed to join them, fire and brimstone gusting in my wake. If I was lucky, I'd stand in the lines next to someone with no sense of smell and be in with a shout of being like all the rest. Normal, that was what I wished for. I had an idea everything must be so much easier for those lucky buggers who counted themselves normal. *Ad Astra*, the badge said. If anyone asked I was ready. It meant *To the stars*.

3

On the first day, there were things. The teachers saw the things and they were good and had to be used sensibly. We were big boys and girls now. They were sure we'd manage *sensible* just fine. The piece of squared paper was for drawing a rectangle, eight by five boxes, using a ruler to keep the sides neat. This would be our personal timetable. We could colour the boxes representing each forty-minute period any way we liked according to the subjects listed on the board so long as each subject had a different colour and we put a key at the bottom to remember which was which. That way, even if the ink rubbed off, we'd be sure what was next. I chose yellow for English because I liked English and yellow was cheerful and chose black for Maths so my timetable looked like a bee. We got nice blue jotters to take home and cover with wallpaper and the offer of a pencil if ever we needed one. We got lovely free books in class, some of which bore the publication date of a previous century. It was all acquisition.

On the second day came commandments, the forbidden and the compulsory in tandem for the greater good of all. No jewellery or any other forms of self-adornment and no running inside school buildings; no rubbers, no pens or other implements powered by indelible substances and no privately owned coloured pencils; no chewing hair, pencils, gum, sweets or fingernails; there would be no chewing in general save in the dining hall where refusal of custard was not allowed; no shouting, fighting, high heels, mini-skirts; no trousers for girls and no football colours for boys. Compulsories included good timekeeping, homework, working sharpeners, rubber bands for Cookery and plimsolls and regulation big blue knickers for PE for in PE one removed one's skirt. Squeals of shock were ignored. Girls our age had no call for vanity or prudishness, Miss Lyons said; the rules were *the same for everyone*. This wasn't true because the Seniors in fifth year sometimes wore shorts or little skirts playing hockey, but we weren't Seniors so what did we know. We were the bottom of the heap. We were to arrive on time for teachers; eat everything given in the dining hall because waste was the residue of the ingrate and people in Africa were starving; stick to the left-hand side on the stairs and above all, wear the Academy uniform with pride. For goodness sake, girls, it's not difficult, Miss Lyons sighed. Nobody's asking you to think for yourselves.

On the third day came our first proper lessons using the timetable and an instinctual sextant for navigation, and by the fifth day, routine was already ours. We dumped our bags at the foot of stairwells where anyone to whom they represented a barrier would kick them out of the way and scuffed our new shoes running to the bike sheds, the toilets, the wooden annexes wherein French was conducted. We ran in all the places where running went unseen by teachers, finding outlets for *joie de vivre* by stealth. Inside the dining hall, we masticated four varieties of dark brown gristle-heavy stew and ice-cream balls of potato unless it was Friday, when Ruskoline-dipped millimetre-thin fish with peas was served as a matter of Christian abstinence and those of us who thought this pattern would be the same every week were thereafter proved not wrong. Yellow globs of fat attached to all forms of meat which I spat out rather than swallowed, covering my mouth in case I was caught. The bread tasted of Nivea. For those with coins to spare, an Italian ice-cream van parked on thc double yellows outside the school gates every day selling sweeties and ice poles and we murdered our teeth taking the taste of lunch away. We avoided drinks for all drinks led to the girls' toilets sooner or later and they were no place for girls with any sense of self-respect or smell. No food or drink of any kind, including medicine, throat lozenges, sweeties or water, were permitted in class. These things were known; expected procedure rather than official rules, best learned for the smooth-running of the school. Only after the seventh day did the tripwires arrive.

I was at the foot of the stairwell with a girl called Sheila from West Kilbride in the last minutes before the bell when a voice behind us shouted loud enough to make Sheila's penny toffee pop out of her mouth and skitter along the polished parquet. The voice wanted to know what moron had put its sodding bag in the middle of the stairs. Nobody replied. We turned to see the speaker, a huge bloke with a braided blazer and a jaw the size of an excavator bucket, red-faced with annoyance behind us. He had one hand clenched and the other clutching a small black coffin by its small black handle. A steady stream of Juniors were trying to burrow past him to go up and a queue, equally stuck, was building behind. The bag was at his feet and he was looking at me. It meant he'd tripped on the bag and *I* was the moron. In his head, the moron and the owner of the bag were one and the same person and both those people were me.

Don't just stand there, he growled. Get the sodding bag out of the way.

I accepted a flick on the head from his monster knuckles and did what I was told, releasing him to shoot down the corridor so fast, the sound of a cork popping was almost audible, the words *moron idiot* trailing in his wake as he disappeared. At the same time, a short, bald man in a black gown came fluttering towards us, filling the space the big bloke had vacated seconds before and without breaking stride, booted the bag I'd just rescued against the corridor wall stage-whispering *Goal!* in the voice of an excitable crowd, then carried smartly on as if nothing had happened. And the bell rang. It was only when I pushed the bag away from further harm and heard something crunch that I realised the kick had been real. Something inside had broken. Glass most likely. The noise sounded heavy, like jagged chunks. I almost opened it to check, then changed my mind. For one thing, I might get cut and for seconds, the bag, however protective I felt towards it, *wasn't* mine. I'd moved it out of the way because someone had to and appeasement seemed better than confrontation. Now things had gone wrong. If I hadn't moved it, the teacher wouldn't have kicked it. The brokenness was my fault. The massed hordes of Juniors rushing to different classrooms made it hard to think so I waited till the bell stopped altogether, the footfalls were past. Eventually there was only whistling silence and me. No one came for the bag. Either its owner had forgotten it or was looking in all the wrong places. Which made me responsible. Abandoning the bag would be thoughtless – what if the real owner showed up and plunged a hand into the broken glass without warning? – but staying beside it was breaking a rule and a different sort of punishment attached to that. *Idiot moron*, I thought. *Sodding bag*. But glaring and name-calling didn't help. I had to do something, and the doing meant taking on three wormy little truths. 1) Being responsible and being obedient were two different things; 2) Morally conflicted time-wasters got on people's nerves and 3) Biddability was what authority admired most in those with none. Added together, they suggested some unknown person's chances of hideously lacerated digits were less of an impediment to the school's smooth-running than my being late. So I scarpered, arriving at class with the excuse, concocted on the spot, that I'd been on an unavoidable errand for Miss Lyons and she sent her apologies. Sheila had lost a toffee, but I had gained an ability to lie on the spot. This teacher might ask Miss Lyons. Miss Lyons might find out by other means. The Big Boy might report me for cheek or the short man remember me as the most likely person responsible for leaving a bag full of broken stuff unattended in the corridor. *Nobody was asking me to think,* Miss Lyons said. But they were. Just more deviously than anyone was prepared to say out loud. In short, obeying the rules would mean *unthinking* a lot of the time, second-guessing, keeping your nose clean and your arse covered. The things that crowded into everything else. I felt naive and sly at the same time. A liar reeking of cowardice. I hoped I was wrong.

Shoulders back, head up, look like something for crying out loud and don't show your mother up. Start as you mean to go on and start from the moment you go outside the front door. People know whose daughter you are. Back straight. Purposeful strides. Look purposeful. Don't even *think* of letting me down.

Walk. Turn right out of the cul-de-sac into Wellpark Road, then left down the Springvale Street cut into Springvale Street proper heading uphill to Argyll. Turn left. Walk down Argyll Street ignoring the Jacks Road turnoff and its bridge over the railway with the hawthorn bushes and keep straight on to Caledonia Road. Ignore the cat at the dairy door on the far side of the roundabout. Keep straight on following the dividing wall behind which are the Plantation trees with the Galloway Burn running fitfully through. Hear birds. Keep going and the junction for Sorbie Road appears. Take the sharp right over the bridge where there's no railway any more and there are the playing fields, stretching way. And on the other side, behind the gates, the school and all it stands for. You can't miss it, everyone says. It's plain as the nose on your face and they're right. You don't.

Ardrossan's chief charms were the Barony Church, the hammered-since-the-thirteenth-century-then-flattened-by-Cromwell remains of a castle, the bus station and a vinegar-scented array of Italian-owned chip emporia. There was a harbour showing the fastest escape route to Arran that doubled as a thoroughfare for sailors, no-goods and prostitutes. Not that I knew what prostitutes were, but the harbour, allegedly, was full of them. The Academy, for all it looked like a brickworks, was a local landmark regarded with pride. In the dim and distant it had been fee-paying: now all you had to do was pass the Qualifying Exam, and its doors were open. My mother had heard of Eton, but had never seen it and never would, but whatever the King's College of Our Lady of Eton beside Windsor was like, it could not possibly be more top-notch than Ardrossan Academy. Education, she said so again and again, made a difference. It was a passport to *getting on* via a dedicated process called *sticking in*, which led by the natural law of fairness to a Better Life. Ardrossan not only provided this opportunity but provided it free. Buying an education, unless it was for children who couldn't pass exams in the normal way, struck mum as proof that some people had more money than sense and ought to be taxed more. *Anyone* could access an education in our country, a training that once mastered and sifted through by the passing of exams would put them beyond snobbery or disadvantage for ever. People with an education could do *anything they damn-well liked*. She clung to this idea like a cat to a plank in a storm-tossed sea, for, if it were not so, life was not fair and striving counted for nothing. And if striving counted for nothing, drowning was better than weakly paddling on. Watching me head off to the fantasy palace of Ardrossan Academy every morning after the ups and downs of Jacks Road Primary must have filled her with wild relief. *I'll make something of you if it kills me*, she said, *and it might*. Every morning, she saw me off at the open door while my sister, French-rolled with her Co-op astrakhan collar up, barged past on her way to the Glasgow train. Cora did not say goodbye to me nor I to her, but mum set off to work at Kyleshill School kitchens knowing her girls would be gainfully employed, at least for one more day. And whatever the meteorological, political or domestic situation, I walked. Over six years of hail, battering rain, lethargic sunshine or roaring gales, the route never varied by so much as a step. I can still close my eyes and trace it as clearly as a lover's face.

Shoulders back, head up, look like something and start from the moment you go outside the front door down a path my mother bordered every year with early snowdrops/primroses/night-stock/Michaelmas daisies, down to the end of our cul-de-sac of squat council flats and Walk. Turn right out of the cul-de-sac into Wellpark Road, then left down the Springvale Street cut with its pits and potholes where I'd once been held by the neck but the man ran away, into Springvale Street proper heading uphill to Argyll. Turn left past the paper shop where Gloria who looked after two little boys who disappeared one day and never came back embraced me, and Walk down Argyll Street where the privet hedges put out tips you pull in summer and scatter like wedding confetti, ignoring the Jacks Road turnoff and its bridge over the railway with the hawthorn bushes where you were chucked in the brambles by a Big Girl called Etta Lynn who demanded money on the grounds that you had a raincoat so had to be posh and keep straight on to Caledonia another name for Scotland Road. Ignore the cat how do you ignore a cat? at the dairy door on the far side of the roundabout where St Cuthbert's overseen by the Reverend Balls and his legions, the pews where the senior choir sat straight as whips in their fashion boots/sling-backs/flat little lace-up Clarks and keep straight on past the smart sandstone semis with gardens out front and the shadows of faces behind curtains as you pass following the dividing wall behind which are the Plantation trees the green-painted railings and the benches, lewd hand-carved messages, love hearts, invitations to believe who did what for how much with the Galloway Burn into which I fell head-first at the age of four and nearly drowned running fitfully through. Hear birds there are always birds and they sing despite everything. Keep going and the junction for Sorbie Road where one day if you work hard and meet the right chap you could live and make your mother proud for once appears. Take the sharp right over the bridge where there's no railway any more but the edge is heady with rosebay willowherb to the rusty tracks, a straight ravine you dreamed was filled with horses and there are the playing fields stretching away as far as your old primary school the place you showed no grace at sporting events and never would. And on the other side, behind the gates, the school. You can't miss it, everyone says, come hell, high water, high winds or snow it's as plain as the nose on your face and they're right. You don't.

Your future depended upon it.

You wouldn't have missed it for worlds.

Second week, the rules gave way to orienteering. We were expected to know our way in the dark. The building had long straight corridors gloomy as mine shafts even first thing in the morning, but subjects became identifiable by scent (Latin smelled of dried-up newsprint, French of lavender polish, Physics of cold, soft lead) so you knew where you were at all times notwithstanding. After a short while, this indoor half-dark was a welcome thing, encouraging touch. I ran my fingers over the polished wood banisters and baize-middled notice-boards, cold painted radiators and dirty glass. Every morning if you looked hard, the sandstone walls seemed ankle-deep in damp with a bath ring line on every wall, while the upper floor lit like buttercups from the lights on the half-landing, even when there was no sun. I learned the time of senior boys' rugby training from the crunch of cleats on the tarmac and the big, bluff PE teacher calling out names; knew long before we went inside whether charcoal, paint or chalk was today's medium of choice from the scent that carried from the open doors. And in every classroom were runic messages from those who had been there before us, every available inch of desk-lid thick with inverse braille. Initials, disembodied eyes, skeletons, spiders and swastikas, bald heads peering over lumpy little walls, and arrows with targets, hearts or trajectory lines. Stick-men sporting balloon-animal genitalia and stick-women ballooning a great deal more we tried to hide under pencil-cases, jotters or the tinny box of a geometry set out of compassion and modesty. It was not to save the teachers' embarrassment. There was no need. No matter what cocked its snook from the desk-lid, the teachers seemed not to see. After a fortnight, we found that we could do it too: a combination of familiarity, contempt and the only way to focus on the lesson in hand. Acceptance got things done. If our classes were rigidly streamed (A to F based on the ripeness of former exam results), it was Darwinism in action, a natural order at work. If we felt uneasy as the F-streamers headed off down the corridor, trying to look blasé rather than bulldozed, we needed to toughen up. *We don't have lame ducks here*, Miss Lyons said, and though the phrase filled me with compassion I did not want to be lame. I wanted very much to fit in. I'd had no luck with the Sunday School Club or the Brownies so the Academy seemed my best hope. If I kept out of trouble I'd be fine.

Mr Peartree wrote the word ROME on the board and turned to face us, radiating something close to joy. He had black brilliantined hair and a black gown, the corners of which stored chalk, which let him swirl its extremities like stripper's tassels as he walked. He wrote the word ROME a lot. Ruthless determination teamed with military order was a Good Thing. So was world domination. The civilisations of the Indus Valley, of the Akkadians, Sumerians,

Babylonians and Phoenicians were nothing to the city of seven hills. The Celts were blue-faced ruffians when the Romans were polishing off Carthage, he said. The thought of it made him beam with pleasure. We wrote SENATUS POPULUSQUE ROMANUS in our jotters and learned a Roman salute.

What came before is what makes us tomorrow, he said. Write that down.

We wrote. What made the Romans seemed largely to have been armies and roads: their routes and tactics, centurions, prefects and tribunes, the generals given to decimation and crucifixion. For light relief, he threw in aqueducts, central heating and suicide. Marc Antony became soft from love for wicked Cleopatra and lost the Battle of Actium. He fell on a sword and she died of a suicidal snake encounter, allowing Octavian to claim a victory and secure Egypt itself as a Roman province. Three cheers for Octavian. Women and anybody with normal appetites and interests made rubbish history. After we'd written enough, we put the pencils down and turned to the living instead.

Did any of us have an older brother or sister here before them? A girl at the front, the only Cynthia I ever met, said she had a brother called Alasdair in fourth year. Mr Peartree said Cynthia looked prettier than Alasdair and we smiled indulgently. Somebody with a big brother in the Navy owned up next, then another with a sister in fifth year, another with a male cousin in year two who was cordoned off with the junior boys for we were now divided by sex. Racking my brain produced nothing. My cousins were mothers with children older than me and the corner shop asked *how's your gran?* when they meant my mother. A late baby whose mother had assumed her the menopause, I surrendered the game to people whose families were less ancient and watched. Mr Peartree caught my eye anyway.

You, he said, pointing. Any relatives who attended the Academy? I shook my head. Sure? he said. Embarrassed, I nodded. He kept looking anyway and the class rustled. Well, you look like somebody to me. Everyone turned. Who is it?

I felt accused. The only person I looked like was dad and where dad had been to school was anybody's guess. Mr Peartree, even if he was in his fifties, was too young.

Nobody, I said. Someone laughed. Keen to please, I flicked a short mental index file of exam-passing relatives and came up with no one. No one except Cora and it couldn't be her. Seventeen years ago was *for ever*, and anyway I didn't look like her. He could not mean Cora. But I had to say something.

I have a sister. My sister was here.

Name?

You don't know her, I said, aiming for definite.

Name?

It was ages, I said. You can't have—

What, he said, enunciating slowly, is her name?

Cora, I said, hoping my stammer wouldn't kick off. Cora. I couldn't remember her surname. She got a new one along with the husband when she got married and even if she had run away, she wasn't divorced. I didn't know the right answer so I gave the first one again. Her name's Cora.

Mr Peartree stood up. You mean Cora Galloway?

Galloway. That was it. Her name was the same as mine. Her married name didn't come into it and I was an idiot for thinking it did. Cora *Doreen* Galloway? His face was shifting, locating something far away as I nodded. Goodness, he said, smiling, shaking his head. Cora Doreen Galloway. Goodness gracious me.

The class were mumbling in the pauses as he scrutinised me over the rims of his glasses, letting the smile spread, and he rested his hands on his knees. I remember Cora Doreen very well indeed.

My shoulders hunched, wondering what he remembered her for.

Bright, he said. Could have done well, chose not to. There we are. He dusted chalk from his hands. Life is full of surprises. And where is she now?

I said nothing, not sure if this was one of the things I wasn't supposed to give away because it was our business.

A dancer at the *Folies Bergère*? An air hostess perhaps? His eyes saw into somewhere far away. I've often wondered what happened to Cora.

Full of surprises. My head was already filling up with them. Cora and mum shouting at each other about nothing you could pin down; Cora in one of her low-cut frocks, twirling, coming home with her ankles bruised and a fag on one lip, her mascara worn down to panda marks; Cora turning up at our door with a vanity case in her hand saying *Christ is this it?* But none of this was sayable. If you didn't tell a teacher you were eligible for a clothing grant, you certainly didn't tell him this. All I knew from telling was that Cora had gone AWOL. Born after a dead son, Cora had been *spoiled* or so my mother said. Then she kicked over the traces, threw her chances away and ran off with a Glasgow boy to get married and not have to live in Saltcoats any more. She didn't write. But when mum left dad three years later and took me with her, Cora turned up at the door of our single room above a doctor's surgery with no warning, only a vanity case, a box of matches and a strong desire never to mention married life again. The last was something she'd done so successfully, hardly anyone knew it had happened at all. I had a nephew somewhere and mum had a grandson. Neither of us had clapped eyes. I had never seen a picture of the wedding day never mind the child. I wasn't even sure what his name was. I had never seen a picture of her at school and certainly not here, in Ardrossan Academy's *worn-with-pride* blazer, as I sat now trying to bring her to mind. It was a lot of stuff to think and know that none of it, not a word, was utterable. Even if it had been, it was not what Mr Peartree wanted. He wanted a story involving progress, a smooth transition into adulthood, the name of a job. Then I remembered the typing qualification. After a stint as a waitress and a clippie on the buses, my sister had taken herself to college and got a typing qualification. She had *distinction.*

She's a secretary, I said. In a big office in Glasgow. Her boss gets manicures.

Mr Peartree's smile sat still for a moment, then melted away.

Given my hesitancy, he might have been wondering if I was all there.

Well, he said. That's a fine thing. It's the secretaries that really run these businesses. Everyone who works in a school knows that! Tell her I'm asking after her. He raised his eyes, looked deep into mine. It would be true to say, he intoned, every word a chime, I was very fond of Cora Doreen Galloway.

Then, leaving me miles from certainty, he turned back to his chalk and his preferred civilisation. The word *Cora* rang in the empty space above my head, the sensation of being hooked to it whether I liked it or not. GLADIUS. Mr Peartree was writing on the blackboard. IACULUM. Down a long double-barrel of confusion, I picked up my pencil and watched. I watched because I could barely hear for the blood in my ears, a low, adrenal thrum. *Fond*, he said. *Very fond*. She might have sat not only in this very room, but in this very chair. My neck was crawling, my eyes steady as Mr Peartree, with the slow deliberation of a Japanese warrior, began some kind of dance. She had been here all right. I could feel it. And I was here in my turn, maybe even in her very place. Mr Peartree held up an imaginary sword against an invisible opponent with something approaching intent. *Take that*, he roared, thrusting one hand forward. Immediately, he became his own opponent, turning to face the space he had previously occupied and coiling an imaginary net over its head. It was gladiatorial combat, I realised. A pitting of wits and dexterity. And while he did it, stalking himself in enthralling slow motion, I tried to piece together what my sister might have been like before I was born. I conjured a girl with double plaits tearing across a hockey pitch in shin-guards like a Samurai; a younger girl drawing a smiling face inside a maths equation, carving a target on her desk so hard she broke the pencil. Younger still, my age, belting towards a high-jump to scissor-kick clean over the top then roll like Cleopatra at the feet of Caesar on a thick rubber mat.

Into his stride now, Mr Peartree flicked the wings of his gown for clearance and lunged at thin air. He turned and parried his own attack but it was all but over. His back exposed, he whirled and struck home, hard.

Cora Doreen. Her whole name. He had not asked for mine.

Oblivious, Mr Peartree was buckling, falling, tangling his gown over his head in a gesture of despair. *Et tu, Brute*, he croaked, sprawling. *Mortuus sum.* And the class burst into spontaneous applause.

Mr Peartree stood and took a bow as I schooled my face to blankness, letting nothing show; not delight, not fear, just empty space. Someone was walking over my grave. If I paid no attention, it would come no further. The teacher smiled till the clapping stopped and told us to write down the following for homework. Heart thumping, I picked up my pencil.

Imagine you are a citizen at the Colosseum. I wrote the words in my best, most careful cursive, silver-grey against the plain white page. *You! Stop drawing attention to yourself and write!* Whoever he was addressing, I knew it wasn't me. I was being as good as I knew how to be. Head well under the parapet, I was turning out my very best longhand, about the business of recording my homework. *Describe the sights using accurate historical detail and the emotions of the crowd.* Strange things could happen in the world, lives turn inexplicably on their heels. I knew that. But I hoped as I wrote, hoping my spelling was sound, that whatever it was that came before would not make me who I was tomorrow. *You may choose to be a slave if you prefer.*

I wrote what he said down slowly, with effortful care. Whatever had happened to Cora, I didn't want it happening to me.

4

Have you homework?

The answer was always yes. Even if it was just messing about, it was writing things down and I was left to do it in peace if I called it *homework.* Anything not homework, housework or paid work was *a waste of time.*

Don't think anybody will help you when you've hee-haw, she said. You have to fight for everything you get. You stick in with the homework. Don't let your golden chances pass you by. Like me.

She headed up the hallway, hoovering, trailing the strains of *If I Loved You* from her mouth like perfume. Mum dispensed advice all the time that I thought I wasn't listening to. Forty years on, it's still there. The homework advice came in various guises, boiling down to much the same thing. Self-sufficiency was the only survival tool you could count on. Years later, I heard the mothers of Barra fishermen did not teach their sons to swim, the idea being that they'd die all the quicker if they fell overboard into a freezing sea, and saw immediately the logic behind it. You could fight some things with preparation, but nature was bigger than you and not open to appeal. In a cold, cold climate, the mothers reducing a child's odds to the inevitable was kinder and faster than allowing them to struggle in vain. Mum's take, because it was metaphoric, was gentler: freezing circumstances were more survivable than freezing water and I could be my own buoyancy aid if I tried. Homework bred self-reliance. The more crushingly boring the effort required, the more it counted as real work as intimated in the word *toil*.

Reading was less impressive than *writing down* because *writing down* looked more like physical labour. Physics was more laudable than Poetry because the inherent dullness of basic Physics made it gruelling. Art homework was *just drawing pictures*, but ploughing through the soul-witheringly formulaic language of a Chemistry Report made Chemistry *brainy*. Biology landed somewhere in the middle of this divide: on the one hand, dissecting things was repulsive enough to win brownie points but you also got to play with animals. Of all the Arts subjects, English came closest to real graft because it included *parsing*: no creativity required, just recognition, rules and the writing of long lists – as morally improving as sewing mail sacks. Best of all was – or more correctly were – Mathematics.

Maths was what inventors dashed on blackboards to show the vast size of their brains and got a massive score on the incomprehensibility and repetition stakes. So far, our class had been treated to Arithmetic (the same as primary stuff with square roots thrown in), Algebra (sums with numbers disguised as letters) and Geometry (drawing shapes and angles and colouring them in). Geometry was my favourite. I lounged on the rug drawing circles with intersections like new moons to show subsets while *Coronation Street* played in the background and all was well with the world. We were doing sets and subsets which meant a lot of colouring in and intersecting circles. *Blue pencils* were a subset of *all pencils; pens* were not. *Pens*, however, might sit next to *all pencils* in a larger set called *things that write*. Some geometrical relationships resembled fried eggs while others made chains. Now and then something made a set with nothing else at all, but such abandoned groups, like everything else in this world, had to sink or swim. Mathematical rules made no allowance for anything's feelings.

Cora used to do that, my mother said. But she drew faces in the wee circles instead of doing them right.

Cora peered over the top of a baby-jacket to see. Wee faces, she said. Haha. Smiles and dots for eyes. I remember.

Haha nothing. You got marks off for not doing it right. Mum was stringing beads.

I did plenty right, Cora said. She cranked up her row counter. Just not that stuff. It's daft. Maths is daft.

It is not daft, my mother said. It's clever.

That's right, Cora said. It's so clever it's completely useless.

You think everything's useless, my mother said. Anything you don't like is a waste of time. *Invented* snobbery, that's what you've got. You're an invented snob.

Inverted, Cora said. The adjective is *inverted*. Godsake.

Mum, oblivious, turned to me. What do you think? She's wrong, isn't she?

Mmmm, I said, responding but saying nothing at all. Mmmm.

See? Cora said. Even clever-clogs knows that stuff's rubbish as well.

She does nothing of the kind, my mother said. Then thank God Annie Walker came on. She wore eyeshadow and lipstick and an affected voice that betrayed ideas above her station. She didn't deserve her husband, Jack, because Jack was content with his life and she was not. Annie, the malcontent, ran a pub.

If I'd had the man she got, mum said, my life would have been different. That woman doesn't know when she's well off.

Marvelling at Annie's ingratitude was the kind of reliable distraction that made it well worth paying TV rental. Due to the thin walls, we had the privilege of hearing two TVs – ours and the Greggs' upstairs – at the same time. The Greggs were going deaf which meant we heard what they watched, especially if it was something loud on the other side. *Coronation Street* was a guaranteed half-hour of harmony because they watched it too. TVs being on, in competition or twinned, was the sound of *normal*. We ate our tea off plates in front of it, ran commentaries on the adverts and heckled comedians till switch-off. Mindful of the walls, we whispered answers to contestants on *Double Your Money* and complained about the smug male lead of *The Avengers*. Writing essays with my ears full of something else was second nature.

Holiday commercials were tense affairs since Sandy, the boyfriend who reappeared between Cora's other boyfriends, had asked her to go away with him for a week and she'd preferred to stay at home in her chair watching Wimbledon. My mother liked Sandy but thought he had *no backbone*.

You should go somewhere, she said. Barnsley. Go to Barnsley and see Jack.

Uncle Jack was a bore and a boor and the mayor of Darton. Nobody except mum wanted to see Uncle Jack. Cora said nothing.

You must have enough money for holidays, mum persisted. You're not giving me much, that's for sure.

Cora lit a cigarette with one hand, the knitting suspended in the other, refusing to play.

I'm only saying, mum went on, if Sandy's your boyfriend, you should be doing stuff together instead of just that pub in Windmill Street. You should be out enjoying yourselves if you like him that much.

He's not my boyfriend, she said. He's a pal. He's just a pal.

The ads were still on. Mum had no reason to stop while she was on a possible winning streak. You should go out and give me and her a break.

Affecting nonchalance, I scanned my textbook for some more pretend Geometry to do, something to make me look preoccupied. Triangles, I needed something with triangles.

I'm not interested, Cora said.

What d'you mean, *not interested*?

I can have a walk down the shore if I want a holiday. I don't. Holidays are boring.

Nobody said anything for a moment or two.

Anyway, she said finally, if I want a holiday I'd want a proper one. Spain or somewhere. I wouldn't go on a pissy bus tour.

Mum rolled her eyes.

Sandy's OK for a drink, Cora said. But that's it.

Well, you should get rid of him then. Mum's lips were tightening. You'll not get another one with him hanging about like a smell. You should find somebody else.

I don't want somebody else, Cora said slowly.

You're young yet, my mother said, tying off a strand of waxed cotton thread. You've your whole life. You should get a man.

Cora snorted as though that was the daftest thing she'd ever heard.

I had a man, remember? Smoke came out of her mouth in little white puffs. Bugger that for a game of soldiers.

My mother lost her temper. You're twenty-nine, she said.

Well?

Well, is sitting on your arse at the fire what you plan to do with the rest of your life?

Cora blinked slowly. *You* get a boyfriend if you're that bothered. *You* go out. I'm not needing to go out because I'm *fine.*

You're a cheeky bitch you, my mother said, but her heart wasn't in it. McKellar Watt sausages were dancing, singing about how meaty they were.

You should find that boy of yours, then, mum went on. Her eyes were on the screen, pearls rolling on her lap like eyes. You don't even know what he looks like. Your sister doesn't know what her own nephew looks like.

An isosceles triangle has at least two equal sides. Mum didn't mention her grandmotherly status which was cunning. She had kept herself in the clear. I was damned if I was getting sucked in. *An isosceles triangle. Two equal sides.* The words juddered around too much to absorb readily and I read the same sentence three times.

Aye fine. Cora breathed out. I'll just drop him a line tomorrow then. He'll be desperate to meet his Aunty Janice and I don't think.

She was in no mood. Up till now, tonight's provocation had been pretty low-key. This one could have turned nasty, but didn't, so Cora must have had a hard week. Why mum kicked off this kind of thing every so often was beyond me. It needled Cora and I got belted round the head sooner or later: there was no resolution. Resolution was not the point: the needling was all. I picked up my ruler and read example 5 again, trying to focus. Everything would calm down if I focused.

Well, anyway, my mother said, looking down at me, *she's* got the right idea.

Cora kicked me in the ribs.

You hear that? That's you being cast up to me.

Don't drag her into it, mum said, forgetting she was the one who'd dragged me in in the first place. Cora wasn't listening.

Creeping Jesus and its daft sums. The day she's got a right idea about anything I'm a Dutchman.

Elsie Tanner appeared on screen clipping on a pair of earrings to the accompaniment of a slow brass quartet. Everybody liked and was appalled by Elsie at the same time so we'd watch. She was too good not to. Saved by the Harlot of the Street. Taking advantage, I offered mum a pear drop from the sugary bottom of a paper bag, implying everything was hunky dory. She took it. Even Cora took one, or at least pointed at her mouth meaning me to do it for her so she didn't have to stop mid-row and make her needles sticky. Grateful, I picked up the confection with the tips of my nails and dropped it on her tongue, careful not to touch her skin by accident. And there we were, back to rights. If anyone had been passing our window at that moment and looked in, we'd have resembled nothing so much as Little Women, each head bent over a separate domestic concern: Cora plying her needles, mum stringing beads, and me, dusting sugar off my fingertips, resettled between them about the business of self-improvement. I had Pythagoras the Greek and whatever his hypotenuse might be to help me. With this stuff on your side, you were never alone. I flexed my fingers, checked the pencil tip was sharp, and drew triangles as though keeping the room from blowing apart depended upon it. Focus on something solid, dissociate from the rest. This was what kept the world turning.

Christmas was a bike. It was time I had more of a sense of adventure and a means of transport so I gave it a go. After a week it was clear I was no athlete. I didn't even have much of a sense of balance. Even if I made the bike go any distance, I scared motorists who could see I had never read the Highway Code. Mum thought I'd use it for school but we'd had notes round warning that bicycles were brought at the owner's risk and I was nervous it would get stolen. Before long, the bike was an obvious error of judgement and sold off to someone who'd appreciate it more than me. Miss Lyons, not knowing, told us to write a thank-you letter for homework. *Use the normal, natural voice in which you would write such a letter at home*, she said, making a strange task even stranger. I'd never written a thank-you letter in my life, but at least its function was easy to guess. The bit that threw me was *the normal voice* suggestion. I had written letters to dictation (*you write it, you're better at spelling than me*) that had been sent to Uncle Willie in Carlisle, but that was it. I'd never sent a postcard and all that went on a Christmas card was your name and, at a stretch, a kiss. In much the spirit of making a Blue Peter Advent Crown, I set about the task without much faith that what I was about to construct was in any way *normal* at all.

Dear Mum sounded crazy. *Mum* on its own looked brusque. *MUM* in capitals looked arresting, but hectoring, so I added an exclamation mark. It looked best. *MUM!* radiated excitement and eagerness to please. That had to be right. I had a start.

Mum! I wrote. *Thanks for the fab present!* Informal, breezy and up-to-the moment. *What a BIG SURPRISE.* This was good. The capitals suggested both delight and the bigness of the surprise and the subsequent sentence – *It must have cost a fortune!!* – was appreciative. Mum liked expense to be appreciated and the double exclamations showed the level of appreciation to be frantic. *I'm not very good yet* – this was teetering close to guilt, which though it was truthful was not up-beat, so I reined the tone back to bright – *but soon I will be!!!* Having already used the device of two, these three exclamation marks added a dash of knowing humour so I didn't sound cocky. *WOW!* I wrote, flourishing the W. *Thanks!* And I was done. I put addresses and the *sincerely* part on then, after some deliberation, added *ps See you in the living room!* for verisimilitude and two *xs* for warmth. The signature I'd been practising in secret to make my name look flashy sat at the end like the cherry on an Empire Biscuit, its curlicued J an Elizabethan ruff of swirls. I thought this letter was just the ticket. Miss Lyons didn't.

My homework came back with three lines of cramped red handwriting – *Gifts can be acceptable or welcome. Fab is not a word. Mention of cost is vulgar* – and no grade. Just an X. The X, unlike those I had appended in the persona of letter-author, was not an indicator of affection. It meant *wrong*. Baffled, I read her comments, then the instructions again. The words *normal, natural voice* were still there. I rewrote the letter in my head knocking anything effusive, vulgar or fab on the head, then imagined handing it to mum. I imagined her reading, reaching *Thanks for the acceptable present* and passing the note to Cora, who would make a sharp and probably physical riposte. Done with imagining, I looked again at the big red X and flushed with huff. *Vulgar* I could take on the chin, but *wrong* was a step too far. Without thinking, I scratched the word *bitch* on my desk in blue pen. My only act of vandalism in six years of secondary education: I must have been furious. Fortunately, Miss Lyons did not often ask us to be imaginative so the rest of the jotter was largely ticks for matching opposites, collective nouns and proverbs which mum would like. Imagination was better given a wide berth: it led only to trouble.

One year of Needlework was devoted to making an apron and

a cross-stitched hairband. We did it teacher's way and at teacher's pace or not at all. Cookery, from a limp beginning making cornflakes and milk, graduated to scones, pancakes and rock cakes using blackboard recipes and brass-weight scales. Not liking currants was no excuse: ingredients went in as listed. The nasal excitements and weighing out of coloured powders into test tubes that was Chemistry wore off quickly when the actual results of our experiments were sidelined in favour of what the textbook said had happened. Plumb-lines and pulleys in Physics were dull from the off. The thrill of French, its written form crawling with cedillas and circumflexes, lasted longer, partly because Miss Brown, a woman with a beehive hairdo, was smaller than a child and nice to us. *Toto est dans le placard,* we chanted in chorus. *Il mange la confiture.* Miss Currie, who taught Housewifery, insisted we watch her demonstrate childcare by bathing a baby doll in an enamel basin with soap, the finale of which included pulling off the baby's head to empty out the water that had filtered in through the leg-joints. She may well have pulled off an arm as well, but that might be embroidery after the fact. Whichever is truer, the uses of borax and bicarbonate of soda as stain removers seemed tame thereafter. Those of us who took Latin got to quit after a single period and we clock-watched for most of it. Miss Currie let us know she had noticed.

The scholars, Miss Currie sniffed as we fled, would do well to remember that household skills will play a far more important part of your *real* future than some silly *dead language*. What kind of wives you expect to be I don't know.

But she did, and we knew it too. Rubbish wives, that's what kind of wives we'd be; foolish virgins who would find out too late that clumsy hospital corners and unstarched ironing led only to misery, ruin and broken homes. It wasn't news, exactly, my mother did a good line in much the same thing when she was in a bad mood, but we slunk off with our tails down and the creeping suspicion she was right. It lasted as long as the walk to Room 202, because that was where Latin itself, and, more to the point, the Latin teacher, took us into her excitable embrace. Dr Nisbet, who taught with such enthusiasm her face bloomed like a sunflower when she conjugated the simplest of verbs, was as baking soda upon the grimy suggestion that Latin was useless. Latin was a way of seeing. Inspired, I read the textbook even when I didn't have homework. Girls were forever *adorning the temple with roses*. Soldiers repeatedly and for no apparent reason *admired the boys*. *Omnia mutantur, nihil interit.* Everything changes, nothing perishes. If every flip from Latin to lumpy English gave me a rush, it was not necessarily because of what the sentences said in themselves; it was because translation was so realisable at all. Words and phrases that at first glance were alien, obscure or downright weird could be broken down into components which joined and split apart like pop-beads to reveal – *meaning*. It was astounding. Unsuspected, there under my nose all this time, language – of all deceitful and slippery things, *language* – was made of *rules*. Grammar was not just rote then, it was a machine which, with practice, had the power to extract sense from chaos, light from dark. And if the *language* could be learned and forced to reveal its underlying order, maybe other things could be learned and tamed too. Maybe all things, even *people*, even off-the-wall sorts and their equally off-the-wall actions, might be skeleton-keyed into understanding. It was a Big Thought, one that opened windows in the cramped quarters of my brain. Also, it proved sour-grapes Miss Currie completely wrong because Latin *wasn't* dead or anything like. It was a wellspring, a source and a means to connection. Some people went to Scripture Union every lunch-time, trusting something called Fellowship would see them through. Others sacrificed their dinner-break to Netball as their chosen means of finding satisfaction. At thirteen, I found Latin declensions, the chime of nominative, vocative, accusative, genitive, dative and ablative as the signposts on the Road that led not only to Rome but Damascus. If it was a choice cooler girls who didn't have stammers laughed at, I didn't care. The body was weak indeed, but ideas were armoured tanks. Whether she meant it or not, Dr Nisbet, with every lesson, was Boudicca in brogues.

The antithesis of Latin was PE. An order to catch or hit a ball, to race, chase or hurdle over, even relatively slowly, was not something I welcomed. I'd been centre-forward for the Jacks Road P7 netball team only because I could throw. In the midst of people who cared whether they won, I blanked. Hula-hoops slithered over my hips and collapsed on the hardwood floor like clown pants and medicine balls banged against the tender spots where breasts had begun to bud. Big Betty Stewart loved the whole thing, even when we learned to dance the *Gay Gordons* with the boys before Christmas, their bare chests cold against our nylon shirt fronts as we twirled beneath resistant arms. Miss McCourt, a PE teacher we routinely called Tanya after a baby elephant on TV, softened for nothing and no one. Strains, allergies and headaches got no one off class. And sensing *periods* (plural, *periods* were always plural) were looming as the next excuse, she gave us an explanation-free order that if we needed a sanitary towel – here she waved a white bandagey parcel the size of a brick over her head to a collective gasp – to march to the medical room where she or Miss Lyons would offer *one pad and no more*, as though anyone might try to sneak off with six for the hell of it. If we thought periods were an excuse for getting out of climbing, sprinting, leaping or forward-rolling, we could think again. You're Big Girls now, she said, finishing the session by telling Linda McCann, a farmer's girl whose coral-coloured nipples already glowed like brake-lights beneath her shirt, to behave herself and buy a bra. Our comfort throughout was in knowing that when the fresh intake arrived after the summer, they'd be the new bugs and we could pose as old hands.

Green no longer, towards the end of first year, we were dulling to *jaded*. When Mr Parker in Geography belted one of our number for not knowing the average rainfall of Dundee, we realised the mollycoddling was over. When Miss Lyons handed me back a poem I'd taken time over with the words *I don't know who wrote this but it certainly wasn't you*, I opted, like Seneca, for stoic and hated her in silence. When Trigonometry launched a fleet of sines, cosines and tangents, my fling with the Magic of Numbers veered at a sharp 90° angle towards the rocks. It had been fun while it lasted, but the colouring-in was over, revealing Maths as a dull interplay of cyphers and nothing more. Even the Romans let me down. An unexpected showing of *Spartacus* on TV revealed Roman xenophobia, ruthlessness, vindictiveness and slavery as the other side of beautifully constructed grammar and I took it hard. Sometimes, life took dark turns. You got older and you lost things. I still loved Latin, but less innocently. I tried to appreciate the value of circumspection in favour of diving headlong in. As luck had it, PE decided to teach the opposite. Next time in the gym, Tanya (Miss McCourt to the timid) set up an obstacle course with things to leap over, squirm beneath, climb and snake between. Diving headlong in seemed to be its purpose. It looked military, painful and designed to sprain. Sylvia Torrance, who had come in looking tearful and thinner than usual, followed the gym mistress around pleading permission to sit the session out. Tanya didn't even look round. If you can stand, you can jump, she said. None of your nonsense. Sylvia's face was the colour of bread dough.

Fifteen minutes later, Sylvia fell halfway up a rope ladder and slid, almost soundlessly, onto the varnished hardwood floor. Miss McCourt rolled up her giant sleeves, lifted Sylvia like a baby and carried her through to the changing rooms. Some girls, the kind who genuinely believed that wall-bars were fun, didn't dwell. The rest of us turned. We watched Sylvia, borne away in the teacher's arms like the dead Ophelia, long hair trailing like an ash-blonde veil. Some swore they saw a smear of blood on her thigh; others, a flat, dark stain on her knickers that refused to hide. We watched till she disappeared through the elbowed-open space between the outside doors, chill gusting in to fill the place she had been. *That could be me next.* Nobody spoke out loud, but you could hear the words. They hung in the air like drizzle. One girl just kept walking across the high beam, her eyes focused on the path ahead; the rest of us stayed where we were, listening. That could be me, the voices were saying. Any minute now, that could be me.

Next morning, it was. I woke up in a henna-coloured puddle and knew but said nothing, just went to wash. When I came out of the bathroom, mum was stripping sheets. She took a KitKat out of her dressing-gown pocket and handed it to me without speaking. I ate it, wishing I could think of something to say. Mum snapped open a fresh top sheet.

Do you know what this is? she asked. I nodded. Right, she said. As long as you know. She smoothed the top sheet flat without looking up. I'll get you stuff this afternoon at Corner Duncan's. See and come home sharpish. That said, she handed me three pairs of school-issue navy bloomers and a paper hanky.

On you go, she said. You're not sick.

But she saw me off at the door. Padded like a hockey player, I waved and felt tearful. I didn't feel good or clean or even defensible. I didn't feel right at all.

The front door was open when I came back at four, achy in places I couldn't pin down. Mum was waiting in the kitchen with a paper bag. She pulled out a cat's cradle of white elastic strips with hooks attached and a white mesh block and started plying them together. The pad attached, she shoved her arms through the holes on either side of the hammock pushing the belt round her elbows and paddled her arms to mimic legs.

See? she said. She paddled again. That's how you put it on.

Since she was mortified enough to be annoyed, I took the pieces she held out and didn't say thanks because it didn't seem to be a present. Right, she said. Off you go. She thrust the box of pads out for good measure and looked at me earnestly, ready to impart an important truth. Hide the packet under the cistern, OK? You don't leave things like that lying about. That's a rule.

OK, I said. I tried to look earnest.

Confident now, she said I should get into bed when I was done and she'd fetch me a drink. I didn't argue. Going to bed when she said herself I wasn't sick was confusing, but a drink in bed was a treat. I did what I was told, stripping out of my uniform, struggling into the stringy contraption she'd given me, and letting my nightie fall into place. She had chosen the orange brushed nylon sheets when I went back through. They sparkled with static and smelled fresh. I got hot Ribena, a handful of Jaffa Cakes, this week's *Bunty for Girls*, a leaflet and a couple of aspirin in foil as a reward for being co-operative. She looked relieved. There, she said. She pulled a loose thread off the valance and settled it back in place again.

All set. At least you don't have the bike any more. White saddle and everything.

I said nothing.

And don't go using the pads up all at once. It's me that pays for them. She stood, sighed in a way that suggested a job well done. Do you need anything?

I didn't, so she slipped back out to make Cora's tea.

Thanks, I said as she pulled the door behind her. Thanks were in order. This was special treatment. I clutched the *Bunty* like a good luck card, then sank back into the pillow to read. *The Four Marys* – one ugly, one bright, one beautiful and one sporty – were being harassed by posh identical twins. You knew the twins were posh because they said *utterly beastly* all the time. To the twins, everything and everybody was *utterly beastly* so at least their world was consistent. An important match-winning hockey stick had been broken and nobody knew how it had happened. Suspicion fell on the twins, of course, but there was no proof. The girls had to uncover their wickedness but didn't know how. *More next week.* My guts were starting to churn. I kept reading. *Wee Slavey* (*the Maid with the Heart of Gold*) was in trouble for a suspected theft of a candlestick and had to catch the true criminal all by herself to escape being taken away by the police. She got no credit because she shouldn't have been out of the servants' quarters at that time of night, so the cook said she had solved the mystery instead. Wee Slavey got more pots to wash and smiled through her tears.

The black and white drawings were starting to spangle. I had a bash at a story about an orphaned swimmer but it was no good. The stories seemed slight today, too ethereal to trust. They weren't real girls after all, just drawings. And, today at least, drawings to fool somebody younger than me. *Bunty* was cast aside for a crack at the leaflet. It was printed on shiny Izal-type paper with two line-drawings and dense-packed, spidery words. Periods went on for days, it seemed. A drawing of half a leg with some bulbous tubes like mushrooms at the top was supposed to show you why. The words said this was growing up and would happen every twenty-eight days from now on, regular as clockwork and probably for ever. I rubbed my eyes, rolled on the pillow and heard the door click, the rush of cold air that meant Cora was home from work.

Coo-ee, she said, perky. Out in her world, it had clearly been a good day. My mother's greeting was lost in a low burr of mumbles and I knew she was giving away my secrets. Right on cue, my sister called from the hallway.

Hoo, she said. Her voice was cheerful. The game's afoot! I imagined her rubbing her hands. Here comes trouble!

The TV button clanked and the sound came up, crackling. I heard the nylon lining of her coat shivering off her shoulders, the metallic scrape as she hung it in the hall cupboard and dusted herself down.

Welcome to the bloody club, she shouted. Then she laughed in her throat, thick and hearty. It's all fun and games from here, chum, you mark my words. It'll be boys next. Wait and see. You'll be chasing bloody boys.

What boys had to do with periods was beyond me. There hadn't been one mention of them in the leaflet and it should know. It was just Cora being a pig as usual. The dragging pain beneath my belly advanced as I curled into the covers, hiding. Already, my sister was passing remarks about the news headlines and yelling for her tea. I was in bed, it seemed, for the foreseeable.

I swallowed the aspirin still there on the bedside cabinet, coughing, then stared out of the window at Mr Gregg's pigeons till they started staring back. The McFarlanes' TV bellowed as they switched it on, then fell back to a low mutter. Ours was promising a bright weekend ahead as Cora switched channels, singing *Delilah* in a jokey voice, which probably meant Tom Jones was on later. Mum roared to ask if she wanted a fried egg. My coloured pencils were in the living room and Bunty's stupid face was grinning from the bottom of the bedspread. Annoyed, I kicked her off and pulled the covers over my head, sparking brushed-nylon shocks all the way down to my bones. Pigeons were crooning. Captain Birdseye was extolling the virtues of fish fingers. Avon called and Ariel with enzymes digested the stains other powders left behind. Mum shouted to ask if I wanted anything to eat yet but I didn't answer. I was holding my breath, refusing, point blank, to cry.

5

This is the Ardrossan Academy Orchestra. First to sixth year without fear or favour, all present save those of us who are not, and who is not is Howat. Orchestra leader or not, he was playing the piano somewhere. Slight and blond, Howat was going to play the piano for a living one day. He knew it and we knew it. It was not a choice, it was a calling. I stared at him tuning up from my lowly place in the back row of the second fiddles, star-struck as a nun. Easily within touching distance though I wouldn't have dared, Howat with his gold-blond hair and beautiful fingers meant there was more possibility in the world than commonly met the eye. He's not in the snap but our confidence in him is. Eager without being able to help it, we're possessed of something akin to hope. Whatever his background, Howat, merely by being Howat before our very eyes, was worth his weight in ivory inlays, for if he could do something astonishing and get away with it, we had permission to at least dream. Absent or not, you can see him on our faces. Look again. He is definitely, radiantly, *there.*

Head of Music, in cahoots with Head of PE, had cooked up a

scheme that made choir mandatory for any boy selected to represent the school in the rugby team. At least that was the rumour, and given the array of burly chaps who sang, we were inclined to think it true. The square-jawed rugby, badminton and athletic sorts are in the orchestra picture too, back row and wearing proper trousers for a change. Dead centre is the huge bloke who called me a moron first week, smiling and without his trombone. He did not remember me so bore no grudges. A third of the row wears glasses and two thirds are growing their hair over their blazer collars. Over six years of pictures, boys in this same back row will model mullets, perms, shoulder-flicks and shaggy-dog fringes, Elvis sideburns, mop-tops, tumbling flick-back curls and one full-blown afro. And beside them, a small core of red-eared short-back-and-sides lads who, at whatever cost to their chances of teen romance, remain above that kind of thing.

The next two rows, closer to camera, are the girls. Here they come, the elfin and prematurely matriarchal, the Mona Lisa studious and not-always-fully-conscious; the earnest, the prim and the full of nonsense, yet none of us, not even gorgeous Joy who looks like a Botticelli angel, wears make-up. Or not much and not at school. Girls with their legs akimbo around the hefty bodies of cellos are not allowed either, so the only instruments on show are violins and those holding them in the main are the pixies in knee-socks at the front. Everyone sports a stringy school tie by which we look willing to be led and some of us already have been.

Mr Hetherington, corduroy-clad Head of Music, has ear-tested every one of us and supplied an instrument to anybody who could hold a tune. Everyone should have a chance to make music, he said, and testing was mandatory for first year with a cupboard full of state-provisioned instruments to put belief into practice if anyone took him up on the offer. The cupboard was full of the glittery metal fixings of clarinets and saxophones, hole-reinforced oboes and pudding basin tympani. It had racks of stringed things housed in matt black coffins and trumpets and cornets with brass open mouths. Narnia be buggered: *this* was real enchantment. Handfuls of broken strings, dented tuning pegs, ancient rosin-sticky bridges lay where they'd been dropped, and loosely arranged in no particular order were the orchestra scores, straining at the spines with use. It was a place for the nervously yet terminally curious, a place to conceal and be concealed while you rummaged and rustled and found buried treasure. It was, at first sight, love.

My violin came like everybody else's in a compressed cardboard case with red velveteen lining, its wooden body light and shiny with newness. What a violin looked like up close was enthralling. The black-painted fingerboard ran down the neck and over the belly like a canopy, above which the strings, only four, were suspended from pegs to tailpiece down the entire length. In the middle, a complicated little wooden gate held the strings away from the wood giving them space to resonate and make the sound. It was clever and simple and every bit of it, including lessons, on the house. It was like winning the star prize on a TV quiz show: the car, petrol, road tax and breakdown cover in one package. Even mum, who had a genius for finding leaden linings, was impressed to the point of tears. She showed the violin to Cora who said *I'm not interested* even though her eyes lingered on the velvet interior of the case before she went to run a bath.

Nobody asked me if you could get that thing, she shouted through the door. Don't think just because you've got it now you're playing it when I'm at home. Some of us have real work. Stresses and strains. She turned the taps up fast so they squealed like piglets. I need a rest when I come home.

But she already knew I wouldn't. I didn't set a finger on the piano crushed against the back wall behind the sofa unless she was out. I knew the drill. She just liked to remind me she was listening behind every door even when she wasn't watching, a reminder I took as something like affection. Everything was on loan, everything temporary: I already knew.

You'll be playing all sorts one day, mum said, loud enough for Cora to hear. She'll not be so sure of herself then.

Before long, mum wasn't either. *Merrily We Roll Along* with plucked strings like a banjo was quiet but dull. Adding the bow not only cranked up the decibel level but added a cat-like yowling noise when you got it wrong. Tucking the fiddle under my neck was easy enough and holding the bow was fine. It was adding the fingering on top of all of the rest that made things turn nasty. The bow slipped, the sound came out rusty and the notes were flat, sharp or murdered. Mr Lyle, my teacher, put his own violin under his chin the way a chef tossed a pancake, without even looking.

Look, he said. He clamped his first finger firmly down on the E string and bowed. First finger on an E has to be F, right? He lifted and raised the finger playing E, F, E, F. It was all in tune. This – he put his second finger down less than an inch distant from the first – this has to be? He played a note as clean as the chime of a finger cymbal and waited. I knew what it was all right. In his hands, it was a G. That didn't mean that when I tried, which was where all this was leading, it would be anything of the sort. At best, I'd get any of the quarter tones buzzing around the Platonic Ideal of G: other times I'd produce a noise like a door in a horror film. After the piano, where the right key always turned up the right noise, the fiddle left no room for bluff. Approximation be damned: violins were beasts of precision or bust. My fingertips calloused and bled, my nails chipped, my neck hurt from tilting sideways and the chin brace hurt my shoulder, and though it did get better, it wasn't quickly. Cora didn't believe in mistakes: there were the talented and the damned. Mum believed in miracles and was hanging on till she got one. A couple of weeks, she said. I bet the penny drops.

That *knowing how* was not the same as *doing* escaped her. It escaped me too.

I don't think you've the aptitude, she said after a month. Do you think you're managing? She watched me stumble with unbearable, crestfallen eyes. When she dropped *My Fair Lady* on the music stand fully expecting I'd be able to roll it out like ticker tape; when she saw less than an A in my report card; when she caught me sneaking another biscuit without asking, those eyes appeared. I'd seen them at school sports days and the ends of raffles, during *University Challenge* when I couldn't guess the answer to a single question. Mum had faith in trying, but the trying alone was meant to produce results. Musicians didn't require to put in effort. They didn't make mistakes. Just as typewriters wrote books by themselves and poetry popped into the heads of poets fully formed, musicians just *knew how*, and the better they were, the truer it became. Mozart, Einstein, da Vinci and Dickens produced their work as though by spirit medium: error and effort were no part of the story. I was no prodigy and running out of childhood. It hit her hard.

We'll have the RSPCA at the door if you keep that up much longer, she'd shout from the kitchen. They'll think there's a dog tied up in here. Can you not get practice space at school?

The walls were thin and she had nowhere to hide. I didn't like the noise much myself. So I worked out a schedule: fiddle practice before anyone came back from work, piano when only mum was in, homework after five thirty when Cora was back from the train. This routine lasted my entire school career. Given whole days on study leave in fourth year, I played music, sang and made frames from cut lengths of dowelling before five thirty: anything quiet was for after six. This is still the case. Letters of complaint, letters to the press, letters of regret and condolence, essays, ink exercises, compositions and interpretations, forensic against-the-grain analyses or accounts, staggeringly dull diaries, Christmas cards, wish-lists and reading are night activities: anything noisy, including housework, listening to the radio, making jam and singing in the bath, takes place by day.

In the end, I never learned to love the violin, but I loved the orchestra, the sum of which was more than the scraping, honking or quacking of its separate parts. At the back of the second violins, and however cranky a cog I made, I had my place. I fit and cherished the fact, the feeling, the meaning of that. I'd been a non-starter as a Brownie and thrown out of Rosebuds and pre-fives tap. Now, even if it was basic, I had something to give. Because my hands were huge, Mr Lyle suggested I try the bigger, darker, less celebrated instrument that filled in the middle thirds of chords. Violins showed off at the top and cellos drove the whole thing forward from beneath. But violas – here he looked at me over the top of his glasses – were the secret ingredient within. Without violas, he said, the whole lot fell apart. Why did I think he played one? The viola, he said, was glue.

It was perfect. It fit my shoulder better and my fingers went where I meant them to without so much of a fight. The only thing that put me off was that the school photo had already been taken and I was holding a violin in the snap.

Your mother won't care what you're holding in the photo, Mr Lyle said. She'll enjoy the fact you're in it at all and holding *something*. Mothers do.

He was right. Instrument irrespective, my mother liked the

picture. It cocked a snook at Kitty saying classical music was daft anyway. It was a reward for all the scrapey practice she'd had to listen to and one in the eye for Aunty Rose because she thought she was *special* and this had nothing to do with her. It was mum's triumph, mum's trophy. They reproduced the picture in the local paper, faces peering as if through a smurr of spotty grey rain, and she showed the newsagent, the McFarlanes and the Greggs, whose rival tellies we heard from up the stairs, and the dinner-lady crowd at work. Oh yes, mum liked the photo. She liked it so much she bought a Co-op frame and put it on top of the piano where it scrutinised the TV repair man and anyone else who wandered through the living room, a banner of family success. Sometimes I'd catch her staring at it when she thought no one was looking, toying with content. Despite self-consciousness, I liked it too. I liked our monochrome assembly, the life-yet-to-live sheen. We are small components of a bigger machine and our keenness on the idea shows. Bright as buttons, green as spring, we're an orchestra.

Angus and Aunty Rose got the flat directly above ours. Mrs McFarlane died suddenly from heart failure and her husband, who was deaf and smiled all the time from some kind of shrapnel damage during the war, went into care. The Greggs, their neighbours on the other side, looked desolate.

He's just sixty-five, my mother said. You think he'd give it more of a go. Not just give up like that. The Greggs are older and they're fine.

The Greggs have got pigeons, Cora said. And they're still a pair.

I suppose, mum conceded. But you think.

No, I don't think, Cora said. She was painting her nails, stinking the living room with cellulose. He's never cooked in his life. He's not gonny start now. Most men his age are just the same.

Mum nodded and remarked that men were not resilient. If they didn't remarry, widowers lived on home baking from Rural Institute coffee mornings and stuff their neighbours brought round.

Wasny his fault, Cora said. It was her. She puckered her face into a mean impression of the deceased. *Oor Bob disny know how to boil an egg because I make sure he doesn't have to.* As if it was a feather in her cap. It was her that made him useless, silly bitch.

Shhh, my mother said. She was a nice woman. Gentle. You think everybody's a silly bitch except you.

And you think everybody's *nice*. Cora screwed the top back on the tiny bottle and fluttered her extremities. Every mug going is *nice* according to you. You'd have ended up looking after him the way you looked after that old pig through the wall till he died of cheap whisky. Washing his sheets, godsake. You're a doormat, you.

Somebody had to, my mother snapped. The way somebody looks after you, you lazy bugger.

He was an old pig, Cora said. Anyway, good luck to him up the stairs wherever he's away to. He's all right. Just creepy.

His name is Mr McFarlane.

Whatever. No harm to him but I'm glad he's away. Men don't cut it on their own.

Mum didn't deny it. Mr McFarlane packed up and left overnight being no trouble to anybody, which made him *a gentleman* in her book. Someone came to pick up the armchairs and a few bits and pieces but that was it. Angus and Rose applied before the flat was officially empty and were in by summer, bringing the sewing machine, their fancy cotton-trim towels and Angus's car. The little green Hillman had coughed its last and been replaced by a little green Cortina and Angus finally had a garage to house it. The Greggs were relieved. Rose and Angus were uncomplaining sorts so the pigeon loft was safe.

I can take you out for a run any time you fancy, Angus said, not just weekends.

They'd been taking me on countryside trips for half my life and the offer to do it more on request was genuine. Angus and Rose were gentle people who meant what they said. They didn't even tease without telling you first. That Cora called Rose *an irritating big sap* and laughed at Angus because he bought Rose a Valentine every year made me like them better. I appreciated the offer of the lifts but wasn't sure I'd take him up on it often. Once a week was plenty. Besides, their childlessness scared me. Something about being with them made me feel on loan. Rose, who never had any idea what I thought and was an optimist by choice, hoped moving so close would be *a fresh start*.

Me and your mum have had differences in the past, she said.

But your dad's a long time gone now. We're here if we're needed. You could watch *Top of the Pops* at our house, she said. She made an odd jitterbug motion with her shoulders. That would be *groovy*.

Mmm, I said. But even that much enthusiasm was a lie. *Top of the Pops* was one of the few things we watched as a family for pleasure, not just because it was the only thing on. Mum, who cheered up at the very sight of Mick Jagger, knew all the words to *Jumping Jack Flash* while Rose thought Rolf Harris qualified as *cool*. Angus was more of a singer of Sunday School songs he'd learned as a boy, which made his taste distinctive and consistent. Rose was tone deaf and anything she sang sounded like a dirge. The idea of sitting through chart pop with them held no allure. I enjoyed them for other things. Rose made clothes and taught me how to use a treadle so I could do the same. She bought McCall's patterns and cut out recipes from *Woman's Own* to keep in a box on her kitchen shelf. She made adventurous things to eat, including a speciality with tinned tomato soup, cabbage, onions, mushrooms, mince and an Oxo cube she called *bolognese sauce*, which she served with spaghetti that, unlike the Heinz kind, required to be boiled from hard to soft. I'd seen her shopping for that kind of spaghetti in the supermarket. It looked like bunches of skinny kindling. Their other indulgence was Tropical Fruit Cocktail, which was much like the usual pears and peach slices but with pineapple, cherries, grapes and slices of brown bendy banana from the Caribbean thrown in. Mum tried chisel-tips of sweetcorn picked by a Jolly Green Giant and a box containing three packets of powder which Vesta, goddess of the Hearth, had ill-advisedly put her name to. The packets, when mixed with water, made a slobbery mess that was nothing like the Chinese food we could buy from the real Chinese restaurant that had opened at the corner of Dockhead Street, but we ate it all the same, choosing to classify it as *luxury* and therefore an acquired taste. If it tasted bad, we'd acclimatise. An appearance of upward mobility depended on it. By some means or other, exotica was arriving in Saltcoats and we wanted a taste. False eyelashes sat like hairy insects in perspex boxes in Woolworths and glitter in gluey tubes enabled our home-made Christmas cards to shine. Before long, we moved up in the world in a way we'd never have imagined. We acquired a refrigerator.

It came in a Co-op van and was up and running in an hour. We knew it kept ice-cream from melting and cold meats cold but had not expected the bonus of entertainment. Hours were spent opening and shutting the freezer compartment to see if the ice-cubes were ready, then puzzling how to foist them out of the frozen-stiff metal tray. Cora bought a bottle of Martini and showed off with an iced drink at her elbow, watching Rod Laver at Wimbledon. A child brought up on state-provisioned luke-warm milk every school break, I found ice-cubes made drinks taste of nothing, but Wimbledon called for the touch of style they gave instead.

Wimbledon was Cora's once-a-year sports fixture. She enjoyed watching the gladiatorial chess-play of it all, its dogged pursuit of slow, ritual kill. Her two-week break from work was for the purpose of watching Wimbledon on the small screen burning smoke from three packs of mentholated filter tips in tribute to heroes of lobs, smashes and volleys. Tennis, like much of the rest of the world, was male. Women strolling onto court were switched off if they weren't Billy-Jean King because *women were only bit players*. Billy-Jean was the exception that proved the rule. Cora's heroes moved through Laver, Ashe and Connors to Dacian-eyed Ilya Nastase as their shorts grew skimpier over the years. Borg was possessed of cool Scandinavian calm but Cora preferred McEnroe's temper. Mum never got to grips with the scoring but watched anyway, complaining when the crowd took to cheering after years of cucumber-sandwich-strength applause. If British reserve crumbled in favour of selfish shows of emotion, who would we become? *Americans*, Cora said. *Better.*

When I fell in love with Martina Navratilova because she was young, dissident and didn't look like Barbie, my sister asserted that Martina was good but only because she was *manly*. Heterosexual women were genetically engineered to come second. Martina being allowed to stay on our TV, however, was a domestic landmark for which I was grateful. Wimbledon was an arena for debate and philosophy; that fortnight was our holiday in the sun. We watched eating ice-cream even if it poured outside, with the feeling of being, at least superficially and for as long as it lasted, enthralled together. The day after the winners went home trailing glory, Cora went back to work with fags that tasted of sailors, nautical rope and tar to a Corinthian-pillared

Victorian building in Nile Street in the heart of Glasgow. Atlas himself held the weight of the building she worked in. Her boss had double cuffs and went to Portugal twice a year to play golf. Away from home, Cora clapped eyes on people who aspired to things we hadn't grasped were aspirations in the first place, and her irritation, never far off simmer, was growing. But she did not move out. She did not move away. She came home every night to her supper on a plate and an open fire as she had for ten years now since her Great Escape. Glasgow itself was too small if the husband and cast-off son were in it somewhere. Mum's idea when she'd taken her eldest in was that the arrangement was temporary. After ten years during which mum had gone through the menopause and I had gone from toddler to teen, her patience was wearing thin.

You're thirty, she said. She said it umpteen times a week, usually serving food. Age, food and care seemed irredeemably connected in my mother's head. I'm too old for this. She served the plate with a tea-towel in case it was hot.

Cora, released from her corset and in her stockinged feet, did not look up. She put her hand out for cutlery.

All I'm saying is it's time you got a grip. You need to find somebody and settle down properly.

She handed over the salt and waited till Cora was adequately seasoned, then took the shaker back through to the kitchen, all the while carrying on with her speech, the words accommodating the fade and rise of the laws of physics as she came and went.

You're far too cosy here, that's the trouble. It's time you sobered up. You're no spring chicken so get a bloody move on.

Cora poked at her food with the tines as though it might be contaminated, unearthing the best bits.

I'm just the housekeeper as far as you're concerned, mum said. Well, if you think I'm fetching and carrying for you the rest of your natural, you've got another think coming. You hear me? It's time you showed a bit of respect, got a man of your own and headed into the sunset.

Nothing.

You hear me? D'you not even want your own place for crying out loud? Do you listen to a word I say?

Cora's usual response was to push her plate aside, reach for the fags, raise one elegant eyebrow and sigh. More irritating than a simple *No*, it helped her save face. My sister cared very much that she came across as aloof and independent, unbreakable. If showing a bit of respect meant running a house of her own, mum could whistle. Sometimes, she'd turn up the volume on the TV to drown out what she did not want to hear. Other times, she'd nod across at me.

I pay keep money. That one doesn't. Chuck her out for Godsake, not me.

Once or twice she thundered off to her bedroom to play pop music loud, shouting *nobody's listening* from behind her closed door, but that was as far as it went these days. Mum's sniping didn't provoke her to throwing punches the way it once had. These days, as if she was tired, she chose to sit things out. Cora the bad, the bold, the dangerous to know, no longer went dancing. If she was rethinking how to live her life, she did not let us in on it. Maybe the offers had stopped coming. Who knew? Family, marriage, career advancement, money, booze, men, a good laugh – my sister's hopes and dreams were anybody's guess.

You know what you'll end up with? my mother said, driven beyond endurance. Damn all. Nobody will look after you when I'm gone. Not a soul.

Cora barely blinked. She sat in the corner, hunched and resistant, exactly like a picture of a soldier in the trenches from the *Children's Compendia*. The soldier, a heavy blanket round his shoulders, was lighting a fag with one hand and shielding the flame with the other as if it was the most important thing in the world, while round his feet a dead horse, two lacerated men and a pile of shovels sat ignored. Maybe Cora was just battle-weary. She was taking a rest. A long rest. As soon as you worked out one theory to explain my sister, orneriness or instinct kicked in to prove it wrong. A bare week later, hints of a *new friend* were scattered lightly on the evening air during the ad breaks. Cora had no women friends, not one, so *new friend* meant only one thing. The word boyfriend, however, was one she avoided. She was toying with mum, cat and mouse spiteful: mum could think what she liked. It was *nobody's ruddy business* came over loud and clear.

The friend was no nearer having a name or a face when Rose and Angus invited us up for New Year. Mum wouldn't go. Every year, she laid out shortbread fingers, sultana cake and ginger wine in case anyone arrived at the door but in general nobody did and the token spread would go under a covered dish in the pantry by quarter to one. This year Cora, *friend* or not, stayed in as well. We watched the bells and midnight cheering on a pre-recorded broadcast from a studio that might have been anywhere before I went upstairs to bring the year in with Rose and Angus. I recall Rose was murdering *Rowan Tree* and Angus doing his song about phantoms in the West End Park and eating a whole jar of cocktail cherries. I remember Cora coming up with a bottle of Johnnie Walker and cans of ginger ale, complaining that mum had gone to bed. I remember Rose mixing a Snowball – advocaat and lemonade stirred briskly till frothy – and Cora handing me what she called ginger ale thereafter. I am told I sang *Danny Boy*. After that, there is only carpet. The texture under my cheek and the hemp smell of carpet.

Next day at three o'clock in the afternoon I was in Rose's spare room throwing up down to the bile. Cora had been spiking my ginger ale, probably with the whisky she had brought upstairs. Rose had worked it out after Cora had excused herself and gone back to her own bed downstairs.

It was days before I could keep anything down and mum was wild. Cora, in tears, packed a vanity bag and left, saying she wasn't coming back because nobody ever took her side. She was just teaching me a lesson about alcohol, which was an entirely responsible thing to do. You're all horrible to me, she roared, banging the door so the frame shook. We heard her crying through the sound of sling-backs clacking into the distance.

You need a warmer coat, you silly article, mum shouted out of the window. It's January.

Cora didn't reply. Mum looked at me with my grey New Year face, stricken. She needs a warmer coat. Where in God's name is she away to without a decent coat?

By the time she found one and hared outside, Cora was gone. No track, no trace. We went out the same night, calling as if for a lost cat. Nothing. Two nights later, she was back with her face puffy, refusing to say where she'd been. *I've got work on Monday or I wouldn't be back at all.* It was the only clarification anyone was getting. Eventually, mum decided Cora must have run to her *friend*, whoever he was, then either slunk home bored or he'd thrown her out. Cora stayed in three Saturdays in a row, then mum asked out loud.

None of your business, Cora said. She knitted several rows looking purposefully blank. Mum looked at me and shrugged. She was giving up. Aware she had shaken pursuit, Cora turned her needles and smoothed the fabric she had woven straight. Bloody cheek.

It must have been at least fifteen minutes and the next ad break before anyone spoke again. It was Cora. Anyway, she said. We turned to see her taking a long, slow draw, the tip of her cigarette volcanic. Her eyes were flat. His loss.

I almost gasped with shock. She meant he'd dumped her. Cora's man friend, the one she'd hidden away to keep him safe, had sent her packing. A sudden rush of heart-soreness welled up in my chest, then died back to irritation. It was none of my business. Why she had dosed me with Mickey Finns then stormed off in the first place was none of my business either. Nothing was my business and nothing in our house was ever explained. She was back, that was all. We were three again, hashing on. I looked at her hard, trying to work out what I felt about this woman who was my sister, curious to see if the blood tie might be something, for once, felt. A fine tracery of lines at her temples, the seamless pale fabric that fell from her amber-tipped fingers, the odd fleck of grey near the temples in that black, black hair. Last stitch, turn. She held the fabric to the lamp, checked the tension was even, her spacing neat. It was never anything else. Cora's knitting, every stitch, was tight-reined and perfectly controlled. Meticulous, she wound the stitch counter on by one more space and dug in her needles for another row.

Jimmy Gilmour threw snowballs at me outside the dinner block and I dodged them all. Ooh, he said. I had no idea you were so *lithe.* He said it in such a way I forgot to dodge the next one and George Crawford got me in the neck with a chunk of compacted ice. It hurt but I didn't care. I was *lithe.* Michael McCartney and his horrible pal lured girls into the more-or-less empty bike sheds to see an air pistol one of them had sneaked into school. The horrible pal tried to make me scared then shot me in the leg to hear me squeal. Not squealing was easy. All it did was break a round, grey-rimmed puncture on the side of my knee like a tiny target. *I think your gun's bust, sonny*, I said, trying to look like Pussy Galore, then limped off to class, bleeding.

Maybe I should have been flattered. If boys hit and chased you, it was a sure sign they were trying to impress, according to a magazine called *Jackie*. *Jackie*, produced by the same Dundee powerhouse that turned out *Bimbo*, *Beano*, *Hotspur*, *Bunty* and *Warlord*, was entirely dedicated to hormonally altered teenage girls. Where *Bunty* advanced pre-teen love of scrapes, docility and pluck, *Jackie* traded on self-consciousness: fashion, make-up, hairstyles and the general wish to alter appearance, picture-stories of girls with sooty lashes surviving flirtations with boys, and *Cathy and Claire* – a problem page for those most in need of tips about life, sex, love, underarm hair and spots. *Cathy and Claire* were particularly keen to reassure that boys were, when you got to know them, *just like you and me*. I trusted none of it, but couldn't put it down. Information was information: make-up tips to recipes for peppermint cremes and sultry lips, I read the lot. The pin-up pictures of male starlets confused me a bit but they had one big advantage over real boys: they smiled back. Harmless, twinkly, pretty as girls, they looked nothing like boys at school who shot you in the leg with airguns or pelted you with snowballs. They looked textbook *normal*, which is to say not normal one bit.

The girls in *Jackie* looked nothing like real girls either. Every last one of them had upturned noses, cupid-bow mouths and starlet hair. Most of all, what they had were liquid eyes. Their bodies, after such luxuriance, were skinny disappointments. Thin-hipped and underfed, they looked more like Bambi than people. The secret, according to *Jackie,* was eyeliner, mascara and a decent hairbrush. The one that mattered most was mascara. I knew make-up was available for purchase but I hadn't the nerve. Not yet. But I knew where Cora's lived. Engineering the excuse of going to find wallpaper to draw on, I sneaked in for a look.

Cora's room was lime and floral, each citrus petal the size of a splayed hand, turning the already small space into a Triffid House. The blinds were down and the air smelled of her. Trying to make good my alibi, I opened the cupboard and reached inside for the offcuts first. They weren't there. I opened wider to scan the padded hangers, the top shelf of book-club books, the brown tile floor. Everything had been moved or changed. Cora's buff-coloured stick-out petticoat, usually the first thing that poked you in the eye when you looked inside, didn't. It wasn't there. The end of rail space where Cora's satin-effect, dirndl-skirted, boned-bosomed dresses had been kept like precious artifacts was a bigger shock. The frocks, the most glamorous frocks in the world when I was a child, were gone. In their place hung shifts, sleeveless high-neck Jackie O shapes in muted navies and greens with matching boleros. Each bolero sported a brooch: a guitar, a rhinestone poodle on a green enamel lead, an arrow piercing a fat red heart. The smell of glue and pollen – roll-on deodorant, most probably – rippled from them in faintly repugnant lines. Beneath were some shoes I didn't recognise, still Cora's pointy-toed style but kitten-heeled, lower. Only one familiar pair – the diamanté sling-backs I thought were genuine Cinderella slippers when I was five – remained; tucked at the back and scuffed. All the rest –

the dagger-tips and knife-points with buckles and bright plastic flowers – were gone. Everything good was gone. My eyes filled up so suddenly I had to kneel on the floor near her fake astrakhan wrap for comfort.

What was missing was more than dresses. It was what I kept in my head as *my sister.* The dresses had meant Cora in a good mood, heading out in the world all brass neck and bottle and not giving a damn. I loved the way she had looked wearing them, the surprising softness of satin beneath the starched-stiff rayon collars. I loved their in-and-out zip-up shapeliness, the way they wrapped her curves in their bold, emphatic, touch-me show. What I realised, looking up at their dull replacements, was that the days of the frocks were over and done. This in turn meant two things: 1) I must have believed the look-at-me Cora would never change and 2) I had entertained the audacious fantasy that the dresses, the times I'd sat at her feet and watched her dolling up, the arts of drag and snappy camouflage were as precious to her as to me. I realised I'd been hoping my sister would one day take me by the hand, open the cupboard wide and say *Choose. No, really – I'd like you to have one. Go on, take your pick.* And when I did, she'd zip me up, show me how to apply make-up and I'd see on her face how transformed I could be with the help of a guiding hand. I thought she'd say *Some kid, eh?* smiling that big, wide smile she gave good-looking boys working coffee machines, the smile she'd given me when she saw my face unwrapping the Mickey Mouse she'd bought me for Christmas when I was five. *Some kid!* I was wrong. With a scale-dropping puff of whatever the opposite of magic dust was, the very idea that Cora would give me a dress or be proud of me looked vain. Something only a child might think. Giving her stuff to me had never entered her head. She'd just needed the space and chucked them out, no second thoughts. And the frocks, the Cora who wore them, the me who adored her in them had been chucked out at the same time. Feeling thick, I closed the door again and drifted to the dresser where I found what I suspected. Her make-up had been overhauled too.

In place of the industrial-strength pan-stick was a nothing-coloured compact with a caked-flat puff inside. It didn't promise to veil her skin in *American Tan* or *Touch of Gold*. It had no name at all, just *Beige No* 2. The lipsticks, *Peach Blancmange* and *Pale Petal*, looked bland. Beside them, a thin plastic tube, the lid of which lifted to reveal a long, thin screw-shaped stick, was her sole mascara. She'd given up the little green spit-and-scrub box for a bottle-brush coated in drippy black gunk. I couldn't see how it was used without making a mess and put it away again, nonplussed. All that remained of her former kit was the bleeding stump of an old favourite, top missing and drying out. *Fire Engine Red*'s days were over. What came in its place was tame. Safe, sober, *tame*. I could have wept.

In my head, Cora was tanned with emerald eyelids, her hair and eyelashes the kind of black that demanded the adjective *jet*. In my head, her nails and mouth were blood-orange, her ears pierced by fat silver gypsy-hoops. Now, while no one was paying attention, Cora had picked another self off the rack, someone more low-key and probably more devious. And thirty. Cora, my sister, was into her fourth decade. It was a startling thought.

I lifted *Peach Blancmange* and extended the bolt of colour using a little plastic slider on the side of the case. Carefully, so as not to break the soft wax barrel, I coated my lips, then stepped back to check my reflection. My lips looked the colour of a tropical disease. Yellow-ochre, palate-knife thick and bursting over the lines where the colouring-in was meant to stop. Inside my pink cheeks and round face, the mouth gave the impression of being slathered with custard. Horrified, I wiped the colour off on the approximate area of my mouth with the back of my hand and put the lipstick back where it belonged. This was my sister's room and I better remember it. It was not mine and never would be. Quickly, I put things back to rights and headed for the bathroom and washed my hands and face, then made for the coal-shed. I could think in the coal-shed. It was the one place to hide. There were only two bedrooms in our flat and one was Cora's. Mum didn't have one to herself. She shared with me: a double bed, a wardrobe, the chest of drawers with my school stuff under the bed. Mum didn't have anything private. I didn't have anything private. Things couldn't stay that way for ever. One of us was going to get too big for her wardrobe space, her drawer space, her boots. Sitting in the coal-shed I understood for the first time that someone, not all that long from now, would have to give. The house was my mother's. It couldn't be mum. Then Cora gave ground to nothing. The picture of the soldier under the blanket popped into my head again, roll-up nipped between his fingertips, standing firm in the midst of chaos. What my sister was doing, clearing space and adopting decoy clothing, was entrenching. She was digging in against siege. And the thing she was entrenching against, the one who'd have to cede and sooner rather than later, was me.

We stayed up for the moon-landings, of course. Long after my mother and sister went to bed, I stayed up watching men in white diver suits bounding on the distant surface of our cold, dead satellite and cosied into the sofa as the fire fell to embers. The moon between the curtains looked no different. It wasn't. Nothing lived on it. No aliens, no cheese, no dead dogs from exploratory flights with no rescue plan. I hoped the astronauts would find something other than rock, but rock was fine, on balance. I fell asleep on the settee, reassured that whatever happened, the astronauts had at least chosen to be there. They were, most probably, safe.

The rest of summer was walking on the shore front and the odd saunter around Saltcoats Museum trying to care about a pickled baby octopus in a bottle, and a model of a clipper, photos, maps, the smell of dust. Saltcoats Museum had been a church and the cemetery remained. The weeping angels that watched over the posher plots had been pulled down recently in some kind of public safety operation, and the less stable headstones laid prone on the grass which made them easier to read. *William McColl died of typhus aged two years* was still there. *His sister, Margaret, aged eight months.* In the whole graveyard, no one occupied a space alone. Maybe it was a space-saving thing, and the singles had been popped in together for company. Maybe being single disqualified you for church burial and the loners had been melted down with quicklime in a council tip somewhere. Whatever it was they did, the solitaries weren't here. It depressed me even thinking about it. I was missing school, and playing half a tennis game against the wall at the end of the road was no help. Playing the viola didn't help. Downhearted, I flipped the orchestra photo face down on the top of the piano so they wouldn't hear me sawing at my scales. Mum put it up the right way. I put it face down again and she complained I was being annoying and Cora belted me round the head. Briefly, it was Old Times. I flipped the picture on its face next day out of sheer forgetfulness and the same thing happened. Pavlov, I thought. Pavlov, bitches and the ringing of bells. Next time I turned the picture down it was deliberate play-acting forgetful. Pissed off, Cora threatened me with a cigarette burn, flicking ash onto the back of my hand as a warning and I saw the possibilities. Cora hated the orchestra picture but had been conditioned into keeping it prominent: every time I turned it face-down, she put it back. All I had to do was pretend I'd learned my lesson and alter the angle of the picture. It was spiteful, devious and easy. I left the photo alone but tilted it outward, just enough so the sun would strike off the glass when it reached the right place in the sky and bounce the glare into her corner of the room, straight for Cora's armchair as she settled in. It would be fleeting, certainly, hit and miss, but that was part of the beauty of the concept: something small and unpredictable nipping at her eyes while she watched TV or tried to decode a fair-isle pattern. And as she flicked her head or rearranged her chair to be rid of the irritation, I'd know what it was. It would be the orchestra with me in the front row with the other gnomes, safe under glass. I was patient when the mood took me. Tenacious. When the mood took me, I was glue.

6

Uncle Angus had naked women in the garage.

Rose sent me in with a black pudding roll on a plate and four of them, from the waist up, were staring into the middle distance from the nearside wall. Bits had been airbrushed out and they were salmon pink all over. Like balloon animals. I left the plate for him to find and steered clear of the garage for weeks wondering if Aunty Rose knew. I didn't want to be the only one with this knowledge. If she *did* know, on the other hand, it would mean she was in some kind of it's-OK-to-have-naked-women collusion and I didn't want to think that either. Bowls of school blancmange pulsated in my dreams, my grandmother's blind eye rolling out of its matchbox to stare at me. The thought of mum or Cora seeing what I had seen was so embarrassing I had nightmares of my clothes melting like candle wax as I crossed the playground or waited for a bus. Nakedness – even allusion to nakedness – was taboo. In our house, the subject was not closed, it didn't exist. And to keep things that way, my mother kept the TV under hair-trigger surveillance.

Kissing, touching of anything other than hands, James Bond,

The Avengers, Catwoman's tight leather catsuit and whip, *Play for Today* and lions sniffing lionesses' bottoms rendered our TV lifeless in seconds. Animals in general were untrustworthy subjects. Primates, unless bowler-hatted and advertising cups of tea between shifting pianos, were given no air-time at all. Baboons, with flagrant red love-hearts where their backsides ought to be, were not allowed past opening credits. If lambs were delightful, rams and the enormous pink shopping bags that trailed behind them were not. Horses, dogs and anything purporting to be a nature programme were suspect. Should the worst happen and the flurry for the off-switch result in sudden loss of picture, asking why, what for or complaining was *cheek*. Adverts, discussions and Tom Jones bypassed mum's strict decency parameters on the grounds of being *entertainment* and jokes, by and large, survived so long as they steered away from the deeper shades of blue. Jokes, after all, were necessary survival tools. Everyone knew that. If life was not a comedy it was a tragedy and the former outlook was to be preferred. Violence, while not exactly welcome, went unremarked. Violence was not shameful, it was unavoidable. Sex, on the other hand – like debt, fear, love and haemorrhoids – was best kept dark.

That Cora, the dancing queen and all-round lover of good times, also drew the line at *smut* I put down to the fact she'd been born at the start of the war. Maybe it was other things, who knew? Nobody was going to ask. If *that kind of thing* had its place – and it was by no means certain it did – that place was not on our TV. Every so often, she'd raise an eyebrow at the screen and *tut*, flicking ash off the top of her current fag like Princess Margaret at a cocktail party. Clearly, one expected better of the BBC. Cartoons, comics and school, however, were dependably sex-free zones. Desperate Dan might make the occasional reference to a sweetheart, but Cow Pie was his real passion and Tom gave Jerry a hug only at Christmas or, more questionably, when drunk. Most dependable of all were the ivory towers of Ardrossan. At the Academy we learned to Strip the Willow with other eightsome reels as backup, not hug-happy waltzes. All touch between the sexes was formal or resented; physical touch by a teacher most often punitive. Then word arrived as we packed up after Cookery on Thursday afternoon that something sexy had happened in Physics.

The messenger, a slip of a thing called Claire not given to exaggeration, pointed at the strip-light over our heads. The labs were on the other side, upstairs. It was possible something rude was going on right now as we dusted the flour from our hands and stared. The scones we'd been making turned pale as we wrapped them in warmed tea-towels, ready for the off. As soon as the bell sounded, we hared upstairs and found the other half of our practical group, milling, smelling faintly of sulphur, and keen to confess. Everything we'd heard and more was true. They'd had something called *sex education.* Susan Battle, a red-faced soul with strict-observance parents, stumped off down the stairs and spoke to no one. She looked harmed. Everybody pretended not to see. The netball centre-forward, a more robust girl altogether, spelled things out. After one period of *bona fide*

Physics, the textbooks had been collected, the lights dimmed and, to the accompaniment of an ancient wall chart and a pointer, they'd been given what she called a thirty-minute talk. Her neck changed colour when she said it. Babies, she said. *You know.*

I didn't but I kept *schtum.* Aileen Wilson, a curly readhead with outraged specs, hugged her schoolbag like a teddy bear.

They can't do that, though. They can't just *give* you sex instead of proper lessons. They have to ask permission. Aileen wanted to be a lawyer. Your parents have to be canvassed and if they don't sign their express permission, you don't have to go. It's a fact. Nobody spoke. Aileen's scattering of freckles turned pale. So I'm not doing it, she said. They can't make me.

The rest of us looked at her suspecting they probably could. Even if it was questionable, we weren't all as lippy as Aileen. Even now, however, the worst had not been revealed. Not only had the sex talk actually happened, it had been given by Miss Thomson, the regular Physics teacher. Miss Thomson, whose Tyrolean jumpers and ear-muff hairdo made us squeal with hilarity; whose demonstrations of mass, motion and gravity never demonstrated anything of the sort; who lost the thread and told long rambling stories about the beauties of Elgin instead, was who the school had chosen to impart the mysteries of human sexuality to Class 2Bii. It was jaw-slackening. The bell rang anyway and we lined up with chain-gang resignation outside room 306, Aileen included. If even the lawyer had lost her nerve, no one was calling the police. A final piece of advice came from

Jan Harris, a crop-headed ragbag of nerves, who called as she left that Miss Thomson had said a fanny's real name was a *regina*, which only went to show how little attention Jan paid in Latin. The smell of scone dough and burnt raisins from my bag was no comfort. Not now. The bunch that had come out looking more bruised than sexually literate had served their sentence. It was us next.

Actually, it wasn't. Instead we got a student teacher who gave us a load of notes on currents and voltage and no explanation for Dora's absence. The rest was silence. Practical group IIA (A-M) seemed to slip the leash of sex education altogether and I ended S2 as informed about my reproductive system as the average Bash Street Kid. Maybe it had been a pilot scheme with section IIB only the guinea pigs. Maybe Dora, having given it her best shot, had opted out and no one else took over. Maybe a lot of things: it just didn't happen. By the end of my third year, it was all a bit stable-door in any case. I doubt Dora's version of sex would have helped. Meantime, I gave Angus's garage a wide berth and crossed my fingers the subject was closed. It wasn't. I was bowling down the last inch of the hallway when I heard my mother's voice, low and soft on the other side of the living-room door. Even over the TV every word came clear.

You'll not believe what Angus has got in that shed.

My back stiffening, I waited at the door to listen.

They're in there with the car. It's not even a calendar. Just pictures. The more her voice fell, the more cleanly she articulated the syllables. *They've nothing on.*

Cora snorted and made a tssk noise.

You can see them through the side window when you're doing the dishes so he's not even tried to hide them. You can't *not* see them is all I'm saying.

God almighty, Cora sighed. And him – what age is he?

Fifty-eight, my mother said. I could hear mumbling numbers under her breath, counting on her fingers. Sixty. Anyway, too old for that kind of thing.

Well, it just goes to show, Cora said. Dirty pig.

It's not as if he's tall, my mother said.

Five three, Cora said. That's how she canny wear heels. She's at least five nine.

She was Rose. The height discrepancy had long been one of my sister's favourite snipes. Angus stood two steps higher than his bride in the church porch for their wedding snaps and Rose had worn flat silver sandals. There was a silence while they mulled over the numbers. Then a spluttering sound, like a car using too much choke on a cold day. It was Cora, snorting, trying not to laugh and failing.

Ssshh, mum said. It's not funny. There's nothing funny about it.

There is so, Cora said. Him five three and the Loch Ness Bloody Monster. She gurgled out loud. Imagine that at night eh? Him and her. You wonder how they manage. She laughed out loud.

My mother tutted, then gave in. The two of them sniggered like girls with a dirty drawing.

Imagine! Cora said. Hahaha.

That was enough. Whatever they were imagining, I didn't want to know. I took a step sideways hoping to escape into the kitchen but Cora called out between bouts of what was by now helpless guttering.

She's out there, Cora said, catching her breath. That takes the biscuit. It's been listening.

Who? mum said.

Creeping Jesus, Cora gasped. Who do you think? I can see her reflection in the telly.

It was true. I turned and there was the evidence, a slice of my skirt and legs sheeny on the dark grey screen. Worse, I could see Cora's face, cambered in the corner, looking back. She was wiping her eyes.

Look, she said, helpless. There she is. Hahaha.

Before mum got up and saw me too, I pulled the catch on the outside door and ran. Cora bobbed at the window as I belted past, waving. I was the joke now, running from nothing while my sister pantomimed behind the pane. Seagulls startled as I picked up speed, parting like the sea as I approached. I kept running.

The swings near the shore front were empty. Past tea-time, they usually were. Nobody was walking a dog. I sat on the flat plastic slats on the nearest one and held the chains that fell on either side, kicking to keep the rocking steady and sulking. It was *unfair.* Everything was *unfair.* And embarrassing. Like sea-monsters, naked bodies had surfaced from the deep and risen, waving their ghastly extremities, into clear sight. I hated the sleazy, secret jokes and the guttural laughter that came with them. I was furious with Rose for packing me off to the garage with sandwiches in the first place; furious with Angus for sticking his airbrushed tarts up in the shed without wondering once who else would find them; furious at mum because she'd acted like Cora and not only been dirty-minded but *sided with her* about such a thing and left me out entirely. And I was furious at the world in general because ageing and the whole puberty shebang that went with it had been built into the contract from the word go and nobody had told me it was coming. Worse, I was afraid of what came next. Of losing who I'd been to become someone else, someone who thought sex and every filthy thing associated with it was *normal*, which was followed in rapid succession by false-teeth, being thirty, being old and dying. I was not furious with Cora because there was no point. Cora with her hidden razors and talent for casual cruelty and her private bedroom didn't care what you thought and that was how she got by. She thumped you when you annoyed her then carried on regardless. And when you got down to it, at least on this occasion, she was right. This wasn't anybody's fault. It was nothing personal. Which meant that what I was genuinely and hopelessly furious with was me. If life was unfair that's what it was, and I better get used to it. Blood and growing pains, bumps and bulges and dark, dank cavities were part of the package of being here at all. I thought about *William McColl died of typhus aged two years*, Granny McBride, dad, several next-door neighbours, pet goldfish and my big brother who had never been more than a very small brother indeed because he didn't last beyond a few hours. It was all beyond control. Whoever we thought we were, we were all one and the same. We were all of us just *bodies*. From the safety of the swings, I held up my hand and looked at the coming sunset through five spread fingers. They were rimmed with red. Sinews showed when I flexed my wrist, a single blue artery, blinking. I stayed out late while seagulls hovered over something that wasn't hiding well enough beneath the water. In all probability something edible. They mewed and circled, their eyes on the prize.

I joined every school choir on offer. Hormones could do their worst but my voice, at least, was not about to break. My diaphragm, lungs and vocal chords were still on my side and I planned to use them every chance I got. Singing was a McBride thing. My mother sang all the time: dusting and chopping vegetables, cleaning the grate, washing the windows, digging up dandelions and scouring, as rhythmic activities, could be performed to Beatles tunes, ballads or sentimental Scottish airs without even trying, and putting the radio on introduced an orchestra or at least a couple of guitars and a drum kit to offer moral as well as musical support. Words she didn't know, she made up, adding fresh rhymes to suit. I sang so much when I was small my Granny McBride called me *Jolson*. All kinds of singing –

well, all except jazz – were ours to engage with: Welsh and Russian male-voice choirs to Bulgarian women's throat-singing, Victorian hymns to Handel oratorios, barbershop, gospel, rock 'n' roll and Christmas carols; opera and bluegrass, folk song and country, laments and nursery rhymes and *gondolieri* barcarolles. We liked cajun music, boy sopranos, torch singers and Gaelic choirs: all they had to do was sing without fear. For the sake of the company and the chance to learn more kinds of singing than I'd known before, I joined whatever the music department provided. We had lots of Kodály and Bartók and Benjamin Britten, Bach, contemporary crunchy stuff and Edwardian church textures – music full of spark and bite like nothing I'd heard before. Bugger *Westering Home* and well-behaved harmony; I wanted music where even the beautiful bits fought back. It was better than medicine and it was free: you opened your mouth and the instrument was there. At the same time, I developed a taste for a more exotic range of reading. The library was all right, but the adult section was not accessible on a child ticket and a child ticket would be all I'd get till I was fifteen. Even the Older Girls selections seemed young. They were about Katy and Heidi or, if a bunch of girls with old-fashioned names got together, *Little Women*. In need of something different, I headed for a stack of publishers' leftovers near the Ladybird baby socks in Woolworths which sold for sixpence each and bought whatever I felt like instead of having to choose from the Suitable Stories shelves. No one at the till asked for identification or made restrictions: all they asked for was the money. Over weeks I acquired histories of the Spanish Inquisition, Celtic belief and witchcraft; accounts of the lives and times of Spartacus, Caligula and Vlad the Impaler, a book called *Stranglers and Rippers* and a manual of death penalties through the ages. I took in myths and folklore, cautionary poems by Belloc and Hoffman, a book of revolting Christian martyrdoms and a history of war surgery. These were worlds in which urine, blood and fingernails loomed large; in which asphyxia, slicing, drowning, scalding, stretching, setting on fire, boiling in oil and application of red-hot implements were deemed important beyond all rational imagining. I bypassed love stories, sci-fi, Westerns and war stories when I had exhausted the gore and turned instead to classics, which sold even more cheaply: *Jane Eyre, Great Expectations, Frankenstein, Dracula, The Ancient Mariner* and *Goblin Market* with illustrations. Sex and Death. Excited, I wrote a play about Flora MacDonald and a scorned Highlander and my mother lit the fire with it. It was not deliberate sabotage, just convenient paper. In Chemistry, we dissected a sheep's eyeball, poked quicksilver along a desk with our fingers when the teacher wasn't looking and dared each other to taste sulphur powder. History hung Guy Fawkes then drew and quartered him without compunction and Geography showcased the wild things of the Amazonian jungle. Sex and Death, Death and Sex: there were no other subjects. Restless and having read every last book in the house, I took to walking. Even with nowhere to go, I walked a lot, needing no dog as pretext. I met the coal man's horse, the corner shop's Jack Russell that quivered all over with excitement at the merest hint of attention and the collie at the Glebe that followed everyone on the off-chance they might have unwanted sausages hidden on their person. I watched out for pigeons necking in trees and crows on guard at churches, cats that bloomed unexpectedly from privet hedges and the ancient grey-blond labrador that went for somebody's *Evening Times* every night at six and carried it home. Things in rock pools didn't count as proper encounters. For a start, they wanted no truck with people and if you picked them out, they died. Crabs, prawns, small fry and limpets – putting them in a jar was all it took. I'd won a goldfish at the fair once and it had done just the same: aquatic things lost the will to live anywhere near people. Sea-birds were another kettle of fish. Noble, enormous and utterly without fear, they were masters and mistresses of their own fates. Some looked as though they'd eat you given half a chance but with no malice aforethought. Like cockroaches and sharks but prettier, sea-birds were unsinkable survivors. You had to admire them for it. Enjoying the gulls took me to the shore front with bread pilfered from the packet in the kitchen, hoping to lure them close. And now and then, in the wake of the gulls, came a less attractive, less clued-in flock entirely: the Mission Church of Christ (Junior League).

The Mission Church might have been about for years, but it wasn't till my teens that I noticed them; a team of young, slightly apprehensive sorts keen to pitch temporary camp on the beach for a barbecue and some soul-saving if time allowed. The larger rocks along the bay were christened with red and black paint – GOOD

NEWS IS COMING, RESURRECTION IS SURE, OPEN YOUR HEART TO JESUS and SAUSAGE SIZZLE ALL WELCOME. Six seemed to be the usual start time, and each session began with them tumbling out of a white van, gathering driftwood to add to a bag of sticks and Zip firelighters they'd brought in case of shortage, then setting light to the whole in the hope of a hearty, witch-burning size of blaze. Then they brought forth sausages and barbecued for Christ. The object seemed to be to lure the lost and lonely into the arms of Jesus with burnt pork links, bottled squash and a singalong. There was a lot of smoke, choking and singed fingers. The unwisely eager lost sausages to the flames while the timid found theirs raw behind the blackened shell, tasting only of kerosene. The sun came down and the Isle of Arran turned blue behind them but they didn't pay much attention to their surroundings. Anemones folding their arms in rock pools, late-scuttling crabs and razorbills preening their shirt fronts went unnoticed while the praying took over. If anyone not already part of the gang enquired after membership, I missed it. All they ever attracted was dogs. By the time the sun was low enough for dark to begin settling, a man with a guitar who'd been hiding in the van came out to strum *Amazing Grace, John Brown's Body* and *Rock My Soul in the Bosom of Abraham* while the missioneers sang and held hands. No matter how lonely or confused I felt – and I did, it has to be said, I often did – the Mission Church didn't seem the place to turn for help. *Kumbaya,* always late in the day, was the sign to push off quick before the handclaps creaked to a standstill like a steam train running out of coke. At the time, I thought the Mission Church seemed only marginally better than food poisoning but looking back, they did put an idea in my head. I didn't even know the idea was there till I saw it in the music shop window in Dockhead Street. It was rosewood, hourglass, so perfectly lacquered it cast a crimson shadow when the sun bounced off its hips. It was more portable than a piano, completely companionable and possessed of six silver strings. My fingers made marks on the glass with longing. I didn't want an invisible friend or a Heavenly Father. I wanted a guitar.

I got it by doing odd jobs for Rose and selling home-crafts to the newly opened baby shop next to the newly opened Wimpy Bar. Enterprise flourished as long as it took, then died from natural causes. I had what I wanted: cherrywood, varnished till it glittered and all mine in three weeks. By the time I owned a dozen chords and hard-skinned fingertips, I could accompany simple stuff by ear. *Streets of Laredo*, *Freight Train*, *Old Man River.* After *We Shall Overcome*, I was ready for the next step, the thing all strolling players, minstrels and folkies did sooner or later. They took a freight train, boxcar, a mule or the downtown bus and headed up, out, on or off into the fading sun and I could do the same. On Saturdays, I picked up my guitar and my Bob Dylan Baker Boy and took the long, lonesome road to West Kilbride. The bus up the coast left every half-hour and Jane, a Welsh girl from school whose dad worked at something near West Kilbride that may or may not have been the nuclear plant, suggested I visit. It wasn't like me, but with the guitar I felt like someone else. In an off-white shortie raincoat from C&A, a pair of moccasin boots and a centre-parting like Joan Baez, I even dressed like someone else. Anything was possible. Clutching the sunset-red guitar neck, I watched the Ayrshire coast roll by windows smeary with sea-salt and bird lime, feeling the opposite of homeward-bound. A cellophane-flat expanse of sea that reached to Arran, Ireland, the Atlantic, America lined the way out – the drystane dykes and Highland cattle of the road back could be ignored. In summer, the finds of basking sharks might appear on the horizon and jellyfish slopped ashore in see-through swathes. By Seamill and the golf fields the bus swung inland and dithered through West Kilbride as far as the graveyard, and the graveyard was my stop.

I could have waited till the bus reached Largs with its views over the firth to the Cumbraes, regular Rothesay crossings and Nardini's magnificent ice-cream parlour, but that stuff needed money. Graveyards didn't. Anything free had its own attractions. I'd grown up next to a cemetery, the tips of its stone obelisks showing over our garden wall, and had never found them frightening. Victorian headstones with hawkish angels in stages of aggressive distress were frightening, but not the grounds. Not the sheepish skeleton grins of eighteenth-century memento mori or the dead. More often than not they were set in shade and apart from the raucousness of everyday life. Some were floral and vivid in summer, tuneful with yellow bees; some were thick with hawthorn and holly bushes that looked best edged with frost. People left things – flowers and books and odd little tokens – then moved on. If the dead didn't talk, they wished me no harm and I did not turn up my nose at their company. An added reassurance in West Kilbride was its distance from home: if anyone did show up, they'd be no one I knew. I could sing without fear of ridicule because more often than not I had the place all to myself. If I drew no great attention to myself, I'd be left alone, even rise to the status of fitting right in. Anywhere cared for was a good place to be, and these places were tended with something like love. I'd seen a graveyard in Yorkshire once and been shocked by its disarray, the tangles of weed and ivy and wind-bitten, fallen-down, nobody-cares-much stones. In West Kilbride, the grass was bowling green trim, bordered with wallflowers, pansies, dahlias and gladioli. There was a tap at the main gate to refresh the bunches people had brought as gifts from their own gardens and, since they weren't here, I did it. I sifted out what had wilted, chipped off name-obscuring mosses, pulled up buttercups for people who had no flowers at all and generally played house. My mother had been a home help in her time: I knew by example how to make even a burial plot look lived-in. Once, I found Edward Galloway in an out-of-the-way corner and my pulse quickened, but it wasn't dad. It was someone who'd been a beloved father and husband with boys left behind, not girls. Wherever dad was buried, it wasn't here.

It occurred to me on my hunkers in front of the wrong man that I'd never asked. *Where is he?* seemed selfish beyond some ill-defined but palpable pale. It may have been that I was afraid of making people angry or sad or furious: it seems more likely I was terrified they'd take me to the place itself and I'd have to stand six feet over his chest cavity not knowing what to say, how to be. Whatever my mother felt about his death she didn't say – not outright, at any rate – and I picked up enough to grasp that revealing one's emotions, even knowing what they might be and keeping it to yourself, was *not done.* I do recall that after his funeral, her asthma got worse so it wasn't all relief. *Kitty's got angina,* she'd say, drawing short, effortful breaths. *It'll be me next.* Looking up in the dictionary revealed angina was not catching and she needn't have worried on that score, but that wasn't the point. She wasn't telling me about angina; she was telling me she was afraid. Sometimes, she'd wake beside me with her skin clammy and her heart thumping, insisting she was *perfectly all right* without being asked. Other times, she'd become matter-of-fact like Granny McBride and issue instructions for procedures in the event of cardiac failure. No flowers, no headstones, no fuss. *When you're gone you're gone. They should burn you up and scatter the dust – end of story.* This was something she wished me to understand as if my life depended on it: the thing to do with the dead was erase all trace. She wasn't seeking platitudes or reassurance when she said these things: what she wanted was a listener. Cora wasn't much cop in a crisis, so the listener was me. Interjections would only have interrupted the flow. The more personal the revelation, the less chucking in my own remarks seemed apt. Besides, questions made my mother uneasy. They turned her cold. The last thing she needed in the course of saying difficult things was to have to summon the resources to freeze me out. I knew the drill.

It hadn't been that long ago she'd swallowed enough prescription leftovers to fell a horse, after all. And when she came back pale as putty with her eyes the wrong colour, nobody mentioned anything had happened at all. *You keep your lip buttoned or else, lady* was all Cora said as we stood at the door watching mum shuffle out of a taxi. *The last thing you do is open your mouth.* I knew already. Of course I knew. Nobody mentioned ambulances, pills or Uncle Allan being hauled out of the pub to try to render her conscious. Maybe she didn't know. And if not, we weren't for telling her. Sometimes, thick, grey silences and pretending if it killed you were all that stopped the world blowing apart.

Now, hiding in a corner of West Kilbride Cemetery, it dawned on me the pit of unasked questions was deeper than we allowed ourselves to think. We turned away from everything that might provoke them. We had not so much as a shoe or his bus driver's peaked hat. Not a single tie. We had no scraps of paper where I might trace the line of his handwriting with my finger, no postcards, letters or envelopes, no betting slips or signatures or receipts. No razors or shaving brushes; not so much as a stub of styptic pencil or a single come-loose shirt button. No wedding snaps. I had never seen my grandmother, mother or sister in a wedding dress, not even in a smart suit holding a bouquet and smiling. We had no snaps of nearest family at all. The only things of my father's were a handful of his book-club choices ranged in a gap-toothed row on top of Cora's wardrobe and a set of rusty cobblers' lasts in the coal-shed too heavy to run away on their own. This erasure must have been deliberate. And this was what my mother wanted too. *Burned and scattered.* Gone.

This was the kind of stuff I thought about on Saturday afternoons. If it sounds dark, it wasn't: it was a search for illumination. Half-clues I'd been collecting over the years began to make an itch beneath my skin. The most disparate pieces could come together if you took your time, applied memory, detective cunning, the rules of enough abstruse dead-language grammar. Meantime, there was the peace of the cemetery and *Amazing Grace* ripe for the singing. Cosied in along other people's floral tributes, my head could turn where it liked. I wanted to take nothing for granted, let nothing simply wash away. Maybe I thought that if I sat still long enough, was patient and thoughtful, a tide of understanding would have no option but to roll towards me.

Your future could depend on this.

Miss Lyons skirled a slip of A5 over her head while a dogsbody from the front row shelled them out to the rest of us. Our futures were at stake, she told us. Serious choices lay ahead.

The life-altering papers turned out to be selection forms: lists from which we indicated what we preferred to study for the remaining years of schooling. Third year would soon be upon us and was already going pear-shaped. This was our finale as an all-girl chorus. From now on, we were high-kicking alongside the chaps.

All I was sure about was Latin. Even if the Romans had been bloody-minded and cruel, their language still thrilled me. That dealt with column one. The rest was a grid like the Littlewoods' Pools coupon with no instruction as to the life or death significance of any one thing in the list above any other. *One subject only per column* was printed in heavy type. I took it home knowing my mother wouldn't have any more of a clue than I did. Those whose parents knew the expected form for this kind of thing were rare as Easter Islanders and most of us would choose what we liked without any notion of its usefulness to something as high-flown as a Path in Life. Asked what I wanted to do with my future in primary seven, all I had come up with was ASTRONAUT, but that was only an essay. I could picture being alone with a glittering instrument panel, an illusion of control under my fingertips and only endless, glittering, people-free space stretching out in front. But that wasn't what I expected to get. Nobody got these things in real life: they were acquired randomly and/or by the Communist system of selection. Most of our families thought the same way: you did what your folks did because they knew the route; all else was fantasy. Mum had been a servant, a mill worker, a bus conductress, a cleaner and a dinner-lady in that order. Aged two, I had handed over packets of cigarettes at the counter and had permission to eat as many penny caramels as I liked. Aged two, serving in a shop had been great fun. At three, I had been allowed to follow her as she had cleaned the doctor's surgery and the waiting room with a duster of my own. Aged three, I had framed us as pixies in the night come to mend and brighten and I liked the idea. Servant was rarified work in this day and age and the mills were in Yorkshire. Being a bus conductress looked heavy work and being a dinner-lady, while it afforded lots of free food, looked dead-end. Cora had been a waitress and a typist. I knew nothing about either line of work. Aunty Kitty's husband, Vince, was a decorator but he said girls weren't allowed. The only thing left was teaching.

Everybody knew what teachers did and mum was keen. It was clean, easy for them that liked books and a job for life. Now all she had to do was pick from the permitted selections and I'd be set for life. Cookery was not allowed with Latin. Art was not allowed with Music. It was impossible to pick a new language, like German, without French and Latin jeopardised both. Maths and PE, both of which made my skin ripple with loathing, were compulsory. Picking the right things to be a teacher looked too hard. Maybe it would be nicer to get a job at Boots the Chemist. She could see me behind a counter with my hair in a chignon; little pearl earrings, a Coco Chanel frock. Cora laughed at the very idea. Nobody was going to buy make-up from *her*, she said. Apart from anything else, she's got a stammer. It was true. It wasn't consistent and it wasn't pronounced, but I had a stammer when confronted with anything new and became completely speechless when frightened. Deflated, mum dropped the subject of Boots and we all went back to the tick-box puzzle, guessing.

Other people don't get to stay on, my mother said. You're getting a favour.

She was annoyed by the complexity of the form, its hint of too much rope. We sat up after the news was done adding French and Music to my already selected Latin; English and Maths because they were unavoidable; and History. There was nothing in the final column I liked, so I wrote the word Art under Business Studies in lettering as close to typewriting as I could muster and ticked that instead.

Godsake, Cora tutted, checking the form for obvious mistakes. Music and bloody Latin. What kind of job is that supposed to get you? That's no use to man or beast.

I like Music and Latin, I said. I'm good at them.

You'd probably like a butler as well but you're not gonny get one. That kind of thing is *too fancy for you*. Who do you think you are? The Duchess of Argyll?

Shut up you, mum said. You got every damn thing going when you were her age, piano lessons and driving lessons and all sorts. You're jealous, that's your trouble.

Aye right, Cora agreed. I'm dead jealous of her getting to do Music and Latin. You've hit the nail on the head there.

Ignoring the sarcasm, mum folded the paper. Anyway, it's done now. That's it sorted.

Music's not a *job*, mother. It'll be that daft classical stuff and opera and that stuff she plays on the piano. It's not for the likes of her for Godsake. You're just encouraging her to get big ideas and she'll get shot down sooner or later. You mark my words. *Music*.

Mum faltered, knowing that Cora might be right.

Well, it's done now. Just leave things the way they are and she'll do something else another year. It's no skin off your nose what she does so stop arguing. This is what she's doing. I'm her mother, not you. It's my say-so.

Cora whipped the paper from mum's hand and checked it with her eyes. You spelled *selection* wrong, she said. She dropped it on the carpet next to me. Sort it, then put the damn thing away. Don't say I didn't warn you.

I got the lot, even the Art I'd added on. Cheek and fancy and guesswork were pushed through without too many questions and the Music teacher, as I found out years later, working behind the scenes. Some poor souls from Largs were forced to do Physics and Chemistry in accordance with some grand family scheme and I was grateful I was not one of those. I got rid of Geography and Mr Parker's knuckle-crippling trick. I got rid of report-writing in Science. I had a burgeoning social life with Janessa and Marion, two girls from the lunch-time choir who were happy to form a trio with me and sing at Old Folks' Homes, hospitals, the Bowling Club and the odd Burns' Supper. One or two of them paid. By the time summer arrived, Cora announced she was done with men and took mum out to the newly refurbished La Scala cinema to see *Ben Hur* in new improved technicolor with Charlton Heston in a thong. In their absence I started writing songs and mum suggested I was *coming out of my shell.* It was news to me she thought I was in one, but I was touched. Maybe I was. Cora gave me an old eyeshadow she didn't use any more and I painted my toenails a colour by the swoony name of *Satin Pink.* I bought ingredients with my pocket-money and made chocolate, coffee and coconut cakes at the rate of three a week, experimenting with frostings and butter-creams till they turned into something you could eat. I visited Jane and her family in West Kilbride without fear. I made friends and one of them was a boy.

Graham was one year older than me and lived at the cemetery gates because he was the keeper's son. Graham liked Kenneth Williams, *Oklahoma!* and *South Pacific* and busked songs from the shows on an ancient upright piano in his bedroom with more enthusiasm than skill, which was strangely liberating. There was no physical contact with Graham other than hand-slaps of feigned outrage and the odd pretend waltz. I did not know the word *gay* then and neither did he. Oddities together, we thought of each other as *old-fashioned.* Once, laughing at a joke, he slapped his thigh like the principal boy in a panto and hooted. *Oh you,* he said. *You're priceless.* It was the second nicest thing anyone had ever said to me and he knew it. The idyll burst forever when a friend of his came round unexpectedly and Graham introduced us. The friend had no interest in musicals but hung around. He turned up next time and kissed me when Graham was out of the room fetching orange squash. Graham found out, of course, and took it badly. I regretted upsetting Graham but not the kissing. I hadn't bargained for it being pleasant, let alone exciting, and it was. I couldn't deny it was. Even thinking about it – my first real kiss – as I headed home on the outbound bus made my tongue and spine go fizzy. When Graham asked me to repent and I couldn't tell a lie, the cherry tree of our relationship was gone forever.

Thereafter, I traded the gentle pleasures of musicals and graveyards for the swings. The swings were in the park next to the housing scheme where Kiss-Boy lived. Boys hung around there scaring little children away and catcalling stray girls onto the roundabout to make them drunk with spinning, tempting them in the woods with vinegar crisps and ice-cream 99s from the van. For West Kilbride, the area had a shiver of *rough* about it but I went, out-on-a-limb scared yet pulled by some magnetic allure I did not understand. In my shortie raincoat and on polished soles, I headed straight for the slipperiest slope on offer, keen to run accidentally across Kiss-Boy and feel that slither in my vertebral column all over again. Part of my brain had already melted – the part that connected boys to men, and men to my sister and not me. The part that had bookmarked grammar and the rules of harmony as what mattered. I didn't do this kind of thing, this soppy stuff. But this kind of thing, the lip to lip contact, was not what I had imagined. I told myself it was interesting, no more. But that only goes to show how much trouble my brain was having with the whole business. It was telling lies. My brain was no longer in control – if it ever had been. There was an unexpectedly frisky array of chemicals at work under my touch-paper skin, ready to catch at the slightest spark. As if I was charged by static and my hair on end, boys noticed. Jimmy, Ben, George, Dennis and a big sap called Ronnie all offered to steal my jotters, draw cartoons on my dinner tickets and walk me home if they were going into town. The body I'd been so wary of acquiring was flexing its extremities, sending semaphore without my say-so. Blood outs, sap rises. Half-horrified, half-thrilled, I fell into line and simply waited for whatever came next.

7

Creating an impression – are you a hit or a forgettable miss? Take our test and find out!

My blazer sprouted Bowie badges. I hooked my skinny school tie into a fat double windsor and loosened it at the hilt. I tied my hair with a chiffon scarf and slicked *Sugar Frost Surprise* on my lips.

Boy-conscious, Cora said. You can tell it's in with the boys this year.

She is nothing of the kind *boy-conscious*, mum said. We're not all like you.

They could think what they liked. I had to redo the tie to get it just right and that took concentration. The scarf came loose before I reached the school gates and the lipstick surrendered to a bag of crisps at ten thirty but I was new to this stuff. Creating a veneer of sophistication wasn't child's play. As my sister had demonstrated for years, serious drag took serious application.

You only get out what you put in, Cora said, flickering her lashes against the mascara wand with aggressive determination.

Lazy cows get damn all grass and some women don't even try. Understand what I'm saying? She looked at me, one eye owl-size and the other still unpainted as she swapped hands with the little wand of black gunge. Nobody hands you nothing on a plate, madam.

She snapped her fingers and I handed her a tissue.

Keeping yourself nice is half the bloody battle. Now bugger off and get me a coffee.

I heard and obeyed. Cora on the subject of appearance had professorial authority. As long as she lived, no one ever accused my sister of *not trying*, at least as far as looks were concerned. Once, all that effort had been for the pictures, the fair, going out on the town. Now, it was all to cement her position as Head of Typing at the Nile Street stockbrokers' office where she worked, bossing Juniors till they reached the status of credit to the firm. Every morning, Cora drew on her eyebrows as she drank her coffee. *Black coffee, two sugars, nothing to eat.* After years of plucking, all she had left of the originals were two little commas, the back halves of which had to be pencilled in to exist at all. I'd seen her draw then erase her efforts with cold cream half a dozen times rather than head off for the train with less than mirror-symmetry brows. A good finish took time but willpower took over in a crisis. Stabbed in the eye with an eyeshadow brush, my sister could suppress her tear-ducts in a fraction of the time demanded by normal women, allowing her to reapply her colour and still catch the Glasgow train without breaking sweat. Malformed fifth phalanxes, bunions, corns and callouses on both feet did not deter her from sling-backs and peep-toes: if personal pride demanded the renunciation of bodily comfort, my sister defied it with nun-like self-denial. Her fondness for buckles, hooks, zips and cigarettes meant she learned an adroitness with denier far beyond the everyday, for Cora's nylons did not ladder. Maybe they didn't dare. No matter how often she crossed her legs with a head-turning slither of nylon, fussing her hem back over her knees, they did not snag. At weekends, she filed and buffed her nails to yellow ovals then painted them with three coats of lacquer the better to withstand the rigours of typing. Other people could operate switches, buttons and lighters for her: stylishness was more important than practicality. Her one concession to what my mother called *extra help* was the purchase of a beauty device called a *Playtex corselette*, which, despite the itsy-bitsy teeny-weeny connotations of its suffix, was not an inconsiderable garment at all.

Pinkish-beige with panel control and extra boning, the corselette looked like an ugly swimsuit someone had forgotten to sew up at the gusset. The top had two seamed near-conical bra pouches with thick straps for extra support, stiff mesh inserts criss-crossing the waist and a lower part like a long vest that stretched to just beneath the crotch. Hanging from the bottom of the whole were four ribbony flaps with rubber button teats from which stockings might be suspended. Here and there for purposes of further tightening were steel clasps, hook-and-eye fastenings and grip-fasteners with stainless metal teeth. Opened, the latter looked like baby shark mouths, waiting for a kill. This thing wasn't for amateurs: it was professional female kit. How it was forced up over the hips was a mystery because Cora's bedroom door was always shut, but you knew she was putting it on because the swearing, huffing and general wrestling noises were impossible to ignore. Mid-corselette, no one was allowed to knock in case she lost her concentration and had to begin all over again. However it was done, Cora always triumphed and the corselette was forced into submission over the hips and into place.

Now and then I'd see the thing at rest through her open bedroom door, cast aside on a basket chair like the cast-off skin of a monster salmon, and marvel at the dedication my sister could muster for her art. If anyone could teach me about the trappings of womanhood, it was Cora. *Keeping yourself nice* was a womanly essential and *making an effort* required more than a fleeting attention span. To be woman enough, I'd have to study, practise, apply.

I read labels on shampoo bottles and hairspray that promised *gloss, hold and shine*. I worried about split ends as though they were a contagion and carried nail scissors in my pocket to cut them off without delay when found. I practised scarf-tying till I could tie a bow behind my head without it being squint, uneven or simply wrong and could tell which materials were more likely to hold a knot all day and not unravel as soon as they met a puff of wind. I taught myself to leave lipstick in place instead of wiping my mouth instinctually and practised eyeliner precision with a fine sable paintbrush on the back of my hand. I insisted on nylons from now on, learning to check both stockings were the same colour before attaching them in the morning. Soon, I was popping into the phone box on the corner of Argyll Street to apply mascara, fatten the knot of my tie and roll up my skirt at the waistband to make it shorter than knee-length. Miss Lyons stopped me between classes and looked me up and down.

I don't know what you think you look like, she said, hauling me by the waist to adjust my skirt back to regulation length as though I was a toddler. Bunching up your clothes like a streetwalker. What would your mother say?

The physical proximity startled me, but the hand she placed on my shoulder went too far. I drew back. When her hand followed, I stiffened and shook her off. It was what I did when touched unexpectedly but it must have seemed deliberate and angry. Maybe it was. Miss Lyons's eyes narrowed.

Let me tell you something. Her voice was low and clipped. Girls who think they can go their own way come to grief sooner or later. These *mini-skirts* and silly ties will not impress your fellows. Other girls, respectable girls, will not befriend you. I looked down at the parquet trying not to stare at her too-yellow face-powder, the fringe of carnation red that had travelled from her lips to her front teeth. She shook me, once. And if you think slathering your mouth that silly colour is a route to anything other than a fall, you are very mistaken.

Cora popped briefly into my head. *Nobody hands you nothing on a plate.* Maybe Miss Lyons's little speech meant the same as my sister's. Maybe it meant the opposite. Frankly, I had no real idea about the detail but I picked up the gist, and the gist was *common.* Without using the word, she was saying I was *common,* enough for other girls – the Largs set, I presumed – to register as *not their kind*. If my slip was not on show, something else was. What she wanted me to do I didn't know. After a moment of what must have been disappointingly confused silence, Miss Lyons sighed.

What class are you supposed to be in?

Dr Nisbet, Room 202.

She looked at me. I could feel the look right through the top of my head. Latin? she said. Am I to understand you are in Dr Nisbet's top stream?

Yes, I said. I like Latin. Suddenly irritable, unlike myself, I lifted my head and looked at her flatly. I helped win a prize for the school last year in a Latin-speaking competition. Dr Nisbet is a very good teacher. I admire her spirit.

Her eyes blinked slowly, like a fox sizing up a dog.

Is that your evaluation?

I nodded.

Well, she said. Doubtless she'll be wondering where her star pupil is right now. I blinked. Miss Lyons tilted her head, almost tickled, one pretty pearl earring appearing beneath her hairline. I can see I need to keep an eye on you.

She inhaled, let a slow smile spread, then flicked a finger in the direction of the stairwell. Go, she said. Before I lose my temper.

I went, thinking her nose in profile was Roman. Like

Agrippina, I thought. Miss Lyons looked like the mother of mad Emperor Nero.

And pick up those heels.

Ashamed without being sure why, I headed for the embrace of Virgil, blaming Miss Lyons for my lateness. Dr Nisbet didn't care. She was knee-deep in Book 2 of the *Aeneid*, taking us gently and one word at a time. So far, the Greeks had built their giant wooden horse with the blessing of the goddess Minerva then sailed off to Tenedos to wait for their plan to work. The Trojans were emerging to look the horse over and, led on by a double-agent, were persuaded to see it as a gift, exactly as their enemies hoped they would. They led themselves to think the war was over. That they'd been left alone.

> *We thought they had gone, seeking Mycenae with the wind.*
> *So all the Trojan land was free of its sorrow.*

But, of course, the Trojans were wrong. Enemies, the cunning kind, don't just disappear: they hide and watch. They lurk. Miss Lyons had her eye on me and meant business. I listened to Virgil and made a mental note to avoid confrontation: confrontation, in my experience, never went well. If I was common, I better be good at stuff or I'd have nothing to fall back on. I felt sure she'd want me to know that. She'd want me to stay sprightly, watchful. On my toes.

We'd had a biscuit tin since the year dot in which my mother stored Bourbons, Tunnock's Wafers and Viscount Creams. The tin was circular and a deep, rich red that went beyond pillar box to carmine with a flat, textured finish that made it feel leathery under the fingers, undroppable. All its edges were rounded, not sharp, with a fine veneer of gold-coloured enamel, patterned to make it look like lace. Hammer-work raised the perimeters of eight fat ovals on the lid, embellishing the pictures inside with the illusion of French knots. And inside each of those ovals was a face, eight perfectly transferred oil-painterly faces of adult men. They had all been real and, despite the fact they came from different times and places, they shared a passion that made the centuries between the first and last an irrelevance. The clue was in the middle of the lid: a violin with a bow like a crossbones missing its skull. Our very best biscuit tin, so old nobody knew how we'd come by it or what exotica it had housed, was a tribute in miniature to composers, each with his name beneath in fancy, curlicued script. Bach like a barrister in a short-cropped wig and Handel in long, white curls. Haydn had a hooked nose like a highwayman. Mozart was powdered till his skin looked see-through while Beethoven looked apoplectic as beetroot juice. The final three were Schubert who wore Billy Bunter specs, Brahms with an Edward Lear beard and Tchaikovsky, Tchaikovsky before the white hair, the depression and the scandal pulled him down, looking young and fine and in the pink. He looked, come to think of it, like the Head of Music at Ardrossan. As a younger man, he looked like Ken.

Ken Hetherington breezed rather than strolled. He wore corduroy jackets and sat beside us to teach, not apart. He taught using eye contact, jokes, anecdotes, asides and elaborations as much as textbooks and could do all these things partly because Music, as *arty*, permitted oddity in its practitioners; partly because running so many music groups entitled him to be a law unto himself; partly because he was Cumbrian (the only other non-Scots in the school were a Chemistry teacher and George Buchan of the French department, who was from Kilwinning but qualified as French on the grounds of stated preference, summer job, staggering fluency, huffiness and Gitanes-coloured teeth) and partly because his orchestra won so many trophies for the school in an age where these things counted that he could teach as eccentrically as he damn well liked. It helped that his S3 academic class were four in total so the attention he could allow each in turn was thorough. I knew right away this was a privilege. What I didn't know was how broad the subject was.

It was the history of the orchestra, of composers, musical styles and forms. It was small-scale engineering, design and technology of instruments and changing possibilities in the production of sound; it was European politics and social history, a study of how national boundaries, revolutions and random wars affected art; it was insight into lives, the ingenious work-arounds of working practice (Czech orchestras were fabulous partly because being able to play an instrument let poor boys off compulsory army service; patronage was largely arse-kissing and lip-biting; viola players were horn players who had lost their teeth and castration and cruelty were the backbone of Italian soprano choirs) and no little investigation of Comparative Religion, Church Latin and smatterings of various European grammars. It was an examination of harmony, modes, pentatonic traditions and the mathematical divisions of Pythagoras in rendering perfect fifths and the cult of whole numbers into conventional Western pentatonic scale. It was folk song and Art Song and poetry, the class system and how to fox it, the permitted connections between individual and state, a testament to collective effort, and a hymn of praise to what human effort tied to talent and the odd lucky break could produce. Almost as a sideline, we learned what music could be and what came together to make it. From the ranges of instruments and their individual colours to the written symbols and cyphers of tablature; the rules of classical harmony, polyphony and the 12-tone system and how to effect them should the need arise. And I loved every scrap. Even working out a figured bass from numbers and sight-reading. Everything Ken touched turned to gold.

By comparison, what English teachers did most of was prepare for exams, the implication being that the only reason anyone had ever written a novel, a poem or a play was to get it on to a syllabus for the purposes of certification. In silent protest, I took to reading the parts of the books the teacher ignored to see what I found. There were two women out of forty-two poets in the book Mr Black, the Nosferatu of the English department, gave out for course work. The women were Stevie Smith and Sylvia Plath. *Nudgers and shovers in spite of ourselves, our kind multiplies: We shall by morning inherit the earth.* The book commentary suggested both women were crazy. Around the corners of Mr Brown's tedious reductions of the War Poets to possible-answer fodder, I also found ee cummings and William Carlos Williams who were crazy too. It wasn't poetry's fault, seldom the poet's. It was the teacher's. I was acquiring my Music from someone who knew it was a way of approaching the world and what it had to offer, not a way of passing tests. Like Dr Nisbet, Mr Hetherington made learning not only desirable but attainable. It was there for us, not the other way round. Teachers mattered more than subject divisions and, in these teachers, I was kissed with unearned, scarcely believable, fit-to-bust luck.

Crazed with possibility and a desire to worm myself into Mr Hetherington's heart, I took in the biscuit tin. He was not disconcerted. He rattled it and took a biscuit. He enthused about the composers and pronounced their names, teaching me how to say Mozart with a t in the middle though spelling it without. Bach, he said, wrote for very little money and no glory with up to a third of his orchestra missing every rehearsal because they were all amateurs or drunk after payday; Handel's father was a barber-surgeon who wanted his son to get a proper job, which meant something that wasn't music; Haydn was a liveried servant with a passion for garden sheds and Mozart was a disappointment to his dad. Beethoven was a bully, Schubert died at thirty-one, Brahms was the son of a dance-band musician who played in brothels for ready cash and Tchaikovsky was depressive and queer. They were all depressed, he said. They were depressed because they nearly all had the clap. Composers, he opined, had rotten lives. Better to be a teacher any day.

Before we lost our teacher for ever, we knew about Paganini's teeth and Purcell's drinking, Dame Nellie Melba's appetite, Robert Schumann's constipation and Wagner's halitosis – unscholarly and even slight things told in passing. Over time, however, these small things, as small things do, suggested something huge. Personal detail made creators into people. Not rich people, not lofty people, not magical or separate. Great work was not something gifted by faeries that *must out* in the way the stars appeared at night. They had health problems, money problems, problems fitting in. They had family worries, personality foibles, could be tedious, annoying or workaday. And some of them had fallen, hit the wrong time or run out of luck, had never bloomed as they might due to – well, *life*. Some were missing or had never had the chance to find out what might have inflamed their hearts. And even those who had, those who lasted, the connected and the tooth-and-claw, were *people*. Which meant Cora was wrong. Nobody could say Music or Art or anything else for that matter *wasn't for* me. Everything was for me if I chose. *People* made these things in spite of obstacles, in spite of their families as often as because of them. And if we were, at the core, all *people*, I counted by default as one of the mass. What Ken taught me along with Music was lust for life, a sense of entitlement to reach. I was *people* too.

Could you defy your boyfriend?
Are you a Sex Siren, a Plain Jane or a Clueless Katy?
What your favourite colour reveals about YOU!

I was a quiz-junkie. The kind that did *Jackie* quizzes knowing they were stupid but not able to pass them by. Laziness wasn't going to lead me to miss any opportunity to find the key to life. Why I thought a daft quiz could provide it is harder to explain. It was too easy to gerrymander the outcome and have the quiz tell you what you wanted to hear. From *Mostly As* to *Mostly Ds*, they revealed nothing worth knowing. *An extremely handsome boy is talking to your best friend at a party. Do you A) walk over to say hi to both and join in? B) swoop there immediately before she gets her claws in? C) hope he'll notice you instead? Or D) turn away – he's out of your league?* weren't even real questions. Unless I was the only one missing out on a life awash with handsome boy dilemmas, they were adult fantasies. If you had time for the quiz entitled *Are you the life and soul of the party?* the answer had to be *no.* Mum had no time for magazines or their quizzes: real life sucked up too much of her time. *Faits accomplis* were more her lot.

The same day there were whispers about lay-offs in the pool of the less senior school dining staff, a letter came from Yorkshire with the address hand-written. She saw the postmark and looked hard at the writing, then took it out into the garden to read alone. Uncle Saul had finally lost out to emphysema and Aunty Pearl wanted her to know. I found her standing in the back green against the washing line holding it. It was not quick, but it was all behind him now, Pearl had written in her dutiful, schoolgirl hand. Sixty-five was a good innings.

We had no pictures of Uncle Saul but he had the kind of face you remembered. Like W. H. Auden only with white hair and bigger shoulders, he was the eldest of the brothers and the only one who sang bass. His hero was Paul Robeson and his big hit was *Deep River.* Uncle Willie, who was a POW in Italy, said what got him through the war was imagining Saul singing and being heard for miles. That was all I knew about Saul. Kitty was second-oldest and I guessed she might be next. What mum was thinking I had no idea.

She went to Yorkshire for the funeral and stayed four nights with Uncle Jock who was a miserable swine so came back in worse fettle than she went away. And while she was gone, Cora seized the chance to disappear too, issuing instructions it was nobody's business. What she meant was not to tell, not to ask, but something made me believe it wasn't far, Troon at most. Cora didn't believe in holidays so it wasn't that. Maybe it was a man with a house of his own. Whatever it was, it meant three nights on my own. I could watch whatever I liked on the telly and even *put it off.* I invited boys to walk me back from the shops and gave them coffee and chatted like a TV hostess. I invited the others round for some Pete Seeger songs and filled the living room with three-part harmony. Testing the limits, I applied eyeshadow in thick blue stripes and banged out Clementi sonatas in my pyjamas. Rose came in one evening to see if we were fine without mum and I lied that Cora was in the bath to avoid a fuss. I wanted to be left on my own. At least, I wanted it till around midnight when the noises of the house settling were louder, the fear of spiders more intense. Reading the fairy tales I loved made it worse: abandoned, lost and mutilated tin soldiers, match sellers to crippled mermaids, the drag of long nails against the window as the Ice Maiden came to collect her own failed to soothe. Sleepless, I thought of my mother in Yorkshire, my sister God knew where and Uncle Saul, the singer of psalms, the corners of his eyes like accordions. Near one in the morning, the clock mechanism in the living room whirred up to strike, but it did not strike alone. There was another noise behind it. Like feet on sand. Dragging. Then a tap.

Someone was outside, at the front of the house.

They were standing on the flower border, fingers tipping against the thin pane of glass. Cora's window. Someone – a man, it could only be a man – was outside Cora's window. I sat still long enough for the sound to subside then waited till Mr Gregg's homers started crooming in the pigeon loft at six, when the light filtering in through the fibreglass curtains made me bold enough to sleep. Outside, when I dared to check, was a trodden patch between the stalks of night-scented stock outside Cora's bedroom and a note. The note, on the back of a cigarette packet top, was tucked between the window and the thick-painted lock. *Just passing by*, it read. *U Know Who.* Small, neat handwriting. Blue. Unfamiliar.

Instinctively, I bolted upstairs to Rose and Angus asking to sleep at theirs. No reason: none asked. They were delighted in the way they always were and I didn't mention the note. Cora and mum came back next afternoon within an hour of each other so there was no need to mention it again. Mum said nothing about the funeral and Cora nothing about Troon or Stirling or wherever the hell she'd been so we were even. I made a coffee and walnut cake for them coming back and Cora chucked me a bag of Edinburgh Rock. Whether the Edinburgh Rock had come direct from Edinburgh was not disclosed. I dropped the folded note onto the carpet beneath Cora's window and hoped she wouldn't sniff it for fingerprints. She might have found it, might not: either way it disappeared and nobody said. If what you didn't know didn't hurt you, we were intent on staying pain-free. Mum gave me two pounds from Yorkshire, with which I bought a Russian Primer and a diary. Mastering the Cyrillic alphabet made a diary, for once, a possibility. The more you learned, the better you grasped how to conceal. Now, as always, reading was all gain. *Can you keep a secret for someone else?* Even without the quiz, I knew the answer. I kept secrets with the best.

A folded paper flicked sideways onto my desk in the middle of French irregular verbs so I picked it up. It had tiny, childlike print inside, each word of its first sentence written with tongue-biting care. And what they said was

You are adorable.

The three words were all I managed before I closed my eyes to cope. Stiff with embarrassment, I felt sure whoever had written it was watching me and stuffed it inside my blazer pocket. It had to be a joke. *Je ris, tu ris, il rit. Il rit* all right. Present participle, *riant.* The note, however, would not take a telling. There was more writing in there, and thinking about what it might say was making me restless. Annoyed, I shuffled the damn thing from my inside pocket, steeled myself and opened it out.

> You are adorable. But I cannot pick up the courage to ask you to go out with me so I'm asking in this note. Will you? It doesn't matter if you say no. I will still feel the same.
>
> Bradley.

Astounded, I blazed through *savoir* and *sortir* and *suivre*, then raised my head in what I hoped was a you-don't-fool-me sort of way. Right next to me, his glasses on a tilt, the boy on my left was peering back. Heavy fringe, blazer, the faint stirrings of a moustache. I squinted across another twice. The third time, he smiled. He had to be Bradley. I didn't even know if Bradley was a real name but that had to be him. I looked again and he smiled again, wider this time. He's nuts, I thought. He flapped four fingers in a secret little wave and I blushed to the roots of my boots. Whatever I'd done to make him write it, he'd done it now. Guilty and excited enough to tremble, I let him walk me as near to home as I dared and he stroked my cheek before he sauntered off. Gosh, I thought. Big shoulders. Even boys had those big, wide shoulders. He was – the thought was dazzling – half a man.

Bradley and me were an item for almost a year. My first boyfriend, loaded with unexpected treasures. I thought boyfriends were about holding hands and kissing. The *Jackie* stories had not prepared me for the best part, which was more to do with being let in on another life. By the end of that year I could respray a car with cellulose paint, kick-start a motorbike, change a gasket set, get by as a passable amateur press photographer and process my own film. On these bases alone, I have no complaints about Bradley.

He lived at the other end of Saltcoats in a bungalow with his sister and parents who were still together but gave the impression they'd be better off not. His dad, Bob, was a school teacher with an interest in what used to be called *glamour photography* and I forget what it was his mother did but whatever it was made her pretty damn cross most of the time. End-of-tether was the general mood of the household, and Bradley's mum coming to the boil while his dad beetled out of the way as though it had nothing to do with him when most of the time I suspected it did. Bob suited him. You were never quite sure where he was. Beattie and Bob both enjoyed a good laugh and I imagined that's what they once had in common. Being alone with either of them could be stressful. Holly, Bradley's sister, seemed to have landed in a holding unit for people with mood disorders and couldn't get out. As a pair, his parents seemed the kind of people who, like children, gave their feelings away every time they spoke. And they spoke a lot. Bradley's folks talked through TV programmes and through each other. They hurled instructions through open windows, up the stairs and through closed bathroom doors. Bob mislaying keys, a socket set, a camera lens or anything else gave rise to a *sotto voce* commentary of the search, keeping the world clued in till the keys turned up where they were meant to be after all. Nobody got hit. They yelled now and then but the yelling lacked genuine killer instinct. Sometimes I felt old beside them, protective and tired and miles away. Most times, I kept myself to myself. And where I did that was Bradley's room.

Bradley's bedroom was a space to himself under the eaves with a small bay window that looked out from almost lamp-post height across the front garden and the carriage-wide sweep of Shore Road. Inside, the view was of a narrow single bed to the right of the door, and *stuff*. Not just ordinary *stuff* but astonishing quantities of *stuff*, including motorbike components, Miró-shaped tools, stacks of *Motorcycle Monthly*, *Exchange and Mart*, *Custom Car* and *Practical Photography*, tins of enamel paint, tins of cellulose paint, Humbrol black enamel and a jar of Gunk. Gunk, on closer inspection, was green gelatinous stuff like alien spawn from a sci-fi movie that claimed to be hand-cleaner though smelled more likely to melt skin than disinfect it. As long as I knew him, Bradley was building an engine, patching bodywork with filler or levering off tyres. If he wasn't, he was watching a

Clint Eastwood movie or developing rolls of film in his dad's darkroom. Bradley liked to build things. Camshafts, cooling fins, rocker arms, adjustment of tappets were second-nature, his visio-spatial ability 3D clear. He understood mixes of chemicals and what *f* numbers and light meters added to the creative framing of a scene. Bradley, unafraid to get his hands dirty, was masculine as only a boy's boy on the verge of being a man's man could be. And men, to one raised in a house of mystery-laden women, were as fantastically storybook as real live dragons. Left in his room while he clonked around with cylinder heads, I fondled his army and navy surplus jumpers, absorbing texture. I poked around the inside pockets of his Belstaff and tried on his leather gauntlets. I took off my clothes to try on his shirts and step into his jeans to feel the differences first hand. Men's clothes were full of pockets. The zips were in reachable places and his trousers, even the tight ones, had slack to stride. Alone in Bradley's room I took to wearing his shirts all the time. He didn't mind. He didn't mind when I painted his fingernails with nail varnish either and tolerated my drawing specs and warts on the big-breasted women he regularly pinned on the walls. *Whatever keeps the little lady happy*, a phrase he learned either from his dad or Burt Reynolds, kept him ticking. *Whatever you say, babes*. One day, Bradley would remind me of his dad, harassed and frustrated by domestic interiors yet saddled with children, keener to escape to the shed than grow up. But I was drawn. His home was not mine and I learned things there. I loved the *otherness* of his skin, the pleasure and warmth of his open embrace. Being folded up by

Bradley was worth any amount of *little lady* rubbish in comparison to the touchlessness of home, and besides, there was all that lust. Not just any old lust but that compulsive curiosity, the hair-trigger responses that fifteen-year-olds find at their fingertips without trying.

I rubbed his jaw wondering if it itched having hair poke through your skin like that; found delight in the hard flatness of his chest and the solidity of his arms. His neck tasted of warm chicken and his wrists of salt. Just the right amount of salt. I touched no part of him that wouldn't be seen by anyone on a warm day but he was patient. He put some thought into things. And what he came up with was a magazine, a single edition of a floppy multi-part encyclopaedia called *The Human Body*. It had an introduction by an anthropologist to establish it wasn't just a load of smut, and a lolly-stick with a joke printed on the shaft had been used to mark the place Bradley had selected for me to see. Together, we opened out a centre-spread of what looked like lost Picassos from the Spanish master's blue period. Coloured, pencil sketched and tinted a shade of noncommittal turquoise so they didn't look obscene, sore or angry, the pictures purported to be of something I'd never seen before. The name of that thing, printed in white rococo lettering across the double-spread, was delicate, Edwardian-sounding, a name like a flower. At five syllables, it required to be spoken out loud to fix its pronunciation in the mouth. *Gen-it-a-li-a.* That's how green I was. *Genitalia*. The word attained, I let my eyes flip the drawings into focus. They were very different. One side showed something funnel-shaped with what looked like layers of ribbon-tie trim around the edges while the other was a series of bulges. I traced the lines that led to the names of the frills and push-buttons and tangled edgings, the curves and snake-head tips till they rose from obscurity into order. Naming was power, I knew that, but these names sounded more like Latin terms for sea-creatures than bits of people and since I wanted to get them right, I took my time. Bradley, to his credit, was persuasive. Engineer to his fingertips, he pored over the technical drawings, explained the corresponding parts, then showed me how they fit, locked, ticked over as one. Then, as he had perhaps planned all along, he offered to show me where I kept mine. Astonishing, what you hold within and never know till someone tells you. I was grateful as sin.

I wish to point out that I did not look at his naked form till I'd learned to enjoy this thing we were doing for well over a month, and longer than that before he was allowed to pull back the sheets. His parents never entered his room without knocking so we were never made to feel underhand except by my own thorough training in shame. That I learned the word *virgin* only after I wasn't one, seems typical. I can't have been the first and anyway, to regret having lost some notional treasure I'd never known I had in the first place seemed churlish. What I had felt was not, would never be, loss. It was learning. And learning, the keener and more dedicated the better, is always gain.

Even at fifteen, it wasn't all *coitus interruptus*. With our noses swathed in bandit masks, we resprayed ancient cars he'd cobbled together out of salvaged components. We hung around in the dingy interior of Dennis Nelson's spares emporium, and developed photos which hung on a little washing line in the darkroom with pegs. We went on walking-distance picnics and trips to the beach and helped my mother with the garden. It was hopelessly domestic and I loved it all. But I did not love Bradley. Scales did not fall from my eyes or stitch them over insisting I was blind. I liked his being there and having someone to talk to. I liked his fascinating otherness and his easy arousal and the sex part was very satisfactory, like being lost and found at the same time only much more physically engaging. I freely admit I experienced Rapunzel-like stirrings of the heart when he roared up to the front door on the big blue BSA, chucked me his gauntlets and carried me off with the wind in my hair and my arms round his waist, recklessly licence-free all the way to Seamill. He was fun and exciting and nice to mum and I was grateful. But for Godsake I didn't want to marry him. And wanting to marry the object of your affections, as any fool knew, was the acid test of *Love.* Love and marriage/horse and carriage: you couldn't have one without the other according to Van Heusen and Cahn, and quality song-writing was an unimpeachable authority. The other thing about marriage – something I knew from repeated telling – was that having anything to do with it meant giving up the rest of your life and people who had their heads screwed on didn't go anywhere near it, which explained why so many songs compared love to insanity. If real love led to real marriage, I wanted to steer clear as long as I held on to any shred of being rational.

Right now, I liked the me and Bradley thing just the way things were. Anything more was greedy, even unnecessary. I said as much out loud in an unguarded moment and my mother straightened her back and stared at me as though I'd hit her with a plank.

Of course you'll get married, she said. She looked stunned. Everybody gets married.

No, they don't, I said. I've got teachers who aren't married and they're *old* for goodness sake.

Pfff, teachers. Teachers prove nothing. Teachers aren't *normal*.

Yes, they are.

No, they're not. Women teachers used to have to stop working if they got married, so they had a choice. They stuck with the job. Which is fine but you can't say it's *normal*. Everybody normal gets married. Everybody knows everybody normal gets married. So don't you start.

Well, it was what *you* did, that's for sure. And look what happened to you. You had to run away and skivvy for one room because you had me and he wouldn't give you any money. You said it more than once. You *kept* saying it.

That was different, she snapped. I married the wrong man. There are plenty of wrong ones – I'm not saying there's not – but it's up to you to pick the *right* one. You're supposed to have brains so you pick the *right* one, Smarty. You're never done seeing that boy. What are you doing *that* for if you don't think you'll get married one day? You must think he's all right.

O for crying out loud I'm just *going out* with him. I was

squeaking now, outraged at her duplicity. It was *you* that said marriage was a mug's game. You said it was the worst thing you ever did. You said—

That was *before*, she said.

I looked at her. Before what?

Before you were an age it made any difference. Before you had a *boyfriend* or whatever it is you call them these days.

I'm fifteen, I said. *Fifteen.*

Oh I know what age you are all right. I was in service when I was fifteen and nobody looked out for me. But I know from her through there – she pointed at Cora's bedroom door – what else fifteen means. Don't think I don't know what happens after the boys turn up. School goes over Niagara in a barrel, that's what. You that thinks you're clever – you know less than you think. You're sixteen near enough and when you're sixteen, if he's still in the picture, you can do what you like. Bradley's a nice enough chap. Her eyes were shining. I'm just saying, if the worst comes to the worst, that's what you do.

Most of what she was driving at was lost on me, but one bit was both explicit and undeniable. Sixteen was legal marrying age in my country. In less than a year I'd still be too irresponsible to drink alcohol or vote but fit enough to commit to matrimony and all it entailed. And mum was giving me the green light. If the worst came to the worst, whatever that meant, it was OK.

He's a bit sure of himself, she said, but he'd be handy round the house. And he'd not hit you. She paused. At least I don't think so. Anyway. A lot can happen. That's all I'm saying. Her voice was low again, conciliatory. I'm only saying what needs saying. I'm your mother. I'm allowed that much. I'm your mother.

Her eyes were brimming. Maybe she was saying nothing more than what was reasonable. She was entitled to say what she thought, and if Bradley was someone she liked I was grateful. He mowed her lawn as part of a deliberate charm offensive the first time she met him so *of course* she liked him. He brought a Chubby Checker record round and got her to twist. Bradley was very good at that kind of charm. It dawned on me suddenly that maybe my mother missed male company. Her friend in the fire brigade, Duncan, had come around a lot at one time, brought her chocolates and stayed to chat. Not these days. Cora said he and his wife had moved to a town further up the coast though how she'd know that was anybody's guess. Whatever happened, we saw Duncan once in a blue moon. He'd have liked Bradley too. Even Cora liked Bradley. At least, she liked him the way she liked most things – from a respectful distance. Now and then she blew smoke rings at him with her mouth in an O to see what I'd do which was nothing. Bradley, she said, was just passing time till he found somebody better and she flirted with him under my nose to make me feel stupid. Cora was annoying, but annoying was better than this searching and poking in of noses. Whatever had got into her, mum seemed to be waiting for something painful to happen. To whom was not clear.

Anyway, mum said, businesslike again, I don't know what the

fuss is about. If you get married these days and it doesn't work out you can get a divorce. You can get divorced these days after five minutes. Your lot don't know you're born.

She headed back to the kitchen, probably hurt and probably clueless, leaving two words spinning on a merry-go-round behind her. *I'm fifteen. I'm fifteen. I'm fifteen.* The exchange had been eerie and all to cock and I couldn't put it into better words. The best thing to do was try and forget it. I had Latin to learn. I had *The Night They Drove Old Dixie Down* to learn so we could sing it at Sheltered Housing on Thursday. I had exams to think about and planning which periods to ask for my instrumental lessons so I could bunk off Maths and PE for legitimate reasons. I had just started piano lessons with Mr Hetherington and he was giving me Mozart and Purcell in perfect little pieces to get my fingers around, the kind of pieces I knew had to be out there when I'd been hacking my way through *The Little Elf* with Miss Hughes, the retired piano teacher from the shore road flats, and I felt things were heading in a good direction. Orchestra rehearsals were beginning for *The Wedding March* and *The Great Gate of Kiev* so we could play them at a Festival and we wanted to win. Being inside so much sound as it swept over the viola section on its way to the back of the hall was like nothing else. The horns bloomed like big brass roses from behind the woodwind desks and a tympani roll shook the floor beneath your shoes. The single oboe, in the desk right behind, could insinuate into the chest cavity without even trying while clarinets smoothed things in treacle. I was in the middle of every rattle, roll and slide of the bows and why I'd give that up escaped me. Bradley was fun. But there were bigger and more stupefying things than fun, things that embraced in a different way. Mum would have to think what she liked. I wasn't giving up Music for anything.

There was no explaining it so I didn't try and in the end, didn't need to. Ken went to Kyleshill kitchens to do it for me. He found mum finishing her shift, one of six middle-aged women in heavy white cotton uniforms lifting the last racks of institution crockery out of the scalding driers, and asked if she'd let me take Music as my main study for S4. She never forgot it. Naked beneath her regulation whites, her hair in a net with the roots needing done, a teacher asked her permission as though she ought, as of right, to be wooed. And though I wasn't there, I didn't forget it either. Someone had singled me out as worthwhile and since teachers were powerful people then, the gatekeepers to futures, she had to listen. She did not say it wasn't a job because there he was in front of her, a musician and employed. Cora wasn't there to say it wasn't for the likes of me though he'd have had an answer for that too. He took her hand and told her Music could give me as good a future as anything else and not to worry that nothing would come of it. He thanked her for her time and wished her well. No gamesmanship. Unused to anything so disarming, she said yes. Was I: Mostly As: Doleful Daisy, Mostly Bs: Clueless Carol or Mostly Cs: Lucky Lucy? Even Cora knew the answer to that.

You're a jammy bugger, you, she said. Who told you it was OK to let that man come round pestering your mother at work? She didn't know where to look for Godsake.

The answer – *it was all his own idea* – was the best bit. My toast had landed butter side up and my yoke was easy, my burthen feather-light. *Lucky* wasn't in it. The only way from here was up.

8

Three vague promises and Macbeth is losing the plot.

Our class were watching the Thane of Glamis unravel before our eyes in Room 42 with Mrs Kidd. The King loved him, the troops loved him, Mrs Kidd thought he was the bees' knees – everything started off so well. A handful of pages, however, an acid-yellow whiff of sulphur insinuates the war-blackened air. Promises of an easy life, the smack of as yet untasted power: any fool can see where this is going. Not Macbeth. He picks up the scissors the witches drop and heedless, far too fast, begins to run.

The Scottish Play thrilled me to smithereens and I read to the end in bed at night using the glossary and tingling all over. Nobody told me Shakespeare would be a thrill. In addition, I was eligible to play in the chamber orchestra and Bradley was teaching me to drive. I could draw the component parts of a motorcycle engine and kick-start like a trouper. My generation were reaping change and acquiring *stuff*, all kinds of previously unimaginable *stuff*. I had a piano – run-down perhaps, but certainly a piano – and a Chinese factory viola on loan from the school. I had a guitar and a boyfriend with big ideas. Wherever dad's grave was, I was sure he was turning in it. Then the life lessons took over.

Bradley gave me the bullet. He was bored with the domestic business of *going steady* and at fifteen, that was entirely reasonable. I could see it was reasonable. His idea of a perfect day was raking about in Dennis Nelson's for throttle slip-ons, clutch covers and windscreen fixing nuts at knock-down prices, then a Clint Eastwood movie with his pals and he was sick of compromise. It came right after we'd spent ages fixing up a rusty little Honda, and the care he'd lavished rebuilding the engine I had taken as a sign of devotion. He had picked the machine for me himself –*125cc is plenty for a girl* – after which I stripped, sanded and resprayed while he did things with spanners. My crowning touch was painting the tank and the mudguards metallic purple with flowers and Bradley sulked. After all that work, I'd halved the resale value and Bradley was a chap with an eye for resale value. Maybe that was what tipped the balance. After the bombshell, delivered as he stood at the door in his Belstaff, he straddled his untaxed BSA and pulled on his gauntlets. It struck me as I watched him preparing for the off that it wasn't just Bradley I was losing. It was my welcome as a pillion passenger. My driving lessons. My other life. Not sure I was doing the right thing, I raced outside and asked.

He'd still teach me to drive, he said. Not to worry.

OK, I said. I looked brave.

Cheer up! he said. It's not the end of the world. And chucked me under the chin, kicked down, and roared into what passed for sunset at the end of the street. That was what struck hardest. Bradley chucking me under the chin. I didn't know whether to laugh or cry.

It took three days for Cora to notice Bradley wasn't around any more and get to the nitty-gritty.

He's got shot of you, hasn't he?

I said nothing. Armed with all the confirmation she needed, my sister reached for what came naturally.

It's your own fault. You know it is. All that boring stuff you like – no wonder he buggered off. You might as well wear specs and a bloody caliper. She stood up and stretched, nice and easy. Take a tip from me and pack that stuff in. There's not a boy in his right mind will take up with you if keep playing that music and reading books nobody likes. You know what boys want? She sat back down, produced her wool scissors and set about her toe-nails not even looking in my direction. What boys want is somebody that knows how to have a good time. Somebody that enjoys a laugh and a dance and a beer, you know? Not a big drink of water with a violin case.

Viola case. Mum appeared with a duster to polish the mirror over the fireplace and joined in.

Whatever. Her priorities are all to cock. *Clever* got nobody a man. Latin Godsake. Boys don't like lassies who do that stuff. Not unless there's something wrong with them. That's how come teachers are all single and ancient. She leaned to cast the clip-pings in the fire where they popped like corn.

You're ignorant, you, my mother said.

Aye right, she said. I know damn all and this here's Mata Hari. Anyway, that's all I'm saying. It's for her own good. Now shift. She put the scissors in their case and crossed her legs. Your head's in the way.

The advice and Romance coaching were over: the news was ready to start. Mum turned the sound up as the tune came to a close and Cora assembled her props for the evening ahead: pattern on her knees, open book on the arm rest, cigarettes and lighter on the stereo. Her interests didn't seem like that much of a good time to me. Soon, she'd drape the fabric of her knitting just so and barely look down. Just knit and stare. I shifted in time to let her see a pub blown to bits in Belfast and mum turned the sound back down.

It's all aggression nowadays, she said. Selfishness and destruction. She shook her head and opened the living-room door, preparing to hive off and make tea. Anyway, there's plenty more fish in the sea.

It took me a moment to understand she meant Bradley. Bradley was one of many, insignificant in the long term. It was a big thought. I stuck a mint in my mouth to help swallow the lump in my throat and thought I'd got off light. It was out now. I'd been dumped. Even knowing it, Cora hadn't laughed and mum hadn't blamed. On the contrary, she brought me tea and a chocolate biscuit and chocolate biscuits, maternally tendered, were a kind of love. It wasn't enough. Still as a dead thing with my face to the wall till mum put off the light, I couldn't sleep.

The dark filled with mum's gentle snoring, but Cora was flipping and turning in my mind, her words swirling like scarlet scarves in a whites wash. What if the things she'd said were true? If it really was my own fault for liking *boring stuff*? If the things I liked were automatically categorisable as boring because I liked them? Worse, that not just some boys, but *any boy in his right mind* would steer clear? What was I supposed to do? A choice between two kinds of loneliness was no choice at all.

I wasn't stupid. I knew I wasn't supposed to beat boys at cards or sport and not to pay my share in a café till we were outside in private. I knew women were tough as old boots really and that men had something called an ego that was easily bruised. But the books thing had me foxed. Why would *books* put them off? Or some kinds of music but not others? Why was *clever-dicky*, whatever that meant, only something to hide? What was her evidence? I thought about the women on Bradley's *Custom Car* magazines, their thighs apart over the bonnets of souped-up Cortinas. True enough, I could bring none, not one, to mind that had been thus pictured holding a book. I thought about Miss World contestants. In interviews, they were happy enough confessing an enthusiasm for world peace, but not Shostakovich or Coleridge. It was more than coincidence. Maybe they knew what Cora knew and to keep mum. Cora read books, but only library books that might be returned and their place, I realised uncomfortably, was always *beneath the bed*. What all this amounted to was hard to say, but unsettling anyway. I remembered the note coming through my sister's bedroom window, its suggestion of secret assignation, and fell asleep listening for a tap on the window that never came.

Bradley kept his word and got me through the motorcycle proficiency test somehow, having sex with me occasionally as *fair exchange*. His words. I couldn't think of a reason why he shouldn't. The emotional and moral paradox at work was not lost on me, but logic comes a lousy second to the only cuddle on offer. His final kiss-off was a copy of the Highway Code and an old copy of *Motorcycle Monthly* with ads for cheap components circled in black felt tip, after which we were, as he succinctly summarised, *quits*. Over weeks, I felt the loss acutely. My face and fingers, my entire skin surface felt bereft. Nothing in *Jackie* offered advice about this kind of thing and books were distraction and consolation only as long as the page lasted. I missed Bradley's little sister, the bustle of his home, the darkroom and its washing line of landscapes etched in light. I missed the socket set beneath the bed, his hilarious taste in country music and the neat dotted line of his circumcision scar. I knew what *quits* meant. It meant written off. It meant *done*.

My mother, mindful that idle hands were the devil's playthings and cousin Peter's wedding was soon, bought me three yards of purple crimplene, a pattern and some scratchy lurex lace for a frock. Peter was Aunty Kitty's grandson, my mother's great-nephew and seven years older than me. I'd been at Galloway weddings when I was small because two-year-old flower girls were in vogue at the time and I was the two-year-old available. What I remembered of these experiences was mixed: clinging to a silver horseshoe while the bride tried to take it from me, being fed up during an interminable dinner, smiling for the record on a hotel lawn in a mini-kilt and jabot blouse. I hoped Peter's – a wedding from mum's side rather than dad's – might be better and cut the frock more in hope than expectation. Two days later, the lurex looked crooked but the zip worked fine so the dress would do. It was cousin Peter's wedding, not mine.

Come the day, my mother chose a smart navy dress suit with a pink rose from the garden pinned to the lapel, new shoes and clip-on pearl earrings that lent a soft glow to her skin. She had a shampoo and set and, since the threat of lay-offs at the kitchens had been lifted, asked them to throw in a pale gold rinse for her now noticeably grey temples. Weddings, she said, ought to be celebrations whatever happened next, and for such a celebration, one made an effort.

Cora didn't do weddings, funerals or silver anniversaries, but she came to this one in an understated shift-dress and a diamanté bag with a lipstick and a tissue inside. She sat at a different table with cousins her own age, women I barely knew. There was a band and flickering disco lights, an expectation of dancing. Peter and his bride, still wearing her white fur-trimmed cape, stumbled about to a recording of Nat King Cole singing *Around the World* as everybody's mother made cooing noises and took pictures. Cora didn't. Head to knee in polka-dot satin, Sophia Loren shapely, she looked more luminous than I'd seen her for years. Her hair was shorter now, professionally curled and shiny with spray under the lights and I watched her from a distance, twirling under someone's arm and laughing with her head back. Curvier than they'd been in their twenties, her hips swayed as she shifted from one foot to the other, pearl white toenails pouting from her blue satin peep-toes. Between dances she held one elbow to help the other bear the weight of a cigarette between the first and second fingers of her right hand, *coo-eed* at strangers and waved. Cora knew how to do parties. Like dad, she could turn on *life and soul.* If the book I'd been reading was true, that made her an *extravert*, one who fed on excitement and externals. My mother, like me, was not. She sat with the same sweet sherry all night and didn't dance, even when pressed. Eventually, Uncle Tommy came over and since he was her brother and wouldn't take no for an answer, she did the rounds of a slow foxtrot whether she liked it or not. Watching her suggested she liked it more than she claimed. He kept her up for a jive while I watched. Peter, the newly married groom, who had been bathed in a sink with me when we were both a lot younger, looked as though he'd rather be sitting things out too. The smile he'd managed all the way through the wedding snaps was still nervous and his vast lapels made his face look overwhelmed. Maybe that's why I liked Peter, always had. He looked like Aunty Marie. His father, bow-tied and tuxedoed, was leaning at the bar like a hit man, hunched over a pint. Uncle Matt didn't do small talk. It showed. In the band break, Hayley, Peter's brand-new wife, did the rounds of guests with her mother, handing out Lego-bricks of cake on napkins.

Leave the marzipan if you don't like it, she said. I asked them to leave it off but they have to stick it on for the icing. It's just what they do.

Hayley was pink and white and highly upholstered while her mother looked sallow and thin. Maybe the lights under your skin just went out eventually and you didn't get them back. Behind them, the floor was clearing for *turns*. It was that time of night. Somebody's uncle got up first. Somebody's uncle always did. He accompanied the band playing *I want to be happy but I can't be happy till I make you happy too* on two sets of table spoons he'd probably brought with him for the occasion. Cheering invited another number after which Allan did his famous Rolling Stones medley on the accordion. Mum came back, flushed and revivified, already slipping the cake into her handbag for later. Between exercise, heat and third rounds of drinks the room had relaxed. The ceremonials were over and the talent parade meant the night was no longer young and belts might be slackened. Soon, someone would come over and ask my mother to sing. At one time, she'd been a star at the Bowling Green Club. I had seen a snap of her with Tommy and Allan, the boys in cravats and mum in a two-piece and smart cloche hat, heads to the sky like wolves to a full moon. Now, she sang only for herself in the kitchen, blaming asthma. Whatever the cause, her voice had weakened to the point where she was ashamed to use it in public and I had no patience with it. Nobody forgot how to sing. Watching other singers get up made her wistful and sorry but she stayed put. When a big woman got up to belt out a substandard *Stand By Your Man*, she looked away. Cora, at the corner of the stage, was rolling her eyes. *Stand By Your Man* was a magnet for the tone deaf. Four bars in, it was already dire.

You not dancing? Aunty Kitty was standing in front of me, peering. She had cataracts. Not the kind of thing, eh? Her voice was steel. I don't suppose this is fancy enough for the kinds of things you like.

I thought about responding, pointing out that turns precluded dancing but didn't. Everything Aunty Kitty said was traps.

That's some frock, she said. Kind of shapeless. You'll maybe grow into it.

I made it, I said. My head ran X-ray plates of every wobbly seam I'd tried to conceal, the rim at the top of the neckline where the lining showed. Kitty looked impressed.

You *made* it. Well there we are. Your mum never mentioned you were clever enough to be making clothes. Do you make her anything?

The question threw me. I wouldn't dream of making mum anything to wear. Mum was a natty dresser. Kitty didn't notice my lack of answer. Well, she said. Here's you in that lovely frock you made just for yourself and not dancing. You should have brought that boyfriend your mum's always telling us about, let us get a look.

Mum was on the other side of the room, trying to talk to

somebody through the rodeo hollering. *Give him two arms to cling to, and something warm to come to when the nights are cold and lonely.* I smiled faintly at Kitty and wished she'd at least sit. It was a pain in the neck looking up.

She says he lives in one of those nice wee bungalows near the shore front. I bet that cost. Worth a bob or two, eh?

Mmm, I said. None of this was really about prices, boyfriends or frocks. I'd hoped the wedding would let Kitty be more mellow than usual but the way this was going suggested not. Sooner or later, she'd get on to her favourite thing and denounce someone for thinking they were *It*. She'd have been a hit at the Salem witch trials, ready to point fingers in an attempt to soothe whatever it was that ailed her. Give Kitty roses and she saw weeds, showing off. People with cars thought they were *It*. People who used trains instead of buses thought they were *It*. People who carried books and visitors to museums and people who chose to watch the BBC when there was a moving object of any kind on the opposite channel were guilty of *It*-crime by default. Whitewashing the front step outside your front door too often was *holier-than-thou*, eating foreign food was *pretentious* and dental receptionists were *stuck up*. Children, if not systematically suppressed, could get *cocky, pushy, too clever by half* or *rotten to the bone*. Kitty had a list of scroungers, layabouts and those in need of a good shake but those labouring under the delusion they were *It* belonged to the seventh circle of hell. Right now, I was being assessed as at least *high and mighty* on the grounds that I knew someone who lived in a bungalow. I knew what I thought was showing on my face because when she chose next to address me, she did it in the third person.

She's keeping him to herself, mibby that's it? Too special to bring here?

Feeling the press of a wall against my back, I did something foolish and lied.

Overtime, I said. He's working. I heard myself saying it. Bradley, who'd dumped me, was apparently *working*. Kitty looked at me sideways.

Your mother says he's still at school so he's not working, is he? Without breaking eye contact, she lifted one arm and hailed Marie like a cab. Marie, mother-of-the-groom mingling near the bar, looked up. Did Beth say that boy this one's hanging about with was at school? Kitty was hollering. The boy's definitely at school – isn't that what she said?

I smiled at Marie hoping she'd stay right where she was and told Kitty the boyfriend in question was indeed at school but he took pictures for the local paper at weekends. This was at least true. Kitty arched an eyebrow as if I'd found a loophole.

Photographer, she said. You know what side your bread's buttered. What's he staying at school for if he can do that?

I had no idea. Engineering, I said. Technical Drawing.

That's what you call manual skills. He's no genius then? Good with his hands?

No, I said. Not a genius.

Are you staying on just because he's there? You can tell me. You are, aren't you?

I showed my teeth and hoped it looked like smiling. No. I like school. I really do.

That's not normal. It's unusual. Your sister didn't stay on and Alma's not bothering either. As quick as she could get paid work and off she went. She's doing part-time at the hairdressers.

I'm staying on to do Music, I said. I need to.

Well. She smiled limply. Your mother was a lovely singer once and she never had lessons, but I'm sure you know what you're doing. Alma says she'll have her own salon one day. She's got a business brain. I was telling your mother only the other day, our Alma says staying on at school is a mug's game. It's not for go-ahead types.

As if she'd been invoked, my mother appeared at Kitty's elbow, bright-eyed and needing her inhaler. Kitty looked her up and down.

Your lassie's just telling us how her boyfriend's a photographer. He's got a job and staying on at the school. She laughed as though doing both at the same time was crazy.

Mum was nonplussed. Why we were talking about Bradley was beyond her. She's doing Music though. That's her choice.

Well you'd never know, Kitty sighed. Doing Music and we never hear a cheep out of her. Maybe you'll give us a song and show her how it's done. The Galloways will get a name for being anti-social if you're not careful.

I'm not singing. My mother puffed and sat down to catch her breath. But she can. She looked at me. You could do that opera thing you were learning the other week. Come on now. Show Kitty what you can do.

My stomach shrank. If singing was what it took to prove we weren't anti-social, to prove doing Music was more than showing off, then I was supposed to sing. It was about mum's dignity now and I knew it. Inappropriate bits of Bach and Psalms, folk songs and other wrong things spun on the roundabout in my head till one fell off. *Where e'er you walk*. It sounded fine unaccompanied and lots of people knew it. They could even join in. Once round the block, no repeats and faces were saved. I nodded.

Sure, I said. I can sing something.

As long as it's not opera stuff, Kitty said. People dying of a cough and jumping off things: you canny do opera at a wedding. It's depressing. Does she not know something a bit livelier? Something a bit modern?

Of course she does, mum said. And she looked at me again.

All the folk songs I knew were about methods of transport, prairies and suicides. Pop needed a backing track. Blues was out. There was only one thing for it. A show tune. I knew everything in *My Fair Lady* forwards, backwards and with repeats.

Well? mum said. Are you going to give us a tune?

Damned if I did, damned if I didn't, I clumped up to the tiny stage in unfamiliar heels and rendered *I'm Getting Married in the Morning*. The band joined in, sometimes in a different key, and I sang for no other reason than that I was honour-bound to deliver. Then it was finished thank God. Blushing, in a badly made purple frock with too-short sleeves and squint lurex trim under the bust, I trailed back to my seat as the guitarist announced a Dashing White Sergeant. Someone shouted *Hooch!* and in the general scurrying for partners, I saw mum wandering off to speak to someone else. Time for dancing. The wheel had turned and I was back with Kitty, on my own.

That wasn't opera, Kitty said. That was from a musical. I'm not stupid.

Well, that's why I picked it. You said—

You thought I wouldny understand opera, didn't you? You're a sly wee madam and no mistake. Did you think I wouldn't know what you were doing? Looking down your nose?

You said you didn't want opera, I squeaked. You made a point of it. You said it was depressing.

So it is.

Well, why would I sing it after that? You wanted something modern!

Nobody stopped you doing what you wanted. She opened her eyes wide. You chose, so don't take a huff with me.

Godsake, I sighed. It came out petty. Kitty being a cow always made my throat tight. Marie bumped between us, oblivious.

Look at you! Free of duty and slightly tipsy, Marie held a glass in one hand. Look at you in this fancy frock eh!

Did you not hear her singing? Kitty asked. She gave us a lovely song. One that was easy to understand.

No! Marie said, looking astonished. I was outside doing the taxis and missed you, hen. Were you good?

Kitty looked smug and I didn't know what to say. Marie laughed. You don't know if you were any good! Don't tell me you're as shy as all that!

I knew I was supposed to laugh and be light but my face wouldn't behave. It felt doughy and unresponsive. It refused to smile. Kitty leaned close.

Tell you who you're like, she said. Your dad. It's just your father standing there.

Marie grinned.

And I tell you something else. Kitty leaned closer. You tell lies. He did that as well.

The cable holding the lift cage of my stomach was in free fall.

You know what I'm talking about don't you? Kitty said. You know what you said. You said barefaced you had a boyfriend and I believed every word. Then I go talking to your mother and she lets slip you've got nothing of the kind. Not any more. Now, here's the thing. She rose to her full height. We're your family. You don't tell your family lies. Not to show off or nothing else. You're off down the wrong road lady, and no mistake.

Mum arrived in a rush, slightly breathless and dusted with cold as if she'd been outside. Somewhere fresher. I wished she had taken me too.

I'm just saying, Aunt Kitty raised her voice, looping the company in. I'm saying you wouldny think a clever girl has to tell lies, would you?

Mum's face, opening to say whatever it was she'd come to say in the first place, fell.

Your lassie here is just after telling me she's got a boyfriend. Then you tell me yourself he's off a week past. Now why would she do that, Beth? Why would she say she's invited him along when she's got nobody to invite? Her voice had shifted to teasing now, a semblance of innocent fun. Is she pulling the wool, do you think? Teasing her aunty?

Och it would be a slip of the tongue, Kitty. I don't think she'd be telling you actual *lies*.

But it's what she said. See, lies always catch you out. Have you not told her that?

I was hoping mum would laugh. I hoped she'd say *for goodness sake* or *who cares?* I hoped a waitress would tip a whole tray of drinks over Kitty and she'd have to be wheeled off somewhere distant to recover with Marie trailing after her, slurring and covered in wine. I wished I was better at knowing how to deal with this kind of thing. But none of that stuff happened and Kitty had mum on the hop. If I was a liar, someone had shown me a bad example. Her big sister was making her feel that she was at fault, not just me.

Do you not tell the truth in your house? Kitty persisted. Reckless, I drew her a look.

That's just snide, my mother said. Kitty looked shocked.

I'm just pulling your leg, she said. It's just a bit of fun.

Aware she was losing something and not sure what, my mother let her shoulders drop. Did you tell lies to your Aunty Kitty? The look in her eyes made me feel see-through.

I forget, I said, too ashamed to come clean. I can't remember.

And Kitty laughed. A dry sound, oxygen-deprived. Maybe she didn't laugh much because her tubes were furred up. Maybe she was ill.

You can't think! I don't imagine you'd be passing all those exams you're so good at if you can't think! She dabbed her mouth with a hanky.

Maybe she was embarrassed about the boyfriend thing and didn't want to say. Is that it? Mum was being heroic but I said nothing. I tried to look like nothing. Well, she knows not to tell lies. This one doesny tell lies, Kitty. So she just made a wee mistake.

It was a joke, Marie said. Just fun.

Kitty dabbed her mouth again and tucked the paper hanky in her watch band. Over her shoulder, Cora came into focus, wondering what the pow-wow was about. She nodded once, stuck out her jaw and swung over, ostentatiously casual.

All right? she said, slipping between Kitty and Marie. Did you like the song? A bit old-fashioned but who cares? Some kid!

Och, we're just saying, Marie said. We were saying it was nice.

Mum was still flat. Maybe she should have played the piano, she muttered. Marie kept smiling into the silence and offered a change of tack.

Well, here we are. And here's the three of you. That's a turn-up: the three of you and not one man between you. That's not the Cora Galloway I know!

Cora smiled slow as butter. Well, since you ask, *no man* is precisely how come I'm dancing. I'm getting danced because I'm available, not like yous oldies over here. Us with no men aren't daft. We get the pick of the boys! C'mon, ma, the night is young. I'll get you a dance no bother.

My mother made protesting noises but her mouth was turning up at the corners.

There's a fella over there says you've got the best legs in Saltcoats, Cora said. Come on over and say hello. Says he hasny seen you in years. It'll make his night. She hooked mum towards her. You'd think that's what you'd want to be doing as well, Kitty. It's a wedding Godsake and here's you like Harry the Horse. You've a face on you like somebody slipped you syrup of figs. Lighten up.

She used to dance, my mother said. Kitty, when she was younger. She used to sing.

Cora looked back briefly at her mother's sister and smiled.

Well, it doesny show. Somebody could mistake you for a miserable cow in the wrong light, Kitty. Get a grip. She clapped her hands and turned back to mum. Come on. Let's you and me leave the old married ladies and trip the light fantastic. You're a long time dead!

And effortlessly as she'd arrived, my sister sallied back into the crowd, mum tailing behind. I tagged along to get out of Kitty's reach. There was a low turn-out on the floor and the band settled into a thumpy four to the bar, which meant only one thing at this time of night. It meant the Slosh, a dance that women did together due to the inevitable shortage of danceable men after a bar had been open for this length of time, a touchless, exercise-routine effort that mopped up children, pageboys, oldsters, teetotalers and any bridesmaids who had not managed to get off with a waiter and were game for the simpler nonsense of a corporate frolic. Cora, mum and Uncle Allan lined up with the rest as the dance began in fits and starts, hand-jiving as they counted time. Under her breath, I could see mum was singing. *Ha ha ha beautiful Sunday, This is my, my my beautiful day.* Cora, touching opposite elbows then twirling on the spot, was no singer and never had been. But she had a big smile. Full-lipped and dauntless. My sister's smile was big, bold and brave. Someone, maybe Uncle Matt, was sitting on the floor with his back to the bar. Father of the groom, he hadn't danced all night which meant neither had Aunty Marie. All dressed up and not a shred of joy in him. Not here, at any rate. As I watched, the reflections of the bride and groom appeared over his head in the gantry mirror. In shadow, but unmistakable even in civvies, Peter appeared dragging a suitcase. He looked more like himself than he had all evening. The ordeal was over. Now all they had to do was escape, avoiding tin cans, confetti, the threat of further fracas, fuss and tears. I watched them embrace then slip like fish from fairground polythene into the wide open darkness. Free.

For what it was worth, I passed my motorcycle test and the bike and me could do as we pleased. My driving was not good and my road-sense lousy enough to be frightening, but I drove: through Ardrossan and the long shore road, opening up the throttle on the stretch to Seamill and all the way to Largs if I felt like it. I let the petrol run lower than was wise and didn't check the oil as often as I should, but my chrome glittered. My head-lamp shone. Rotten priorities. With nowhere special to go, I stayed out late. Out was *out*, after all. That was its attraction. It wasn't *in*. Coming home in the pitch black well after eleven, with nothing else on the shore road, the engine cut unexpectedly one night and left me free-floating in darkness, the echo of waves and distant sheep. This was the downside of independence: the possibility of having to bunk down in a ditch. Unable to see my own hands, I took the top off the petrol tank and peered inside using a lit match. That I didn't blow up like the Ardeer explosives factory still strikes me as remarkable. Then, I had no idea. Something shimmered inside the tank before the wind caught the match and I had another go. All it took was flicking the reserve switch and four kicks. The miracle I'd got home at all didn't strike till I parked up for the night. Heedlessness from missing Bradley, even when I admitted it, led to missing common sense. It wasn't just boys that made your brains go to hell in a handcart, it was lost boys too. Once this thing started, it didn't go into reverse. I stole books out of Woolworths not caring if I got caught and was lethargic even at school. Heading in on the bike to an evening orchestra rehearsal with three sheets of music in my back pocket in a howling gale ended as anyone sensible knew it would. The sheets worked free and cast themselves adrift. I didn't notice that they'd gone till I reached into my pocket in the assembly hall. Handwritten in Ken's scratchy pencil-point sticks, this music was the only music. New-composed, unique. I had had the only parts and now no one did.

This was what letting people down felt like.

It was the worst feeling in the world.

I found Ken at the back of the rehearsal hall and turned myself in. I could write the whole thing from memory, I said, trying to mitigate the dreadfulness, but meantime there was no music. Till I'd done that, we were hamstrung. I hung my head and stammered. I apologised and the s's dammed behind my teeth. I'd rather have been eaten by bears.

Ken said nothing to begin with, just let the air settle. A frost fell. Cool, then cold. He expected better, he said, looking out of the window. He had thought I had qualities. Maybe he'd been wrong.

Maybe he had. Keen to make up, I took to skipping lunch and practised. I was too anxious to eat in any case, and hoped some punishing hard work would help my neurotransmitters behave. It worked a little, but not enough. Eating only chocolate biscuits made me jittery with adrenalin, so I tried out a flute, a cello, a lever-action French horn to use up the energy and worked through pages of harmonies to improve my harmony skills. Desperate, I asked Miss Lyons if I could swap something to take up another instrument to make myself more valuable to the Music department. She took her glasses off, put them on the table and sighed.

For goodness sake, girl. Half your timetable is Music lessons of one kind or another. You go nowhere near the PE department because of one rehearsal or another and already miss Maths. You look as if a game of netball would do you the world of good. But what you want is more music. Who do you think you are? She was not exasperated. Her mood was level, her voice under full control. Who exactly do you think you are?

It was a good question, one that brought me up short and kept me awake. I had no idea. None. Lying in bed, I remembered my parsing skills and pulled what I could find apart in the hope of finding an answer. What I found was not reassuring.

First, I was obsessed with getting back into my Music teacher's good books and had not kept myself under strict enough surveillance. I had drawn attention, not kept a close enough eye on how I sounded. Second, I was Goody-Two-Shoes and Creeping Jesus. Even if I could handle being those things, they were not nice names. Third, I looked like my father. Everybody said so, even Kitty who had never mentioned him before, and everybody knew he was a waste of space. Fourth, I was a liar and an anti-social black sheep. I was my mother's *staying-on-at-school* burden and simultaneous showcase, fearful of failing an exam or getting a report card that blew it all sky high as my sister, allegedly, had. Further, and in no particular order, I had gone from keen-to-please to someone Miss Lyons kept an eye on, who bunked off Maths and who had, at least once, bunched her skirt about her waist like a streetwalker. No one would befriend me. My boyfriend had got shot of me because boys liked girls who knew how to have a good time and I'd never get another boyfriend because *clever* got no one a man. Worst of all, I let people down who had expected better; who, after the trust they had shown, were wondering whether they had made a mistake. I thought I had belonged in the Music department. I was sure of it. And now I was scared. Maybe I had no grasp of what mattered and what was real. Maybe Cora, who had saved mum from the jaws of Aunty Kitty with a lightness that bordered on genius, had a better grasp of all that stuff after all. I was not Mata Hari, not Liberace. I was a long drink of water with a fiddle case. I was an arse.

I also knew this kind of thinking was called self-pity and that was worse than all the rest put together. Lying in, awash with refined sugars and not much else while my mother slept, I felt dizzy. Something brackish rose in my throat now and then and my eyes were watery. In a bid to think other things, I revised the day's lessons in my head but Lady Macbeth's insomnia didn't help mine. Her hands, her hands. Her bloody hands. I remembered, dimly, my period was late. Not very late, but late. I knew that what Bradley and me had been doing, now and then and only if he felt depressed, was risky, at least in theory. But the stuff he'd shown me in the magazine looked million-to-one odds and we'd been careful. Careful-*ish*. You had to go all out to get pregnant because some women, according to Rose, had to try for years and even then weren't always *lucky*. Lucky. That was a big idea. Around three in the morning, I crept out of bed and headed to the bathroom in search of something to knock me out. I had school next day for crying out loud. And there was the aspirin. Aspirin was humanity's best friend. It cured pain, colds, sleeplessness and intestinal disorders, nausea, excess, cuts and grazes, inertia, shock and sadness, on account of which we usually had a lot. Just not tonight. I found one tablet under a clump of cotton-wool and one was not enough. Aspirin needed company: you took them in pairs. I set the loner aside on the rim of the basin and foraged. There were Askit Powders and Fabulous Pink Camay, corn plasters, fag-ends of metal ointment tubes and a half-empty packet of razor blades. At the back was a single blade smeary along one edge, taken out of the razor and abandoned. The bulbous pattern punched in the centre to accommodate the handle was rimmed with rust, but one cutting edge was pristine. I touched it to see and tiny berries of blood appeared on the pad of my thumb though I hadn't felt a thing. That was what razor-sharp meant. Impressed, I tucked the blade behind the cabinet, balanced above the nearest holding screw to keep it safe – what I was keeping it safe *for* I wasn't sure – then drizzled the tap quietly to gather water in the cup of one hand. The one aspirin was all I was getting. I sipped, swallowed and downed it feeling cheated. There had to be something else. There was, of course, but it was all prescription stuff, some well out of date. Tiny bottles with instructions to not share. You didn't share medicine because it was dangerous. The wrong thing had you leaving the house in a stretcher to get your stomach pumped. This must have been what mum did – I counted on my fingers – four years ago. She must have come in and looked, the way I did now, then knocked back whatever had come to hand. She must have needed a cup, a steady source of fluid, a firm hand. My Blind Aunty Lottie had jumped off a low bridge in front of a train in only her underskirt and everyone had been shocked except Jock. Her husband of forty years said she'd only done it to draw attention to herself. Lottie had been funny and kind and interested in all life had to offer; she had danced a cancan with her bloomers on show at the fireside and laughed in a Yorkshire accent. Nobody mentioned Lottie these days. And nobody mentioned what mum had done. Magic beans from the doctor put to wicked use. Not then, not ever.

The bottle in my hand was translucent. Yellow tablets no bigger than split peas with lines down their centres to make them easy to break tumbled inside. God knew what they were. Maybe she had taken something very like these.

Mrs Elizabeth Galloway ONLY.

I opened the bottle and sniffed. Acrid. Sour. I pulled away the cotton swab and tipped one out. A stomach pump sounded like something that could make your periods come back. Either that, or it would take them away for good. I wondered when jumping in front of a train had occurred to my Aunty Lottie, how you reached such a decision. Whether disappearing had been some kind of contrition, and if anybody knew, anybody cared what for.

The bottle was turning in my fingers, rattling the pills inside against the bars of their cage. They looked inoffensive. Easy. What, I thought, would mum do? I thought so long, my arms grew goosebumps and my toenails turned lilac. It was cold in here. The tiles and the whiteness. Next door was bed, mum, my space still warm. I put the bottle back in the cupboard where I'd found it, then brought it back out again. On impulse, I unscrewed the lid, left six inside in case mum needed them in the morning and knocked back the rest with a slug of tepid tap water to make sure they went down. My face, in the bathroom mirror, looked just the same. My thumb had stopped bleeding, the light cut already allowing skin to do that gratifying thing that skin did without your say-so and mending. Setting itself to rights. I closed the cupboard gently so as not to make a noise. I went back to bed feeling weightless, light-headed, almost reassured. My feet barely touched the ground.

9

I was not underwater, just deep somewhere else. I was not in Rose's spare room. It was not New Year. I came to the surface slowly and found I was exactly where I'd been before.

What did you take? My mother kept asking the same thing. Do you hear me? What did you take?

Aspirin, I said.

Liar! She waved the bottle, tumbling the cache inside like scatter-shot. They were her asthma pills. What did I think I was doing touching her asthma pills? Now it was three o'clock in the afternoon and she'd had to go to the phone box and call in sick and she hadn't enough asthma pills for herself when she needed them. Had I the faintest idea, the remotest idea, any realisation of all the bother I was causing?

I realised bits. Most of all I realised denial would only make it worse. So I coughed up. I said I'd only taken the pills as a last resort because there was no aspirin and I couldn't sleep, which was true. I had no idea what they were. That was true too. I said I thought they were codeine.

Codeine my arse, she said. She shook the bottle again. These are *asthma pills* for Godsake. Take a look at yourself. Go on. She held out the Snow White dressing-table mirror set I'd had since I was five, pressing the flaky gilt frame into my hand. You're a sight.

I could see, however fuzzily, what she meant. The albumen part of my eyeballs was the colour of urine, the blue of the pupils gone grey as old cheese. When I lay back down, she held up her fingers and made me count them, then gave me a cup of tea and the instruction to stay put, as though I looked lively. She opened the window to freshen the room and went out. For the time being, I had no plans to do anything else. She clattered about in the kitchen, then clattered about in the bathroom, sorting something. She went out of the house and twenty minutes later came back in humming, clearly calmer. I got up despite the nausea and dizziness and brushed my hair, hoping to pass for right as rain then stumbled just as she came round the door.

You look horrible, she said. Sit. Still wearing her hat, she held up an industrial-size bottle of willow-derived, tried and trusted acetylsalicylic acid and pointed. *This* is aspirin. She opened the top, pushed the cotton aside and hooked two as exemplars into her hand. Look. That's what they look like. Codeine as well, exactly the same. Now get back into bed and I'll bring tea. You've got to drink.

The tea, when it arrived, was insipid enough, but I was in no mood to swallow. Not yet.

Water then. You're having something.

Yes, I said. She fetched two glasses, waited till I sipped from one then sat on the spread, somewhere between intimacy and exasperation.

Was it a mistake? she said. And before you open your mouth I want the truth. Well?

Yes, I said. It was a mistake.

She looked at me. How many?

I can't remember, I said. Enough so the back of my throat still tasted of bleach and burned more than a little, but I didn't say that part out loud. Maybe four.

Four nothing. How many?

I didn't know.

Well, I'm bloody annoyed. You'd no right. How do I get another prescription for these? I can't tell them it was you. They put that kind of thing on your medical records and get a psychiatrist in to sort you out. They'll put you into care. I dropped my eyes lower and took another sip of water. You hear me?

Yes, I said.

I'll *yes* you. I've got to tell him something. What will I say?

Say I thought it was codeine. Tell them I made a mistake. The bleach-taste was moving around in my stomach now, swirling. I sighed. It doesn't matter what you tell them.

She looked as if she was thinking about hitting me then changed her mind.

Say a burglar stole them. I closed my eyes. I don't know.

These weren't the kinds of things I said. Caught more by shock than offence, she didn't know what to say and neither did I. We heard Cora coming in, the shake of an umbrella and some muttering about *bloody rain*. It was streaking down the windows now I looked, the sky going dark. It was tea-time. I hadn't noticed the day disappearing, the weather. I hadn't noticed a thing all day.

Well, I don't know either, mum said. Her voice was low and tight. I'm buggered if I know a damn thing these days.

Is she bothering you? Cora shouted. Christ almighty. As if today's not bad enough. The umbrella noise rattled again. I'll come through there if I have to.

You know what *she* says? Mum hitched her head in the direction of the hallway. *She* says you're all out for number one. Stop her music lessons and that'll sober her up. That school's putting ideas in your head, she says, and she's right. You were never like this before.

That's what school's for, I said. Too floaty to care, my head was ceding control. Giving you ideas, I said. It's what school's for. Joke.

You're an ungrateful so and so, mum said.

I know, I said. It was not a kind thing to say. Driven beyond restraint, mum's cheeks made points against the whiteness of her skin and she hit me with her worst.

God forgive me but I wish I'd never had you.

I sighed and nodded. You've told me before.

Wisely, mum went out, banging the door behind her. There was a clattering of dishes and Cora saying *I warned you*, the sound of a pot hitting one of the electric rings. *I wish I'd never had you* was still ringing in the bedroom, little lines radiating in space. She'd said it too often now. Six words that had terrified me to the roots as a child, filled my head with the sensation of being alone in the woods with the sound of wolves, had rubbed down to just words. It was the way your head dealt with things. It found a way round. And the way it had picked, had been working on for some time now, was to harden the heart. If I slowed my breathing and kept it shallow, the blood took on a useful chill. You could almost hear the sound of ice, cracking, as it steeled around anything soft, helping it cool. *I wish I'd never had you* was nothing but noises. If you got cold enough, you could numb it away. *Well you did*, I'd think, stone-faced. *Too late to wish for that now.*

It wasn't as though I couldn't see what she meant. A middle-aged woman with a toddler who had run away from her husband with no money, no back-up and no place to go was a middle-aged woman over a barrel and that indignity, that need to ask strangers for help, had to be somebody's fault. Never ask for damn all was a motto she cherished. And I had forced her to ask. I knew. Maybe I didn't really believe she meant it. At the same time, it went too far back to mean nothing. Now my head had come up with this idea, teenage and effective. Freeze. Go dark. I finished the water and saw she'd left a couple of aspirin on the sheet. Pills. I almost smiled.

Mum slept in the living room that night and nobody hit me in the morning. Although it was Saturday, Cora refused to summon the energy or even put that purposeful look on her face. She did not refer to me, my outrageous cheek, the pills thing, not at all. She behaved as though I had fallen down a rabbit hole and was invisible to reasonable gentlefolk. The sister who had given me cigarette burns, scratches, scars, scuffs and a broken nose, who had cracked my ribs and knocked my head against an iron bed frame, a sink and every wall in the hallway, refusing to react was dreadful. It left me alone with the guilt. What a cow, I thought, jaundiced. In the self-control as punishment stakes, I still had a lot to learn. Mum came and went with tea, biscuits and toast, saying nothing much. Family tradition.

Sunday was much the same only Cora spoke. She ordered me into the living room to watch TV and keep my mouth shut. There was something funny on and it would do me good. My eyes were still yellow but my brain was clearing. I took the advice. It was Tommy Cooper thank God, an absurdist in a fez doing sleight of hand that repeatedly failed. Medicine.

By Monday afternoon, having written an absence-note citing allergies, I headed back to school. Mr Hetherington seemed to have forgotten I was an irritant and waved along the corridor. I waved back. No Music on Mondays was a good thing: no scrutiny, time to let my eyes return to more normal colours. Susan told me I looked tired but did not press. At lunch-time, I stared at my hands in the practice rooms, amazed at the signs of life in my fingers as they sat on the piano lid, not playing. I stared at them in Mr Blakeley's Latin top-up sessions, curled around the see-through stem of a leaky Bic which appeared to be making notes on the sack of Troy all by itself. The cut on my thumb was only a trace and my nails needed trimming. The body had a logic of its own. It fought back. That evening, my period arrived with little warning and I felt bloated, sore and for the first time in days, hungry. I had no real idea why I'd done what I'd done and saw no need to puzzle it through. Get tired enough and all you want is sleep. That was all I knew. My body, knowing better, was already streets ahead, doing the thing that bodies do. The stupidity of imagining, even for a moment, that I could outfox it made me burn till I felt I'd spontaneously combust. I'd failed. I'd cocked it up and my vanity had taken a knock. It was that simple. Everything came back to vanity in the end.

Don't get me wrong. I was not depressed, or not so I'd have noticed. Nobody was. We could be lethargic, tired, blue, flat, miserable, not up to the mark or needing a good kick up the arse, none of which was as medically classifiable and therefore *bona fide* as piles or a rash. *Not coping,* whilst *not good,* was not serious. If my mother went to bed some days immediately after work, too lifeless to cook or even watch TV, she was *tired.* If Cora stayed awake all night listening to any damn thing on the radio in preference to the silent dark, it was just what she was like. If I had swallowed a handful of pills out of the blue, it was *young people nowadays.* Cora took it personally nonetheless. She got huffier and I became more annoying.

Stop reading books, she barked. You're not sitting in this living room a minute longer reading like a nun. This is where the telly is.

I come home to watch the telly, not to watch you reading bloody books.

It's school things, my mother said. You can't tell her not to read school things.

I can tell her what I like. It's me that's the taxpayer here.

This is where she does her homework.

Well she can do it somewhere else. Don't tell me she doesn't drive you daft as well because she does. It's that stuff she reads that's making her a bad bugger. It's books that's giving her her daft ideas.

It's school stuff. My mother was incredulous, her voice at the top of its range. She disny pick it.

But she *likes* it. Nobody else likes stuff they get at the school, just her. If it's not *Macbeth* it's Harold ruddy Pinter or the Punic Wars or some other carry-on. That Mozart's *Requiem* thing she likes, by the way – it's for dead people. What kind of interest is that for a lassie her age? It's morbid.

I tried to look absorbed. Saying nothing with my nose in a book drove her crazy.

Look! She just does that to annoy me. Tell her to pack it in and just behave. You're not doing her any favours.

Mum sighed.

I mean it. Cora wasn't for letting it drop. What she doesn't understand, what you don't tell her, is *that stuff's not for her.* It's all very well pissing about with it, but it doesny earn you a living. She should stop showing off, watch the telly like everybody else. No wonder she's single.

It was too risky to get up and head out of the room, so I stayed put, figuring out her argument. It wasn't hard to get. She saw no value in what I liked, which was fair enough but didn't explain why I wasn't to get to do it either. It didn't explain why she thought I'd be spending my time just thinking up things to annoy her. That which Cora did not wish to see, did not wish to like, did not wish to see the point in, did not exist. Maybe I reminded her of everything she didn't want to know.

That's hobbies, she concluded. For lassies that aren't you. You're not at Cheltenham Bloody Ladies' College, you daft arse.

Away you go, my mother said. There's nothing wrong with reading. It's perfectly normal.

That stuff she likes isn't *normal*. Cora's voice was cracking. It's for exams. *Nobody* likes that kind of stuff. Not really really likes it. That's a fact.

Plenty of folk like it, my mother said. *I* like it.

Cora snorted.

You're prejudiced, that's what you are. You're jealous because she's clever and she's not giving up the way you did. And another thing, you huvny got a boyfriend eithers, so don't start that *single* rubbish. She'll get plenty of boyfriends when she's older.

That's how much you know. Cora sat back, suddenly relaxed. You're wrong because actually I *do* have a friend. If it's anything to do with you. Which it isn't. She put a fag on her lip and flicked her lighter. So there.

What *friend*? My mother was genuinely astonished.

Never mind. Cora was puffing. Drop it.

Since when?

Cora was colouring up. I'd never seen that before and stared. That's my business, she said, exhaling. Not yours.

Mum looked at me. Did you know about this?

What are you asking her for? She doesny know nothing about me or my business. She doesny know nothing full stop.

I hope it's not Sandy again, mum said, oblivious. He's round here like a stray every time I think you've got rid of him. Is it Sandy?

It's not Sandy. And even if it was, it's up to me who I pick. She spat ash off her tongue. Now leave it. I never opened my mouth.

Mum was about to make another suggestion for the mystery beau but Cora saw and cut her dead.

Enough. *Silentium est aurum.* You hear that? That's Latin for *drop it.*

We watched *Dad's Army.* It was a comedy series about a group of men ineligible for active service trying to pull together as a unit of the Home Guard though they'd nothing in common. Each had a different life outside the platoon and everyone, even the ARP Warden, was good-hearted under the skin. My sister's favourite was Private Walker, the platoon spiv with a girl on each arm and pockets full of black market nylons. Private Walker was Cora's type. I could imagine them both going out on the town hooting with laughter, and Cora coming home with her eyeliner squint and her underwear rearranged. Cheeky boys, light on their feet boys, boys your mother warned you about, were part of her idea of happiness. Short-lived was best. No complications. Boy-withering bookishness and speccy-four-eyes even in the absence of specs were stamped all over me. No wonder I got on her nerves. Apart from the fiddle case, what gave it away? It had something to do with my appearance. Miss Lyons saw it too. More than once she had hauled me up for too-short skirt length, uneven hems, my choice of shirts (*nylon looks yellow in sunlight*). Further, *get that look off your face* and *you look like your father* repeated in my life like a chorus. Appearance sent radio waves. People picked them up.

On-screen, Captain Mainwaring put on a wig to look younger. Everyone laughed. He tried out new faces under the wig. It was funny because the very fact of the wig made him take on a face quite unlike his usual one. He smiled and looked whimsical, kittenish, proud. When he took it off and became the same again, two words popped over my head like light bulbs. *Hair dye.* If a change of hair could alter a great deal without much effort – and it could – I could change my hair too. Wicked black like Cora; copper like Ann Margaret in *Viva Las Vegas*, Grace Kelly blonde. If people judged books by their covers – and some of what Cora said came down to exactly that – you could wrong-foot the judges by sticking on a different dust-jacket. A simple enough thing to pass unremarked: appearance could make you disappear. A track built itself in my head like a domino ripple, spilling bravely out into the distance past tumbleweed, wizened cacti, the sun-bleached skulls of horses. Nothing real need be lost, just the way it seemed. It was the way out of the desert and straight ahead.

A week later, I was a strawberry blonde in a black velvet coat from C&A and since Black Watch tartan looked like school colours, a mini kilt too. Mum was pleased I was *bucking up* and we had a fried egg roll and a coffee in a Glasgow caff like normal people. Caught by the ordinary romance of it all, I said I'd buy her a coat in return one day, fine-woven wool dyed scarlet with matching gloves and a turquoise scarf and she laughed out loud. Out together on the town felt grown up. Without Cora felt like release. This was how people formed futures and saw them as attainable: they went out with their mothers and talked about life over hot shop-bought drinks and didn't give two hoots if people saw them having a nice time. Gratitude, I thought, watching her chewing the second sugar cube from her allocation in a Trongate café, was better than guilt. Given the choice, I'd opt for this any time.

Restored to the local with recharged batteries, I talked Dennis Nelson into a discount on gauntlets too small for his regular customers and foraged two kipper ties and an orange shirt from the bargain bin at Duncan's. If men wouldn't pay good money for these colours, it was my gain. The assistant measured me for a bra while I was there because whatever I was wearing, it was wrong. 36B was the only size my mother knew about. Cora, mum and me as a trio wore 36B despite our age and shape differences out of blind trust. What the assistant gave me to try after the tape-measure session was a revelation. In the right size, a bra had a function.

The band braced your ribcage and made the cups earn their name. Supported for the first time, my breasts rose up like coconut castles rounding my jumper instead of creasing it. Just take it, the lady said, laughing at the expression on my face. It's old stock. On the house.

Unexpected kindness was as good as an embrace. I gathered together what make-up I'd acquired and the appropriate *Jackie* tips on how best to apply it and felt ready. Stocked for a change that was not for the faint-hearted, all I had to do now was pull it off.

Over time, I learned to carry blister plasters for bleeding heels and crushed toes and tissues to fix wind-damaged mascara. I knew to check periodically for lipstick on my teeth and never to rub tired eyes in public to avoid resembling a panda. I left behind the childish thing that was the freedom to turn my face up to the rain and watched how big girls coped with cobbles, potholes and gaps between the paving slabs, how they coped with their hair on windy days. This stuff, stuff I assumed Cora had known by instinct, could be studied like a language, taking as reference not only magazines and advertising but keen observation of girls who'd already got the grammar off pat. I watched women in chemist's shops, trying out scent and closing their eyes with pleasure if it appealed; women holding dresses in the Co-op's only mirror, adjusting their posture, their lipstick, the angle of their chin; women checking the backs of their legs for mud marks, re-bobbing their hair in case. They corrected pendants and reattached clip-on earrings, aiming at better symmetry and blood flow to the lobes. Some women were open while others stole their glances. Almost all of them, especially those of my mother's generation, aimed for their best. My granny, who never used a mirror save to brush her hair at night, would have wondered what in God's name they thought they were doing but I knew. I adopted and adapted. First time, with different hair and a kipper tie as big as my shirt front, it felt like acting but that was the point. Holding hard to logic, I sallied on as ginger as a chestnut mare with my head high. Ken laughed and hardly anyone else bothered. Of course not. Strangers, reliably, couldn't care less. That has to give you confidence.

Miss Lyons cared a bit. For a while she stopped me in corridors between classes to complain about the knee-high boots, the orange shirt, the kilt. But a thing bought is a permanent fixture and these were my wardrobe now. Though she hauled my mother up to school, no one was paying for more. Exasperated, Miss Lyons had a word with Mr Hetherington who said he didn't care what I wore so long as I was presentable. I passed my exams, had more or less complete attendance, was involved in extra-curricular stuff that helped fill the trophy shelves. What more, he had asked, could I do? If she replied he didn't report that far. Miss Lyons, gracefully, gave way. After decades of service, senior staff had a lot more to think about than dress codes. The landscape of the whole school was on the move. Comprehensive education had brought a different intake and money had been thrown at the ancient infrastructure: new soundproof practice spaces, a *language lab* (a room with tape recorders), new cookers and a Biology Greenhouse appeared in a bright new building, though English, Maths and History stayed put. On a daily basis, Miss Lyons, Head of Girls and fast approaching her seventh decade, was discovering the existence of pupils who would never learn to love parsing, who thought *Flower of Scotland* was about thistles and that football was a religious system instead of a bread-and-circuses substitute for a meaningful political forum. This was not the career she had given up marriage to pursue, but it was the career her masters had given her and, teacher to the last, she was damned if she was taking early retirement. By the end of my six years, as I dropped off her radar entirely, I admired Miss Lyons. I wish I'd said.

Mr Osbourne of the Geography department was another matter. He gave out the free dinner tickets on Mondays to those he called *waifs and strays* and I'd been just another open hand in the line for the past few years. This time, he looked up. Maybe it was the luminous hair-colour, even the eyeliner. The Cosmonaut badge on my lapel or the CND logo on the other side. Whatever, it stopped him dead.

We're a bit of a rebel, are we?

This was new. I wondered if he was making fun.

Do you usually get these tickets? he asked, drawling like a TV copper. I've not seen you in here before.

I wanted to remind him he'd been handing me dinner tickets for years now but didn't, just in case. I told him I was sure he'd find my name on his register under G. He did. This time the look went down as well as up, counted five tickets, then held them up by the tail like a fish in front of my nose. When I tried to take them, he held on.

Young ladies do not snatch, he said. It's not polite.

Our arms were in the air with the tickets between us, as though we were about to engage in a minuet. Arm still aloft, he asked if Miss Lyons had seen my boots. I didn't know. I ask, he said, because they look cheap and make-shift. By which I mean *not approved school wear.*

Since he wasn't giving me the tickets and I felt like a fool, I let the arm drop. Mr Osbourne looked at me like a lawyer.

Is the clothing grant I see your parents also receive being used as wisely as it might?

I almost laughed. Whatever he was suggesting – and it's depths were something I hadn't fully plumbed just yet – it was not his call. He was being deliberately confrontational, deliberately arch.

Let me tell you something, he said. He pressed his buttocks against the table edge, the buff-coloured ticket roll still aloft as though forgotten. I want you to listen and understand. All right?

I nodded.

Free dinner tickets are provided by the local council. They are provided to allow you one hot meal for each school day so every week, there are – how many?

Five.

Good. Now – he leaned forward and swallowed – if I find out you have not used every one of these tickets, if you do not go to the dinner hall every day and use them faithfully to repay the trust of the taxpayer and the local council, I will know. He leaned closer. And if I find you have *sold* them for your own gain, I will come down on you like the Walls of Jericho.

I said nothing and felt uncomfortable. This seemed to perk him up. Oh yes, he said, I can check. Now. He dangled the ticker-tape line. Take them. Use them *properly.*

Some teachers smelled of drink. I could think of three without even trying. Mr Osbourne didn't. From the corner of an eye I saw him looking at my shirt buttons and I wondered if my clothes were next. His eyes were watery blue and his smile, not a smile at all, waned as he saw I'd noticed. I could do two things. I could opt for wholesale bad girl and say *Are you looking at my bra?* in front of the rest of the queue. Or look ashamed, take the tickets and slope off hoping he didn't have another go. My usual recourse was the latter. This time, I couldn't haul it out of the drawer.

Mr Osbourne. That was my voice. I heard my own voice saying it. I'd like *you* to have the tickets. He met my eyes. *You* paid for them and I don't want them. You have them. Excuse me, I'm late for Music.

He called as I walked with my ginger hair in a cloak behind me, but if he wanted me to come back he'd have to run. For the rest of the day I ignored all other classes and hid behind the piano, pretending to practise. I pictured letters home and dressings down, my mother's downcast eyes as Mr Osbourne dialled for the janitor to remove us from the premises or I was ritually stripped of braid and expelled. But Mr Osbourne didn't come. He didn't gun for me that day or the next. Maybe he was embarrassed I'd caught him eyeing my buttons or maybe he simply couldn't be bothered, but without the tickets, lunch was history. I spent the time in the music rooms instead, sight-reading harmonies with Susan and delicate little Sheena – pert and pretty Largs girls who got by on crisps – making the room our protectorate. Within a small number in a small room, making light of errors as we headed to the final chord, I was home. Now and then I caught sight of us, all three in the brass plate of the practice room piano, our faces turned to gold.

A big bloke in a suit and a quiff followed my sister through the living-room door, ducking under the lintel. It was ten o'clock at night and we had toasted cheese. I had been eating it watching a documentary about Victorian child mortality when they stumbled in and mum sat up as if it might be bad news.

This is Francis, Cora said. He's just in for a minute to say hello. Cora's chin said *want to make something of it?* but her mouth was uncertain. Say hello, she chimed, trying for bright.

The man said hello and my mother said nothing.

Daresay Francis would like a cup of tea if anyone was offering. Cora made big signals with her eyes. You'd like to make it, mum. You make the best tea. No point me doing it haha. I'll have a coffee, thanks.

Mum drew her eldest a look and went out to clatter saucers.

Godsake, Cora said, rolling her eyes. The man shushed her with his finger to his lips and sat on the sofa, his weight tilting me sideways. In the all-woman household, we forgot how enormous men were in a confined space. And this bloke was huge. He held out his hand and I shook, limply.

Where's your manners? Cora tutted. You have the big chair, Francis. You're a guest, Godsake. I'll sit next to her.

I bounced again as he stood.

Put that bloody book away and say hello properly.

Hello, I said. She tipped the poetry book on the floor with her foot as she moved, looked down to see what it was and sighed. As per bloody usual, she sighed. This is my wee sister. She put an arm rcund me and I drew back instinctively. Excuse the book. She likes books.

Francis tried to look enthused. Poetry, he said. Read it at school. Gerard Manley Hopkins, eh?

I had no idea who Gerard Manley Hopkins was. In the silence, Cora poked the fire then sat back down. Francis coughed. If it's awkward – if your mother's on her way to bed—

She's fine, Cora said. Just not used to visitors. She looked at me and smiled. She's not been well, has she, pet?

I tilted my head wondering what that was supposed to mean.

Usually, she's making cakes and everything. So, Cora said. This is Francis. Everybody nodded. He's an old friend, Cora said. Way back to when I worked on the buses. How long ago was that, doll?

Doll smiled. We never shared a shift, mind, he said. Just worked for the same company. I knew your grandad. I looked at him, clueless. Your dad's dad, he said.

So did I, Cora said. This was news to me. He was an aggressive auld swine.

Mum came in with the tea and the interesting revelations stopped. Hot milk since it's bed-time, she said. It's in the kitchen. On you go.

Bed-time. I hadn't had an official bed-time call since I was ten, but I took the hint. Something was up. Cora didn't have friends. Though there were women who worked under her at the typing pool, she never saw them outside. She had no women friends at all. Francis had to be a boyfriend but what he was doing in the living room was anybody's guess. I picked up the movie star autobiography mum had left on her side of the quilt and tried not to listen for their conversation. Movie star biographies were all the same. The people in them went to Hollywood with a *dream*, then they got *a break* which meant a small role then they became a star. Their friends were all famous. It was boring. With the poetry gone, I unearthed Enid Blyton and disappointed myself with that for a while till mum came through, full of whispers.

The man was Cora's boyfriend. She'd known there was one about the place, but finding out it was *him* surprised her. She met him on the buses years ago, she said and rolled her eyes. I pictured the big bloke in a bus driver's uniform, looking lighter and thinner. It brought to mind a picture I had of my mother, the ticket machine strapped over her chest and her driver all set to go. Dad was in it as well.

I told her Francis had known my grandfather and she looked surprised. If he had known her or dad, she didn't say. In bed, she was restless: her book failed to engage. With the light out, she sighed and fussed. Eventually, she rolled like a seal and put her specs back on and stared at the light coming in round the curtains. We were both wide awake. For a while it was just the two of us being still, then she did something unusual. She started talking out loud, low, but audible enough, as if to thin air.

Francis was married. The word *married* spangling in the air, unwholesome. Not just married, she went on, but married and living with his wife. Not separated. She sighed, took the specs off and sighed again. Well, she said. If she thinks she's bringing that fella here to play at tea parties in my house, she can think twice. All her life, Cora did what she damn well liked and never listened to anybody else's opinion, and she'd done plenty in her time. *Plenty.* This, though; this was another league. Another slip down the ladder. Wherever this was going it was nowhere good. She regretted the wife's position. The woman, allegedly, knew, but that was probably tripe. She was being drawn into a web and made an accessory. It was a bloody cheek. There was a long pause while mum considered her response. On the other hand – her voice came slowly, very slowly – that was probably the only kind of man Cora was going to get now she was thirty-three. I listened to her breathing. He doesny hit her, she said. I asked.

Did dad hit you? The question was out before I knew I'd formed it. In the sticky darkness, the only sound was static, like a radio in another room. She ignored my question.

He's a Catholic so he'll never leave his wife. She's got another think coming if that's her game. She's stuck here with me till I die.

For a moment I thought she was crying, then she turned on one side, preparing to sleep.

You get a boyfriend, hen. Before all the good men are gone. That's all I'm saying. She's wasting her life. Don't do the same.

She was asleep by the time I heard the door-catch release, Cora freeing someone else's husband to go home. The rays around the window swung like a searchlight as his car turned at the junction. I heard it pulling away for miles.

My mother raged at Mr Heath and the National Union of Miners but doing my homework by candle-light was no bother. Outages resulting in no TV were trickier altogether. Cora without distractions, unable to see her knitting, was either resourceful (*we might as well play cards, then – Pontoons with a match worth 2p, who's in?*) or broody as a starving vulture. Blame gave no satisfaction: that electricity, our lifeline to the outside world, was as subject to strike as anything else came, paradoxically, as a shock. So far as I recall, school was untouched. We wrapped up warm if the heating was off and took gloves. Music and the making of it remained reliable. Mr Hetherington must have worked to make that the case, but Music got the glory. It didn't let you down. Burrowed in beside Lexie Millar who played first viola in the chamber orchestra and never seemed to put so much as one digit wrong, I would close my eyes from sheer enjoyment and be told off for not paying attention. It was the tic that made me one of the flock. The chamber orchestra was my favourite and not only because it let me stay on late. I loved the repertoire. The viola parts for stacks of Purcell, Scarlatti and Lully got to shift under my fingers while Ken conducted from the keyboard shouting out instructions at the same time. *A harpsichord has no way to sustain a long note,* he'd shout as we played; *that's why I'm wearing my fingers out here playing all these trills. If you can't hear the cello playing the violin phrase back at letter B, the cellos aren't loud enough – it's supposed to sound like question and response, not an echo bouncing off the Matterhorn. Do it again. Do it again.* I had played mostly alone as a child and my Music teacher was one of the few adults who taught me by showing, side by side. He gave me piano lessons, placing his hands over mine to let me feel the shapes, crooking my wrist to find a better sound. It was the kind of thing I imagined dads did. Expressions of kindness from adult men pulled the rug from under me every time. Once, when he told me I played well, I had to leave the room before the sudden welling-up behind my eyes gave me away. This was the strange thing: reassurance, a thing I craved despite the weakness of character it betrayed, was never unalloyed. The pleasure of praise caught in the chest like pain. I didn't want it to, but saying *thank you* as though I deserved it seemed vain. The best, like the boy-wonder Howat who had already gone into the world and taken his piano fingers with him, knew how to accept these things with grace. And that way was *lightly.* Self-possession, you called it. Balance. An ability to accept criticism in exactly the same way. You either had it or you hadn't, and I hadn't. Hiding compliments away like stolen chocolate was more my style, running off to unwrap them in secret and alone before they had the chance to be snatched right back. Here in rehearsals, one of many, compliments were digestible because shared. It was the same with the music: the clockwork beauty of standard chamber orchestra fare (*polyphony is like synchronised rally driving – one crash and we're all dead in a ditch*) were there for the taking. This music was as reliable as it was surprising, made by people long gone yet whose voices were there on paper *for the express reason* that people like us could own them too. It would have broken my heart to know I'd lose one day, more thoroughly and sooner than I imagined possible. For now, it was my beacon and my constant, a gift no one would ever steal. If it ever came to a toss-up between a boy and this, there was no competition. I'd have signed on a dotted line while the Faustian contract smouldered in my hands.

Between times, rehearsal-free, assorted Largs boys took me for strolls along the beach and made low-key sallies into my cleavage out of what seemed duty more than enthusiasm or genuine intent. One lad nestled me down in the sand dunes and whipped out a copy of *Mayfair* to show me soft-focus pictures of naked women for reasons of his own then kissed me like he'd been dared. These episodes were as reassuring as they were dull: Largs boys needed too much looking after. Friendship was not on the cards. Restless, I drove around at night for the pleasure of going somewhere without needing to stop and admit there was no one to meet, enjoying the familiar transformed by neon pinks and yellows, the bright white glow from chip shops and penny arcades. And on one of those evenings, ticking over while the traffic lights held me at red, I met Phil. He didn't meet me. Tall, good-looking and blond, he was crossing the road with his eyes straight ahead; a man on a mission in an RAF greatcoat, smiling. His hands were in his pockets and the scarf under his chin suggested a predilection for warmth. Maybe he'd been walking his girlfriend to the bus stop. Maybe his mother had made a soup and it was waiting for him at home. Maybe he was a Buddhist and benign was his usual expression no matter what. Whatever the reason, he was smiling as he crossed the road and disappeared in the direction of the harbour. It suited him, the smile. It looked like the right thing. After that, the lights filtered to green and I forgot about him. Though not entirely. One year later, we were engaged to be married. Life: full of surprises. QED.

10

My sixteenth birthday came with Tarot cards, money, a tape recorder and legal permission to marry without parental consent, all of which I recorded in an otherwise unused diary for their pleasurable suggestion that the world was my oyster. Only the last – the marrying bit – depended on someone else's co-operation: the rest were things a girl could make the most of all on her own. The Tarot cards were an unexpected gift from a tall chap called Dennis who sat at the back in Latin and studied Greek. Fortune-telling devices in traditional medieval designs, they could be enjoyed as pictures: the Sun and the Moon; the High Priestess, the beasts on the Wheel of Fortune resigned as hamsters to eternal rotation. I didn't care about the approved way to decode them: their mystery and promise was what mattered. Besides, seeing the Future was the same as Tempting Fate. Sooner or later, like Croesus led astray by the Oracle of Delphi, fortune-telling revealed itself as less use than no use at all. Besides, I already had a Future hidden in the slippery cardiac organ aft of my ribcage, and hidden was what I wanted it to stay. This Future was not Home, Hearth or the Bosom of a Family. It wasn't Love, Marriage or the joys of Blessed Union. It wasn't even Latin. But one ship was anchored in my heart and the name about her bows was *Music*. One day, I'd play for a real orchestra. Or I'd be a session singer, a composer, an arranger or even a tuner – so long as it was music, it didn't matter that much. That something else might make rival claims to my desire never entered my head. Till it did, of course. It did.

Phillip was more sandy than blond up close and up close was where I liked him. I saw him in the playground and knew him right away: the face from the traffic lights, same blond hair. Some detailed research let me fix a rigged collision at a party and we were an *item*. Instant attraction. I couldn't believe my luck.

Phillip played no instruments and did not sing. He had no enthusiasm for the Greeks, the Persians or the Romans but had an idea he might join the Air Force in much the way his dad had joined the Navy and his mum, more fleetingly, the WAAFs. Uniforms, order and spit-polished shoes were in his DNA. We had nothing, not one thing, in common and I didn't care because Phillip was good looking. A stunner. When they gave out the looks he'd been at the front with a barrow and they'd simply tipped them in. Lean, six foot, grey-eyed, long-lashed and with a vulnerable smile, Phillip smelled of shampoo and toothpaste and leather belts and brine. I took to him so much his colouring imprinted, and identikits had me turning my head for years. We were lovers in a matter of days, callers at each other's doors in weeks, then a school fixture. Not that attendance was Phillip's strong suit, but we were obviously a pair.

My mother was never less than pleased to see a fresh-faced lad with ironed jeans turning up at the front door and being *a prospect*, but I didn't want him seeing too much of Cora. She was likely to tell him I wet the bed for the pleasure of pissing on my parade. More often than not, we opted for the cinema or the newly opened Chinese restaurant, where Norman, head waiter and polite to a fault, let us order the cheapest stuff every time without complaint. More often, *out* meant outside. The beach pagodas and the turrets built into the shore wall gave some shelter against howling gales and a degree of compromised privacy. After a while, his parents regarded us as *steady* enough to allow the tiny dining room of their upper-floor flat to be our bolt-hole, giving us coffee, a record player and a lockable door behind which we might canoodle to our hearts' content. There was a lot of canoodling. They got David Bowie, Lou Reed and Marc Bolan on continuous play through the wall as they watched TV and since it masked the secondary noise that was part of the whole canoodling process, didn't much mind. And we canoodled every day. How this was accomplished was both straightforward and shocking. We skipped school.

I was not a natural truant. Not at all. Phillip, despite being named for royalty, was. The first time he showed me what to do, steering me behind the school buildings in what felt like plain sight, I was shocked by how easy, how alluringly *so-what?* the procedure could be. Mastering its skills took little effort and not even much will to succeed. I'd won attendance medals. I knew the importance of sticking in, that truancy was wrong and that something this easy to get away with was plain lazy. To cap it all, it occurred to me that this was probably how Cora had started her life of school-leaver crime and if I was caught my mother would crumble to dust from sheer disappointment. But knowing all this was nothing to the heavy-lidded promise of sex in an empty flat for the whole afternoon. More to the point, it was sex with Phillip, the kisses of whose mouth were both sweeter than wine but more degrees proof than allowed common sense a fair fight. I told myself I wasn't hiving off every day. I told myself my pass rate of exams was higher than average so nobody had any cause to complain. I told myself I could learn French faster on my own than in French class and *L'Amour peut soulever des montagnes*, but these things were the dregs of the sophistry barrel and I knew it.

That said, the depths of my weakness were not limitless. I did not lose my integrity entirely. Once a week was the most I truanted and Music and Latin retained full attendance. All rehearsals and section practices, each choir run-through and every line of Virgil remained sacred. I could easily spend hours in Phillip's purple-painted attic room then head off to school for a single lesson sure nobody knew or cared. My handwriting improved. My homework was meticulous and polished with care. In fact, after years of unspecific guilt, heavy as original sin, being able to pin down a genuine wickedness made me feel much less guilty than before.

Touching in our house did not express affection and no one

but Rose, whose sentimentality made Cora laugh out loud, ever called me *pretty*. Phillip did. And how much sex might be packed into one afternoon with only tea and biscuits to fan the flames was an education in itself. *Collige rosas.* I read bits of Latin poetry aloud as we curled in his sheets, braced against the future. *Carpe diem quam minimum credula postero.* I wrote poems in foreign languages and sent them with sweets and flat-pressed flowers through the post. I penned his name on the inside leaves of jotters and wreathed it in stars as though I was six. What else could this be but *love*?

I want to make something clear. Phillip did not resemble my father. My dad had looked like a wide-boy fallen on hard times and Phillip was radiant, a sexier swap for the angels in the churchyard I'd watched over the garden wall when I was three. He had a settled home life, a normal family and his dad, ex-Navy through and through, was salt-of-the-earth, not a liability. Phillip resembled his own male parent, not mine. In fact, he resembled both his parents and seeing it moved me every time: his mother and father made and unmade his face every time the light shifted. I looked like nobody he'd ever see so he didn't mind or notice. And neither did Jacob. Jacob and Phillip, one for each chamber of the heart, and me for both to live in. It was how I always ended up sooner or later, one side of a triangle. We were, at least in my eyes, three.

Faery wishes, French Hens and Musketeers.

Blind Mice and Little Piggies. The Witches, the Fates, the Graces. The Wise Men and the Patriarchs. Past, Present and Future; the Merchant's Caskets, the Bears in the Wood, the Oak the Ash and the Mighty Thorn. Me, mum and Cora for years and years. Sometimes you can't see the wood for the threes.

And what does he have to say about it? my mother asked. I bet he's got something to say.

I sighed and made my parting straight. Who? I was being difficult on purpose. I knew who *he* was perfectly well.

Phillip. Who do you think? Phillip must get fed-up with you going round to Jacob's house all the bloody time.

No, I said. He doesn't get fed-up.

You're a bloody liar, God forgive me for swearing but you are. No boy is going to think that sort of thing is normal.

What sort of thing is normal?

You having pals like that. That kind of pals. Boy pals. Going round to another boy's house. It's just not what people do.

It took effort to keep my face clueless. This was fencing. The crucial move was the parry. I lunged. He's my *friend*, I said, wide-eyed. Why would anybody not want me to have a friend?

That'll be right, Cora said. No such thing as *friends*. Not between men and women and that's a known fact. Platonic friendship is a fallacy. It was on the radio.

You shut up, my mother said. That's not what I'm meaning. I mean it's time somebody stuck up for that boy.

Which boy?

Phillip. It's Phillip I'm thinking about. Jacob should know better than gadding about with you when you're Phillip's girlfriend. It's not on.

I sighed. Phillip doesn't mind because he knows who I'm gadding about with personally and he has no doubts Jacob is my *friend*. Having *friends* is perfectly normal. They know that. Everybody knows that. Except you.

Everybody knows nothing of the sort, my mother snapped. Not if you've a boyfriend. I wasn't allowed friends at all when I married your father. You got to visit your mother and your sister in my day, that was it. If you had women pals in when he came back, he sent them packing.

Ignorant, Cora said. She was talking to the rug. Whether she meant me, mum or dad was not clear. Just plain ignorant.

You wait, lady. Mum was beginning a slow simmer. If that boy takes his hand to you one day nobody's going to blame him.

Cora laughed like a little bell. I put one hand over my eyes pretending to be in pain. In some ways, I was.

And never mind the amateur dramatics, mum said. You know what I'm saying. You can't just do anything you like now you're sixteen. You're near as dammit a woman.

Look, I said. I have a nice boyfriend. I have a nice friend as well. Phillip is my nice boyfriend and Jacob is my nice friend. We go for walks and talk about school. I like him. That's it. There's nothing wrong with liking someone.

Cora snorted.

It's not about *like,* my mother said. He's a *boy.* People will talk. They're probably talking already. I'm telling you. You'll get a name about yourself hanging about with two of them. Make up your bloody mind and just see *one.*

Ach, save your breath, Cora said. She's just arguing for argument's sake. It's not even her ideas she's chucking around here. It's that stupid book.

What book? My head was racing. Even if she'd found my diary there was damn all in it. What book?

You know fine what book, she said. She gave me her no-nonsense stare. The book with the filthy cover. Like a swimming costume with bare naked bosoms on it – what's *that* supposed to be? Women's Lib tripe. Don't think we don't know it's full of mucky stuff.

The Enoch, my mother chimed. The *Female Enoch* book. It looks like a dirty magazine. There's not even any such thing as a *female enoch.*

And her supposed to be clever. Cora was in her element now, plain sailing with a light breeze. You know damn all if you think a mucky book by some woman with hairy armpits is the kind of thing a girl your age should be reading, that's all I can say.

It's called *The Female Eunuch,* I said slowly, letting the black cover materialise in my head. And it's not filthy. Breasts aren't filthy. They're normal as well.

That's *enough,* my mother said. You listen. Nobody's saying Jacob's not a nice boy. He *is* a nice boy. But the point is – here she slowed and spoke the words with single stresses – *you don't get to see other boys if you've a boyfriend.* Everybody knows that. That's what's normal. You don't get to do what you damn well like. Do something *normal* for a change.

Like the rest of the family? We're as *normal* as ninepence in here and I don't think.

Cora slapped me hard on the back of the head. Don't be sarky, you cheeky bitch. Your mother's talking.

I'm not being sarky, I said.

She hit me again. Stop speaking back as well. I'm warning you.

I drew a long breath and hoped it steadied my heart-rate. I was being sarky and I was being obnoxious and I knew it. But mum was driving me crackers. The TV was irredeemably off for the foreseeable due to unacceptable conditions in coal mines and I was less than an arm's length away winding the last of a skein of wool. When it was done, I'd be a sitting target. Irked or not, I had to shut up.

Anyway, Cora said, who'd want you for their friend if they had any choice in the matter? There must be something wrong with that bloke if you're the best he can get.

There's nothing wrong with Jacob, my mother said. He's got lovely teeth.

Well, how come he's hanging about with her if he's not some kind of lame duck? Any boy in his right mind disny hang about with somebody booked unless he thinks he's in with a shout or there's something funny about him. Am I right? Cora put down her needles and met mum's eye in silence. Mum looked stumped. See? Cora said. You can't deny it. There's something wrong there, you mark my words. Anyway – you with the stupid dirty book that thinks you're smart, finish that ball then get out of my sight. Hop it.

Godsake, I muttered. Cora hit me again. I rushed the last of the wool and stood up and tried to look composed. OK. I'm off.

Again? My mother was crestfallen. You're never in these days.

I'm hopping it, I called, already in the hallway, my raincoat half on. I'm teaching Jacob to play the piano.

They huvny got a piano.

No, but he's thinking about getting one. This was rubbish, but she'd never be round there to know. Rubbish prevented arguments. Rubbish was not lies it was a safety mechanism. Everyone benefited. Right, I said. That's me away.

When are you back? She appeared in the doorway, pale as an abandoned child. Late, I said. Her irritation seemed to have melted, at least temporarily.

When's late?

Eleven. I don't know.

What if Phillip comes? Will I tell him where you are?

He knows. He's coming later on. Phillip will be there and we'll all sit in and play music or something. The guitar's there. It's just fun, mum. *Fun.*

This bit was not rubbish. Playing music or Scrabble or watching the TV was all we ever did. Everything about the trio was more innocent than she seemed able to grasp.

You could do that here, mum said suddenly. She was knotting her fingers now. You and Phillip. We could do dominoes. There's a box in the shed.

OK, I said. I'll think about it.

But we both knew I'd do nothing of the sort. The idea that either me or mum could invite friends round and relax over the scratchy Mario Lanza and Liberace hits with Cora's approval was too crazy to answer, a surreal edge to an otherwise sad exchange. Cora's boyfriend was due round later and she didn't want to be alone with the sticky feeling it gave her, the dark, unspoken things under the stilted exchanges. There was almost an air of menace when he came round, a power shift that made mum a *fait accompli* accomplice, a seedy landlady of otherwise unavailable rooms. I saw what was wrong. But staying did nobody any favours. I wasn't being dragged in to their fight.

Right, I said, limp. See you later.

Their mothers must be pig sick of you by this time, Cora shouted from the safe distance of the living room. Their hearts must sink.

Mum rubbed her eyes. Don't do anything that'll get you talked about, you hear?

No, I said. Of course not.

I was already walking away. Between the threshold and the end of the street I focused on the sound of my own footfalls, counting to ten then back to zero. I was going to my friend's house. Whatever was going on here was not my concern. Cora did not have friends, not real ones. I toyed with feeling sorry for her to see if contempt made me feel less angry but it wasn't Cora I was angry with. I was angry because my mother was more concerned with this *people would talk* rubbish than me. Because when Cora started pot-stirring about what I was reading, she joined in. Because she could be interested in what I read and wasn't: it was all just grist to the family mill wheels which seemed to exist largely to grind. Cora was just Cora but a mother was supposed to know better. Somebody had to set boundaries and mediate difficulties, keep the cart from consistently veering off the rails. I was still counting, the corner in sight. Our house, I realised, had no grown-ups. Like children, we bickered about what was *normal* because we had no idea. Maybe no one had ever shown us. I wondered if there were books that might help, that shared the secrets of how things were done more properly. I imagined buying such a book and it becoming the centre of another pointless row about what was *normal*. In which case, like the unbaptised, we might be like this for ever. I did not look back as I veered into Springvale Street and out of sight because that would look like I cared and I did not wish to give my feelings away. I did not want to feel sorry and stay. I wanted to keep on walking and not come back.

The road to Jacob's house was seaward, towards the gull cries and spray. If I picture him in my head as he was then, he is standing on rocks and waving, one arm of his padded jacket a blue billow, the colour of sky. In reality, I almost never met him at the shore so this is mythic casting. The way I met him in the first place I forget. Why this should be is difficult to explain, because Jacob, from the off, was distinctive. In an era of patent platform shoes and casually induced foot disorders, he strolled to school in fancy desert boots, thick-soled and laced like the Start Rites children wore in primary because they were *comfortable*. In an age of glam and camp rock, he sang tenor in the choir and liked barbershop. In an age of Bond-smirks and granite-jawed leers when guns, cars and Old Spice were the mark of a man, Jacob smiled and practised yoga. Our paths most probably crossed when I was co-opted to join the tenors and I chose him to stand beside. Also, he was the only boy in school with an Afro, a home grown bearskin of thick, deep pile. He walked back home from school the same way I did as far as the dairy at the church junction. I liked him because he was the kind of boy who could walk beside a girl without looking hunted in case other boys saw him and called him a pansy. His mother had a big house on the shore front from some kind of compensation from the accident that killed his father, so Jacob had his own room, a brother with his own room, a sister with a husband and two girls in the flat upstairs, and another sister elsewhere who came round every other day from choice.

The main household included three cats, a handful of kittens, one nervous Jack Russell, and a tankful of mollies, catfish, angelfish and flashy little neon tetras, all Jacob's. His mum was hardly ever in for reasons of her own and he had the run of the house. He liked Carole King, James Taylor and Barbra Streisand so where we were most was the living room, with access to the record player, the easy-chairs, the sofa and a big fur rug. The bay window of this room had a changing view of Arran, the sea and, if I stayed long enough, the stars. I thought Jacob had it made. He fought with his mother but who didn't, and whatever had killed his father, he didn't say. Our idea of a Good Time was an afternoon in Woolworths for cheap paperbacks then the pet shop to gawp at guppies; an ice-cream on the beach, a net-hunt for starfish, sea-slugs and shells then an early evening trip to the Melbourne for lardy chips spangled with too much salt and golf-ball size silver-skin onions to eat on the sofa watching the tide go out. With his own room, some money, a small library of Erich von Däniken books and his animals, Jacob had the keys to what looked to me like a very good life indeed. Now and then, we embraced the way he and his sisters embraced. We patted each other on the back and, crazed by red fizzy pop, occasionally made cheek-pecks of the kind exchanged in *The Grand Old Duke of York* at a primary school party. But that was it. We liked each other. Maybe he was my missing brother, the one who occasioned a marriage then died at birth, leaving others to the consequences. Maybe he was a better sister than the one I'd got. Whatever he was, I loved him in a way I'd never love any member of my family, which is to say I loved him because he made me happy. I didn't fancy Jacob and it never occurred to me I might. Jacob *liked* me. That was the important part. To find someone, despite all the odds, who *likes* you is particular. You didn't cock about with *liking*. *Fancying* was Phillip's territory. Both were, arguably, love but they were different. How different went without saying. Sixteen, flushed with idealism, arrogance and teenage synaptic overload, everything then was cold-water clear. Still smarting, I told Jacob what my mother said about boys not being friends and expected him to be incensed out of loyalty if nothing else. He wasn't.

She's just old-fashioned, he said. I mean your sister's fucked up but your mother's just saying what she knows. They're not going to change in a hurry at this stage in the game. Just ignore it.

But it makes me want to burst. It's just round and round the same things all the time, chipping away for its own sake. What's it *for*?

Jacob laughed. It's to make you scared of what's outside the front door. It's a tie. It's how families work. They like to keep you close and nervous. I do yoga. Calms you down. You should try it.

But they're telling me not to see you! Does it not bother you they're telling me not to see you? I wanted him to be cross. I wanted to stoke the dreadful injustice of it all so we could feel martyred together. What if they say right out I can't see you?

Jacob was having none of it. It's what you think that counts. He shrugged. And I know what you think. I think you'd see me anyway.

He was right. I'd have gone round to his place for the sleeping bag he kept beneath his bed and camped. You could choose your friends but not your family and Jacob and Phillip were who I'd chosen. I had no idea how you got people to behave better, but I had a good idea how to make myself a solid block against them. Now and then, I imagined setting up a home miles away from this place, somewhere I'd never be reminded of my family and I'd have a go at pretending they'd never existed. It would be a *dreifreundenhaus* like in the song from the musical *Cabaret*: my two mates and me. Ideally, it would be a cottage in an open fen with an apple tree, a chimney with smoke and a cat on a mat at the door. It was what I'd drawn as a child when asked to draw a house and therefore best as imaginary, but I could picture it in detail all the same. Inside, we'd be three, the number of the shape which endured for ever if, like the Egyptians, you built it right. I wasn't stupid, or not entirely. I knew the house was nursery fantasy and that practical pitfalls – rent, acquisition, the need to shift a piano and tanks of fish, most of all how to talk the other two into it – didn't bear scrutiny. And of course, three didn't live together. It was an outrage to decency and would get us *talked about* even more if anyone was really bothering to do that in the first place. But practical pitfalls were the only pitfalls I could see. Misled by books with the best of intentions, I forgot you couldn't plot reality. You didn't get to pick your own ending or what your characters felt about each other; you didn't get to reach a goal and stay there, suspended in amber. Most of all, you couldn't ignore what was in the blood and marrow, the dance of habit and the deep-sewn seeds of upbringing, something as obvious and easy to overlook as simple mistakes. What was hidden in plain sight was always what tripped you in the end. I had no idea.

11

Saltcoats shopping drag, despite itself, was applying eyeliner.

Woolworths was selling T Rex singles, shiny eye make-up for both sexes and Ziggy Stardust T-shirts with our hero in lipstick on the front, daring you to think he was engaged in fellatio with a guitar. There was a vinyl merchant where one might trawl openly for Velvet Underground, Lou Reed and Frank Zappa, welcoming to the camp, the streetwise, the theatrical, the sleazy and the heaviest of metal. A Wimpy Bar set up on Dockhead Street selling Chocolate Bowlers and dinky little buns filled with what they billed as pure beef. Modern girls and modern boys even in this donkey-rides town, we discovered there was more on offer to the teenage market than you saw on *Top of the Pops* and more directions than down-the-line straight.

In Largs, several miles up the track from our end of the shire, the smart set were throwing parties after their parents had gone out, and at these parties what went by the vague soubriquet of *getting off* was not only permissible but compulsory. Couples were assumed to be sexually active because the assumption was trendy, and those who left alone felt this as failure. Even at the time, I suspected everybody hated the rituals, the ear-withering level of noise from lousy speakers, the lack of dignity upon which the whole thing was predicated. But we went, disliked it, and went all over again, desperate to fit in and find out the after-effects of downing three different liqueurs in ten minutes. We postured, pawed strangers and said things we regretted, keeping our fingers crossed. Much the way we dealt with contraception.

We were not ignorant. Not completely. We saw nakedness in the cinema and knew *French kissing* had a lot to answer for. Most of us knew mass-produced chemical and barrier devices existed and that the responsible thing to do was seek them out. But we suffered from shame, fear and feather-brained priorities. Condoms were uncool, passé and suspiciously soft (*that's a woman's problem, doll – all those mean to me is loss of sensation*) and IUDs were for grown-ups who didn't mind being punctured by internal metal hooks that all too easily failed. The Pill, however, its name uttered in hushed tones with a capital P to show respect, was the Princess of Preventives. Pretty-pink and sugar-coated, it promised a girl could have her cake without the consequences by the simple expedient of swallowing. It seemed too good to be true and in some ways was, but modern boy and modern girl, Phillip and I discussed our relationship, as we understood modern people were meant to. We acknowledged our hopes as a couple and our default choice of last-minute withdrawal as frankly not good enough for clued-up trendsetters like us. The responsible thing to do – we'd read it in *Cosmopolitan* –

was to head to a clinic which, if the scandal sheets were correct, handed out contraceptives like sweeties even to underage tearaways. We were over the age of consent, a stable unit and well intentioned. Being frank and easy to our parents was still a step too far, and though we were sure they had at least a clue, the etiquette of the place and times was to pretend the opposite. Our doctor still occupied the practice my mother had cleaned when I was three so we ruled him out and Phillip made the appointment with his. His doctor was solid, he said, St Peter. Our case was cast-iron. He had every faith that Dr O'Flynn would be sensitive and kind.

Phillip was already in the waiting room in his greatcoat by the time I arrived. He'd had a go at shaving and his face was pink with a cut under one ear. I wore school uniform: no make-up, no earrings, no nail varnish. Instinct had gone for bland. We agreed not to make an outright demand of the doctor in case that was rude. We would infer. Inference was deferential and doctors like deferential. Obsequious and dewy-eyed seemed the safest route. Phillip went first. After a couple of minutes, he came for me.

Inside the tiny surgery, Dr O'Flynn was writing on a piece of paper attached to a blotter. He looked like W. B. Yeats, wild and grey, with a creased handkerchief blousing out of one jacket pocket and since he was cleaning a fountain pen, didn't look up. He didn't invite me to sit.

This young man tells me you're here on an errand. He kept his eyes on the tissue, expecting a blue emission some time soon. Out of eyeshot, I smiled. Very specific advice. He swung in his chair to hold his pen over the bin where it threw up ink. Sit. I sat. He put the pen back together and turned to look at us for the first time, the rims of his fingernails livid.

And the errand involves contraception. He lined his syllables up like soldiers on parade. Is that the case?

We're engaged, Phillip said. We want to be responsible about this.

We're not getting married any time soon, I clarified. I've got exams and anyway, we want to take our time. Phillip took my hand.

She means we're still saving up, he said. We're trying not to rush things but not take chances either.

And you're telling me this because?

We looked at the doctor trying to work out what wasn't clear. Well, Phillip tried, we were hoping you'd tell us how we get the Pill.

The Pill, Dr O'Flynn intoned.

Contraceptive pills, Phillip explained.

Phillip is allergic to latex, I said. We ought to get something else.

Dr O'Flynn looked us up and looked us down for a long moment. He gazed at our enmeshed fingers. He ran his eyes over my school tie, my viola case, my patent leather boots.

Both over sixteen?

We nodded. He drew a sharp breath through his teeth, hissing. Well, he said. Well. He raised the pen and laid it delicately on his blotter, smearing each side of the nib as a final check of its readiness for use then set it aside carefully. This done, he turned to us, settling one hand on each knee like a guard lion before a jade temple.

You do not ask directly for my advice, but I will give it anyway. He switched his gaze to me, straightened, and spoke very slowly. My advice is to abstain.

There was a pause.

If your eventual intention is marriage, you should be capable of waiting. If not, marry sooner. That alone might keep you on the straight and narrow. It served my generation well enough. The doctor, assuming something finished, crushed the top sheet of the blotter into a ball as he rose and moved from table to door. That is the voice of my heart and my convictions.

It was then I noticed the picture of the pope on the wall near his plain block calendar. This was a doctor with a prominent picture of the pope on his surgery wall. Noticing my noticing, he threw the blotter ball at me.

I will not collude in this business. He opened the door to a waiting room full of waiting people, his cheeks reduced to match-head red spots. My advice is *Ab. Stain.*

I forgot, Phillip said as we stumbled up Dockhead Street in shock. He's an old friend of the family. I forgot about the pope.

That we hadn't seen it coming was more than embarrassing, it was a serious setback. *Abstain* wasn't advice: it was judgement and I wasn't even sure he was allowed to do that. Either way, he had and doctors, like teachers and every other keeper of keys since the world began most probably closed ranks if you went to another of their number and had another go. *Abstain* was the only advice we were getting. There were Family Planning Clinics, but I had no idea if they dealt only with adult women or where you found one. The chemist had no leaflets and most of the ads carried London phone numbers. We did what we could with abstention but within a week I landed a part-time job as a singing waitress with a company putting on docile Burns Nights for Americans and our celebrations returned things to business as usual. We resorted to paper-tissues, not prophylactics, kept calm and carried on.

It remains a thorn that our legitimate attempts to procure synthetic hormones with which to avoid pregnancy should have been subject to censure when we went to the pub illegally every weekend and nobody said boo. Under a carcinogenic fug from all manner of fags – Hamlet cigars, slim panatellas and golden Virginia roll-ups – we could order anything on offer behind the gantry with no questions asked about our age. Phillip liked Guinness. I had vodka on the grounds it tasted of nothing if you put enough mixer in it. The fact there was nothing I much liked to drink except tea I kept to myself. Permission to sit in the warmth of the pub rather than be blown along the windswept sand required regular buying of alcohol and besides, pubs were a sanctioned part of British culture. Pubs, like football, were as near as dammit sacred. Training yourself to drink alcohol was *natural*: the desire to avoid pregnancy was simply cheating. Looking the part was all it took to be served at the bar and sometimes not even that. Fifth and sixth years at school regularly went to the shore-line guest houses at lunch-time to buy pints and play darts wearing full uniform and it was all a bit laddish, chuckle-worthy fun. We didn't know what to think about our experiment in being responsible going AWOL, so we thought nothing. Sex was bad and booze was good. Tradition. *O tempora! O mores! O Caledonia.*

Where there's love there is life. The mahatma said that so we did not despair. We decided to act on the being engaged thing and plough a steady path to savings and eventual union. That was the least we could do. To get a crack at life beyond this place and its ruddy annoying doctors, we had to make some money. Phillip wasn't what you'd call a practical sort so it was up to me. I put the bit between my teeth and champed.

The Clydesdale Young Saver was my first venture beyond pocket-money in a cup under the bed. It came with a piggy-bank, the slit in his back hungry for acquisition. Friday and Saturday nights were not for horsing around any more. They were for taking the Ayr bus as far as two stops after the pig farm at Monkton with my friend Christine, where the company minibus gave us a lift to an ancestral seat of sorts which put on allegedly Historical Banquets to startle Japanese, English, American and Canadian tour groups. The songs rehearsed and ready, we changed into chaste satin and tartan frocks and sang while dishing up ethnic dinners – Cock-a-Leekie soup, haggis and crowdie –

then put on a short entertainment involving a local actor as Robert Burns. We sang between courses as well as before and after – light opera, Scottish standards and folk songs rendered Radio 2-harmless by a man in a beard from Edinburgh. With a piper and a fiddler to lend colour, we served mead, wine and whisky and drank enough ourselves to cope with songs about the repeal of the tartan laws.

We got free tickets for the first show and Cora heckled the master of ceremonies twice, which meant she was enjoying herself. *That's my sister*, I said in the changing rooms after, the wine freeing up words I'd never confessed with pleasure before. I was still scraping off stage slap while she was heading home on the bus in preference to waiting, but I had felt something when she'd chipped in, shiny and smiling, undaunted by the crowd or the po-faced MC. I liked her cheek. *That's my sister*, I crooned to the Ladies of the Household choir and they didn't believe me. My mother was thrilled with the whole show and staggered by the thought of pay for singing: three kid-leathery single pound notes in a small manila envelope, folded once with a slip. A wage packet: a ticket to being someone in the world. It wasn't Equity minimum, but it was three foldable, sweat-scented promises to pay and my mother welcomed me home with a plate of soup as though I'd spent a day down a mine. Supplementing orchestras for local school productions paid too – not much, but something – and the experience was valuable. Ayrshire being Ayrshire, the Bard offered January employment at Burns Suppers.

In tandem with Arthur, a musical refugee from another school who played whatever piano was available at whatever clubs, societies and scout-huts had booked us, we did those too. Sometimes, I was the only woman in the room, there to turn a trick for the lads before they did their Batchelors Club thing, whatever that was. Other women were waitresses and dish-washers, hired hands to make the evening flow, which was what musicians had always done too. Being for hire was something I could do with confidence. I saw more spiced-oat-and-offal-stuffed sheep's stomach piped in and ceremonially stabbed than you'd believe and can still recite *Address to a Haggis* if required. I have sung more versions of romantic, cheeky, humorous, tragic, dramatic and outrageously filthy love songs than seems likely and remember every cadence, every octave-leap, every place a breath can be stolen in my now neglected lungs. I heard more speeches – infuriating, boring and even moving – than was mentally healthy but the whole thing, every last stick of it, was adding to my store of secrets. This was, and I knew it, the time of my life; a time when disparate pieces were coming together like the separate parts of a cathedral roof, ready to meet and hold fast. Some songs I'd known from before I could remember, the gifts of accordion-playing uncles and singing aunties, countless school competitions, the Ayrshire Music Festival and misleadingly kilted Kenneth McKellar on TV – almost a family tradition.

Now they were mine. How they stitched together with opera and bleeding chunks of Welsh male-voice choir didn't have to be defined. I wanted my craft in all its guises. Left alone with the music-room LPs, my ears hoovered up every brass band arrangement, string trio and piano miniature they could. At home with my guitar books, there was never enough John Lee Hooker, Woody Guthrie and Peggy Lee, no quantity of protest music, traditional ballads or North Country working songs that counted as too many. Janáček and Vaughan Williams gave me folk tunes while madrigals could be unpicked and made new with friends in the practice rooms, Sheena and Susan and Christine, sopranos as light-voiced and lovely as wheyfaced Elizabethan boys. I learned rock music, blues and thick-textured German chorales, plainchant and devious sleight-of-ear baroque arias, sea-shanties and Victorian music hall. Even with mum and Cora in the living room, *Top of the Pops* – the one show for which my sister downed her knitting – allowed chart-fodder, pop standards and even small nuggets of the startlingly original. I wanted it all. Phillip played me David Bowie and Jacob taught me loving Carly Simon was the right thing to do. I didn't buy records: other people did that. I had my friends, my school teacher and my song books and the extraordinary thing that was the BBC, shovelling learning into my living room. Singing banquets were corny, but they paid and taught me audience etiquette. My ears took in lyrics at a single hearing and recorded them in a place that never wore through like cassette tape. I saw no pressing divisions between types of musics and still don't. The whole point was richness and variety, the calling home of delight. Some songs didn't even need to be sung, for well-made words in the right order had music too.

Poems, novels, plays and histories, biographies, lyrics, folk tales and putative non-fiction held sounds inside them on the page or off, rhythms and landscapes that meant you were never entirely silent in their company. And in keeping with my newly permitted wicked streak, if I loved a book enough to want to read it again, I stole school editions without compunction. The words would slip through my fingers if I didn't and how else were such books to be possessed? The local shop sold mostly magazines and Ordnance Survey maps, phrase books and *Observer's Books of Allsorts* thrown in. They had the *People's Friend Annual* that read like rotten birthday cards, but nothing that induced *lust*. Nothing you burned to own. Where poetry books were found was anybody's guess. I imagined them buried, leather-bound, in pirate chests on palm-fringed islands; sealed in warehouses at the ends of tall-sided lanes in the grimy parts of big cities where headmasters applied for a forbidden stash in hard cash with a free bottle of malt to sweeten the deal. The books I purloined were hidden in the coal-shed in a plastic bag, free from every eye but mine. The talent for deception, begun with hair dye, had developed in ways I could not have foreseen into second nature and I felt lucky to the marrow. I had everything.

I had a trusted boyfriend, a pal who gave me houseroom, two orchestras and two quartets to feel part of and the best teacher in the world. I had secret books and permitted books, a drawer full of make-up and my sister was too busy with her own life right now to be throwing punches at mine. I had sold the old Honda to begin my savings and knew the bus routes out of town. I sang for money, could make my own clothes and was hardly ever in. I had good grades and for all my mother knew good attendance. The rest was nobody else's business. The night we played the sixth of the Brandenburg concertos, the final concert of a series for the worshipful parish of Ardrossan, I walked home under the stars thrilled with life. I was David Niven ascending the stairway to heaven watching Arran laid out beneath the clouds, the gulls in the harbour, the prom road glittering and the great grey roll of the sea. Just as the sea would always be there, washing towards Arran, Ireland, America and all beyond, all I had now I framed as everlasting. My mind took a snapshot I could taste. Then I went home.

Cora answered the door, all made up and ready for the off. Och, it's you, she said. I thought it was Francis.

The concert was great, I said.

Whoop-de-doo, my sister said, deadpan. That's made my night. Now shift. I want to see when the car comes.

I shifted. Inside the living room, my mother was sitting on the edge of her armchair with one eye closed and the tip of her tongue protruding, trying to thread a needle. Beads were scattered around her slippers, buried in the fireside rug like tiny snails.

Honest to God, she said. I just got these. She meant her specs. You look and tell me. Is that thing threaded?

I put the fiddle down and checked. The thread bypassed the eye by a full eighth of an inch.

It's the cotton, I said. It's too thick. You'll need a bodkin.

You're not getting the bloody bodkin. Cora poked her head round the edge of the door. That's mine. I paid for it. You leave it where it is.

Mum waited till she'd gone again and put one finger against her lips and reached for Cora's knitting bag.

Don't, I whispered. Let me do it. Leave her stuff. You know what she's like.

Are you talking about me? Cora called. If I have to come in there, I'll not be thrilled.

Nobody's talking about you. My mother let her voice coarsen, exasperated. You think everything's about you. That's a disorder, that is. Megalomania. She leaned towards me as she spoke, dropping the pieces that had been in her lap into my cupped hands. I held pearls and frayed, grey thread, the marcasite clasp and the nylon cord. It was her best double-strand. A woman of a certain age, she said, should wear pearls to cast light on her face and she'd had this one a long time. She'd had matching earrings as well but the pearlescent paint had flaked showing the plastic beneath. That was what you got when you bought cheap imitation, she said. Always buy the best imitation you can get. The nylon she had given me was unusable. Bust three times, it was too short. If I soaped the thread however, it might stiffen enough to string the beads without having to use a needle at all. We'd been threading beads at the fireside, her and me, since I was a tot. She didn't need to faff with it on her own like this. All she needed to do was ask.

I'll do it now, I said. I like doing your beads.

Her eyes were soft, genuinely touched. I need them for tomorrow. There's a dinner for the servery team and I want to look nice. I would have asked, but you're never in.

Well, I am now, I said. Shamed by gratitude for such a small thing, I hunkered on the rug the way I had when I was six and turned towards her. I'll show you.

I sorted the five sizes of pearls into groups, then dabbed the end of the thread against the fire tiles with the stump of a candle till it was firm. After that, each bead fell into place in graduating sizes so the biggest ones sat in the middle of the strand. Mum cleaned her glasses then put a hand on my shoulder the way Ken did when I'd handed in good homework, a full wrap. I smelled Victory V lozenges, the scent of face-powder. We hadn't bunched up this close since she'd pulled the tugs out of my hair before I went to bed. Her hand stayed, restless, till the top row was completed and I looked up at her, triumphant, ready to tie the fixing.

I can't even see the holes when you're doing that, she said, never mind what beads go next. My eyes are getting worse. You can't teach an old dog magic tricks, I suppose.

It's *new tricks*. She looked at me. It's *new tricks*, not *magic tricks*. Anyway this isn't magic. Try. Just do what I did.

Francis's car was drawing up, his tyres crunching. I lifted the next thread and held it up for her to take, but she ignored it. She wasn't listening to me any more. We heard footfalls on the path, Francis's by now familiar tap against the glass door, his nails against the pane. The suck of the ball catch loosening, some kind of kissy exchange.

Was it a good concert? Mum was suddenly close. Was it Bach?

Mhm. Last one. Small crowd, but you're lucky anybody comes, really. It was good.

Did you make any mistakes?

I smiled without turning round. It's not that kind of thing, mum. It's not an exam.

I know, she said. I know that. But did you do it properly?

Other people did the big parts. It's more to do with – but I couldn't think of the words. Becoming like a thread in a tapestry was what it was like, not really about being right or wrong, but saying that wouldn't make sense. There was no describing what playing as part of a group like that was like. It's more about the joining in, I said. We all get it right or wrong together.

There was a thud against the door and Cora saying *Oh you!* in the hallway in a French farce voice. Mum was still peering at me. I think you'd have liked it, I said. The soloists were good.

Well, she sighed. You know I always come to the school things. But somebody had to stay in. That one through there was off out and didn't know when he was coming to get her. She canny be relied on to lock a door, her. And if somebody needs to stay in to make sure we don't get burgled who do you think it is?

I said nothing.

She tells you damn all. I said when are you away and she says *later.* She thinks she's Princess Bloody Margaret, doing whatever she likes.

Cora had acquired the Countess of Snowdon tag only recently after she'd tried it on me and it didn't stick. It referred to the good-time girl the queen's sister was turning out to be. I wasn't anybody with much degree of regularity except *lady* as in *you better watch your step, lady* and mum sometimes fancied she resembled QE2: same perm, same gauzy turban hats on Sundays, a love of three-quarter-length sleeves. We were all *grandes dames* in my mother's head, but one of us wasn't pulling our weight.

That's my life story, she said. Waiting hand and foot on that one and being told bugger all.

She rearranged a cushion and sat back, tired. Those vertical lines she'd always had above her nose, lines to which she had once applied strips of Sellotape in the hope they'd smooth overnight, seemed deeper. Like *pi* in an algebra equation. Runes made shapes about her eyes. Outside, at just the wrong moment, Cora giggled and my mother rolled her eyes. That's my life right enough.

Something was overtaking me. Full of concert and belonging and mum's awful separation from either, I wanted to give her something. Some sort of present that wasn't just fixing her beads. I wanted to give her a confidence. Mum, I said, pushing out from shore. I've got something to tell you.

She looked at me.

Me and Phillip. I stopped, panicked.

What? She was all attention now.

Me and Phillip. I put the beads down, risking the whole lot

unravelling. He's going to ask you if it's all right that we get engaged. Then we'll get a ring and put a notice in the paper. But we want you to say if it's all right. It's only if you say it's all right.

Is this soon? she said. She looked nonplussed. I imagine I did too. *Getting engaged* wasn't something you set a date for. All I meant was we were saving up, then we'd tell people and maybe get a Congratulations card. I'd seen them in shops.

You're not getting married right away or anything? She looked horrified.

No, I said. Of course not. I thought I could take her hand then didn't. We're just saving up. We're not – I couldn't say *getting married* yet, even though that was the ostensible objective – not doing anything in a rush. I just wanted to say we are thinking about it. I thought you should know.

The door swished on the carpet pile like a zip and Cora was at the open living-room door, eyes bright. I'm just in to say I'll not be late and you, don't dare touch that bodkin. Leave my stuff alone or else. She stole another look at my mother and double-took. What's up with you?

This one's getting engaged, my mother said. Her lips perked at the corners, trying hard.

Jesus Christ, Cora said. I bet you didny see that coming. Here, Francis! Francis poked his head round the door and I felt my stomach was sliding. Guess what she's done? Francis tried to look intrigued. My wee sister's getting married. Hahaha.

She is not getting married, my mother said as Francis dropped his jaw. She's getting engaged. She's getting engaged for as long as she likes and saving up. Aren't you? They're getting a ring first and waiting. It's nothing else.

Christ, bells and whistles, Cora said. Nothing gets by you. I never had an engagement ring.

You hadny the time, mum snapped. She's not you. She turned and looked at me then, near tears. I don't suppose you'll have anybody else but Phillip eh? So it's the right thing. If it's what you want, it's the right thing.

Do you love him? Cora caroled, twirling the tip of her finger into her cheek like Shirley Temple. Do you really really and truly love him for ever till you die?

Leave the lassie alone, Francis said.

Mum smiled properly now. I could feel it even with my head down. If she's made up her mind, that's good enough for me. She leaned and kissed my cheek, her lips dry and awkward. I'll get us a sherry and you say something nice for a change.

I'm always saying nice things, Cora protested, wide-eyed. And don't get me any of that bloody awful sherry. It tastes like laxative. Mum was already gone. It's been in that kitchen years, Cora said, making a face at Francis. He laughed and said *Good for you, wee one* as though I'd won a pub quiz.

Look, Cora said, tell her when she comes back we couldn't wait. We're off. I'm not holding up a night out for this. She nodded at the window to indicate the great outdoors and started buttoning her coat. Is it cold out?

It's May, I said. It's not traditionally cold in May.

You stop being cheeky. Cora pulled on a pair of thin nylon

gloves to match her eyeshadow. I bet you think you're the bee's knees now.

No, I don't. I sighed and picked up the strand of beads again and tried to look busy.

Yes, you do. I can see it all over your smarmy face. Well, you're pushing your luck, lady. You're showing off and heading for a fall. Even if mum's buying this engagement stuff, I'm not. Cora came a step closer and looked down at me. What do you think your father would say?

My shoulders stiffened. She hadn't had one of these moods for ages and I'd got sloppy in the interval, not prepared. Francis hunched at the door, looking puzzled.

Do you think for one minute if he was here, the Big Shot Big Man I see looking out of your face every day, do you think if he was here he'd not knock you into shape? I said nothing. Her voice steeled up. Let me remind you before you even open your mouth, it was your father that left you the money for that piano. Do you not care about what he would think? Is that the kind you are?

Even for Cora, this was bizarre. *Your father*, as Cora persistently called the man who was her father too, was not a subject. He never had been. His saw and rusted-over vice were still in the coal-house, but no one touched them. It was *not done* to summon him back. Cora hadn't gone to his funeral and before now, hardly mentioned his name. We had no pictures of him on display and nobody wanted any. I could picture the line of his features if I forced myself, the face on the white hospital pillow when he was dying. But to conjecture *what he might think if he was here* had no precedent and no purpose. It was just weird. Wherever this was coming from wasn't good. Neither was it for letting go.

Do you love your daddy? she said narrowing her eyes. That's all I'm asking. It's a legitimate question and this is the right time to ask it. Behind her, Francis looked like the stooge in a routine he didn't know the lines for. Tell us, she said. Tell me and my friend here what we want to know. Do you love your daddy or that boy? Who do you love the best? Is it your daddy or a stupid boy? Is it your daddy?

There was no way to jump. Instinct reached for the least vulnerable option. No, I said. I could barely remember him. No. The sound of mum clanking around in the kitchen and singing *Wooden Heart* sailed into the silence like a paper boat.

Cora smiled. Did you say *no*? Francis slipped out away into the hall. Look at me and I'll ask you one last time. The smile widened. Did you say – *no?*

I swallowed, hard.

Well, that says it all. You that's so grown up. I am shocked that you would allow such a sentiment past your lips. Because you know what? Her voice stretched out like elastic, making the words into a drawl as she knelt beside me to let them push, like nails, into my ear. *He. Loved. You.*

I winced.

You were the only one he had any time for. He loved you, you were the apple of his bloody eye, and what does he get? You don't love him back. That's a mortal sin.

Francis called from behind the living-room door. Come on, Cora, he said. Here's your mother coming. We better get moving.

Coming, she called, rising. Then she looked back at me, the whites showing round the outside of her deep, dark pupils. Because you committed a mortal sin you'll rot in hell. You and anybody that touches you, anybody who ever helps you, will rot. In. Hell.

Mum came in with the sherry glasses on the ends of her fingers, the ancient bottle under one arm.

That took ages, she said. But I got four the same. Four of those daft wee glasses so we can do it properly.

I'm not wanting that, Cora said. She sounded affable, almost chirpy. You like that stuff, not me. I'll just say Good for you, little sister! Cheers!

Mum put the glasses on the mantelpiece, ready to insist.

No really, Cora said. We're in a hurry cheerio. And she shimmied off twinkling her fingers at the window as she went. Mum watched till the car had gone round the corner, the bottle still tucked tight.

I don't know. Her and him. Did they say where they're away to?

Still dizzy, not grounded, I shook my head.

No, I thought not. There's nowhere they can go is there? Where can they go that nobody will see them for Godsake. They must sit in the car all the time.

I didn't understand for a moment. Then it dawned. She meant

they couldn't go to local pubs or the pictures, couldn't even walk out along the shore front because somebody might see. This man had a wife. He had a wife and kids for all I knew and this thing between them was already a talking point. They had to stay out of sight like thieves.

Imagine sitting in a car all night. She popped the sherry cork, sniffed and poured two small schooners. Well at least she's not through *there*. She nodded back to Cora's room. That's a damned disgrace what she thinks is all right, going through there with that man.

My drink looked thick and brown as cough mixture. Feeling queasy, I waited till she collected hers.

Here's to you then, she said, raising the glass. I hope the two of you make a proper go of it. Not like her. Cheers.

Moved, I took a sip. The drink was warm and sweet as demerara. Still shaken but wanting to make a good show, I set the rest back on the fire tiles and hoped it would evaporate before I'd have to touch it again. Mum, who thought Harvey's Bristol Cream was what posh people drank, sipped and looked into the middle distance. Sherry soothed her. So I poured another. Protesting, she took it anyway. She was light now, restored. The moment I had tried to make, a moment of giving her something good, was restored. She made a tipsy mime as she finished the second glass, then smiled.

Will we finish these beads?

Sure, I said. I'll finish them. My arms were risen in goosebumps, someone walking over my grave. You watch and see how it's done. I put six more on one strand, tied it, then fixed the second clasp in place so the strands sat as they should as the finishing touch. Mum took the necklace in both hands and tried it on in the mirror over the fire, tilting her head this way and that.

What do you think? she said. Do I look nice? She did. Mum always looked great in a string of beads, even cheap ones, and nobody ever told her but me. I put my music away, the fiddle case. We were done for the evening.

Heartburn and the possibility of being damned for all eternity meant I was still staring at the ceiling when Cora came back in the small hours. There was muffled laughter, glutinous kissing, the door, eventually, closing. Even with my ears on stalks, I did not hear her turn the key. I waited till I knew she was in bed then slipped into the hall and found the keys on the hall table, still warm. Somebody had to lock us all in. Safe and sound. Cora was thirty-three for Godsake. Old enough to get one of those council flats in the new high-rise, put a down-payment on a car or something. In three years mum would be coming up to retirement and sure as pigs would never fly, Cora would still be here and I'd be gone. A flash of anger hit me like electricity, sudden and shocking. Who did she think she was, my sister? With her voices from beyond the grave and her horrible ideas? And how come mum was saddled with it, saddled herself with it, would not, no matter what, chase her away? Out of sheer rage, sheer *something*, my eyes were watering. And it was cold here. The hallway, irrespective of the month, was always cold. The door was cheap and a gale blew under the damn thing every night. It needed some kind of draught-excluder. I could look in the ironmonger's, find something suitable. There were enough tools in the coal-shed and that clutter of obsolete medicines in the bathroom could do with clearing at the same time. The leaky tin of treacle in the pantry. If I wanted to, I could tidy the whole house. The idea was cheerful. I might change my mind tomorrow, but for now, it was a good thought. Mum turned in her sleep, catching my restlessness as I went back through. I caught a glimpse of pink hairnet, a glimmer of what might have been pearls, and touched her hand in the dark, hoping she wouldn't wake.

12

School unveiled its exam leave with a great flourish but I didn't want it. A fortnight off regular lessons reading illegible notes at home held no appeal. It wasn't studying that put me off, it was the part of the deal that wanted me to do it at home. I didn't want to be at home and school chucking me out felt like punishment. Domestic surroundings were for tidying up, not studying in. I'd given up doing homework at the fire since I was too tall to fit the available floor space. Essays, when required, were accomplished elbow-down on the bedroom quilt with a notepad on the pillow, but the competing noise from three televisions each tuned to a different station from the adjacent flats was distracting. The bedroom, in shadow all year round, was usually cold. In winter, you could scratch the word HELP in the ice on the inside of the windows and see number 20's pigeon loft, bird breath rising in tiny plumes through the grille. Exam leave was not a winter thing, but the light level said nine o'clock at night all day in there which was not conducive to enthusiasm even if the TVs were off. The kitchen had no table, the living room was cramped and the bathroom didn't count. The little flat was perfectly adequate, but where I wanted to be was inside the practice rooms, tiny, soundproofed and private, or in the main music room with its single table for the whole class to sit around and Ken, working through his breaks as our secret ally, a teacher-in-cahoots. Sneaking into school instead of out of it was an unusual solution, but entirely logical. To avoid detection, wear civvies, go nowhere near the goody van or the dining queue, do without drinks to forestall any need for the toilets: easy planning, none of it hard. For a lot of senior girls this was normal. Dining hall food was notionally fattening and since bottled water was a cash-cow yet to be milked, not eating ensured the casual consumption of carbonated sugar. The toilets were awash with naughty girls smoking and demanding cash, cruder-than-average drawings and puddles: risking cystitis was a better option. To keep us on our toes, a hard core of cretins hung around the toilets laughing at the imagined inadequacies of every girl who passed as though competing for a prize. They threw used chewing gum at plain girls, swotty girls, girls with buck teeth or freckles, bow-legs or bony knees, girls with built-up shoes, unfashionable shoes, unfashionable tights, ankle socks or horn-rims. The tall, the skeletal and the Junoesque got the worst of it, but no one was safe. Sylvia Sagan, a pretty senior who had fallen off the wall bars in second year, had something horrible called endometriosis so they called her *Ghost* on account of her pallor. Even Dorabella Ricci, the school siren with bee-stung lips, smoky eyes and hairspray who looked like a madam waiting for a court case, was catcalled, but more apprehensively because they were afraid she'd turn round and bite them. Hiding, not eating, drinking or being seen, was something we did all the time. Given the choice, Dorabella wasn't in school if she could avoid it and Sylvia, at the mercy of her own treacherous blood, wasn't able. Not me. Last out of rehearsals and sloping in every day to the end of every term, I was also, so far as I could make myself, hale as a Clydesdale: absence due to illness was rare.

Illness meant doctors and doctors entailed fuss. Also they asked too many questions. The aversion had nothing to do with any physical pain the doctor might inflict so much as my family's express desire to avoid explaining certain kinds of injuries. Mum visited the doctor for her asthma and her nerves, while Cora, so far as I remember, would rather perform her own amputation than go near the local practice with so much as a sprain. Then Cora seemed impervious to common ills: conjunctivitis, inflammations, infections and leakages, rashes, warts and bronchial malfunctions passed her by. Fitted with a full set of dentures at twenty-two, she had no truck with dentists either. Any aliens ignorant enough to abduct my sister for the purposes of research would find out sharpish they had made a big mistake: no one advanced on my sister with an unauthorised probe while she was conscious. We were not the kind who sought medical advice. In the run-up to exams, however, the heartburn that had been keeping me awake at nights was becoming unbearable. Lack of sleep made me lethargic and I couldn't think in straight lines. It was this part that caused most worry. I wanted to pass my exams.

Exams weren't frightening. They passed the time, and peace

from outside interference was guaranteed while they lasted. The fourth-year tests had been a routine plod and this year's, while tougher, weren't dire. Halfway through my English paper, however, I'd taken a dizzy turn. Maybe I needed to eat more but by now even the smell of food made me queasy. Eventually, worried I'd fall at the hurdles for no good reason, I made an appointment with Dr Hart. I was seventeen and surely entitled to medical discretion. The last thing I wanted was mum knowing. Anyone knowing anything tended to make things worse.

Dr Hart poked spatulas in my mouth and nudged me in the guts with his fingers. He checked my notes, asked me to lie on his couch and held the cold stethoscope over my abdomen, then palpated his hands in the same place as though he was corralling a jellyfish in a rock pool. I was fine, he said, almost irritable at the waste of his time. I put my blazer back on. There was nothing wrong with me in the slightest. Eat fresh fruit, nothing greasy, nothing spicy and try Alka-Seltzer. He bet I had a rotten diet. I smiled and agreed. Not till I was on the way out of the door did he ask, in the manner of a joke, a grasp at thistledown, if there was any chance, any chance at all, that I might be pregnant.

These gym slip mothers you hear about, he sighed, washing his hands at the surgery sink. Any missed periods? Just thought I'd ask.

I held the farewell I'd been forming in my mouth in place and stayed very still. No, I said softly. I managed a snort of dismissal. No.

Didn't think so! He was drying his hands. Give my best regards to your mother from Dr Cameron and myself. How is she, by the way?

I was aware of standing there, looking at him. Before long, he was aware of it too. He put the towel aside and looked straight back.

As a matter of fact, I said. He kept his eyes steady. Actually, I said. Being strictly factual. There is, now I come to think of it, a lateness in that – department. He kept looking. It all depends what you mean by. Any. Chance.

That you might be pregnant? The last of the sentence was down to Dr Hart. The word *pregnant* was not manageable in my mouth for the time being. It didn't mean anything real. Sticking with science and the statistics of possibility only, I conceded pregnancy was feasible, if unlikely in my opinion, by nodding. Twice. My face was very still. My brain, meantime, was pillaging its filing system for a definitive rebuttal. I did not want to talk about withdrawal as a technique since it would sound both naïve and rude. I did want to tell him about Dr O'Flynn and make him see a responsible citizen and not a tart. I wanted to throw in a word about latex allergies, the legitimacy of the liaison that would doubtless now be emerging in his mind and the fact I was sitting exams and hadn't time for this kind of thing right now. I wanted him to know I was really a nice girl and this was some terrible mistake but I couldn't open my mouth.

Dr Hart rummaged in a drawer and handed over a perspex bullet. And though I took it, I walked out sure that if the doctor thought a big girl like me was peeing into a bottle then handing it back, he had another think coming.

I recall walking away from the surgery and down Dockhead Street past the music shop, the newsagent, the baby shop, every step reinforcing the moment he told me there was nothing wrong in the slightest. Fruit and milk. I trusted that part of the exchange. The rest was the strong suspicion I was actually unconscious and making it up. Testing my memory for confirmation, all I could picture was the doctor's face, a room my mother had once cleaned behind him, his V-neck pullover and a fuzzy drabness from the window behind him with no hint of a view. My feet, when I looked down, were in black suede boots despite the fact that MAY had shown on the red and black calendar attached to his wall. The calendar was important. If it was indeed May – exam and cherry-blossom time, one leap beyond the cruellest month but not yet wandered into flaming June – I would not be wearing boots. I would not be strolling down Dockhead Street feeling as if I had drunk too much limeade with my guts fizzing; I'd be at home studying for my Higher Certificate exams. I had one more year of schooling then I was going to Music college. Or something. Those boots and these vague plans for the future were what I clung to as real. If they were correct, this whole doctor episode was nothing to worry about. Or not too much. Something was jumbled somewhere – a time-warp seemed one rational idea – and it would all go away. The plastic bullet stayed hard in my pocket. *Urine.* He had said it twice. Fat chance.

I didn't go back to school, but home. Straight line. With no key, I forced Cora's bedroom window with a screwdriver from the coal-shed, prised the hinges up till their paint cracked and gave, then wormed my way up the pebble-dash wall to launch onto the rug. My tights tore but it didn't matter. I was indoors again, where flights of fancy were at their least likely. I made tea because tea mended all things and dug out the navy-bound *Home Medical Encyclopaedia* that left blue marks on your fingers every time you touched it. There was nothing under *pregnant* so I had to think of other words. Not far away, *pregnancy* revealed a page of white, caterpillary creatures against a dark blue ground that I dimly recognised as newts. Not newts, embryos. *Development at three months in the womb.* It didn't explain what a womb was but if this little knot of rubbery sprouts lived in it, it was hidden somewhere deep. At no stage – worm, ganglion or dolly on a stem – did it look human. It looked like a grub, a blasted fruit on an unfamiliar tree. It did not say the only thing I wanted to know about pregnancy which was how to know if it had caught you out. Being *caught out* was all I knew about the condition. You *fell* and were *caught*. If you left it alone, it took up residence and blew you up like a tyre. It was a sign of spoiled goods in the unmarried and something to keep out of sight even if you were. Left long enough, you burst. Eve's punishment, Eve's pain, Eve's verb. *Fall* as in *fall by the wayside, fall into a trap, fall into the wrong hands, fall foul, fall in the mire, fall into a den of thieves* and *fall flat*. Like the walls of Jericho, Humpty Dumpty, Icarus and Dinah Matheisson's lassie in Sharphill Road. I grasped the possibility it was me as well. Sobered, probably paler than I'd been for some time, I closed the book, checked I'd left no fingerprints on the cover and slid it back where it belonged. I washed the blue from my hands with a nail-brush and looked into the mirror. My mascara was still where it was supposed to be, my lips outlined in baby pink. Maybe I was fine. One blue stain from the encyclopaedia had travelled from my fingers to my cheek. I wiped it off, checked my hands again in case there was anything I'd missed and there it was: one smear on my index fingertip that wouldn't budge. No one would know how I'd acquired it, I thought. They'd just take for granted it was a leftover from an exam-issue Bic. For all I knew, that might even be true. One thing could look like another. It happened all the time. A straight face and enough nerve could get you through all sorts of things. I'd done it before and I could do it again. This thing, the thing we called *getting into trouble* at school in horrified whispers, was not happening to me. There was still the test to go, but tests usually turned out the way I wanted them to. If willpower had anything to do with it, I'd be fine. That was how people got through: they wished it so. Hedging my bets with God, I spent evenings translating Virgil for the still-to-come Higher Latin with the TV no more than a murmur through the heating vent. No entertainment for me. No one was going to be hurt or disappointed, no one's peace of mind troubled one jot. This was nobody's problem but my own. I had to allow nothing, not a word, a hint, a whisper, to reach mum or school or the wider world through which whispers trickled like poisonous drops of mercury, and to kick the whole lot off I had to aim at the doctor's bottle and not miss. It was time to give up on dignity and do what I was told. To submit.

For a week I said nothing to anyone, not even to me. My dreams fought back, unveiling a scene of horses strewn on the disused railway track beneath the Sorbie Bridge on the way to school, dead things thrown there as if on purpose among the ragwort and cow-parsley and curling ferns. Creatures nobody could see but me. The dreams were so vivid I looked over the bridge on my next walk to school, my hands clutching the drystane edge in case, but the horses weren't there. I checked more than once. When the week was up, I went back to the doctor. I was ten weeks pregnant.

Of course I was.

Ten weeks. I wondered what in God's name had I done ten weeks ago knowing perfectly well there was an obvious answer and that whatever had been different didn't matter now. It was just your Donald Duck. What's for you not going by you. Statistical probability. Dr Hart was within his rights to look smug but he didn't. He stuck his nose into some handwritten notes in a cardboard folder and looked uncomfortable. He'd known me since I was a baby and probably felt tainted.

Well, he said. Well. What do we do now? I noted the word *we* and found it redundant. Given no response, he tried again. What do you want to happen now given the available options?

Wary as a rabbit, I assessed this question for traps and found it wanting. For this question to be a real question he'd need to tell me what the available options were. The most likely interpretation of his words was that he wanted me to engage in guesswork under the guise of open choice, which might limit my possibilities before he had to do it for me. Maybe the less I knew, the more he'd avoid telling me. Maybe he had a preferred outcome and was letting me in on no other.

Dr Hart sighed as if bored. As if he wasn't sure I was just playing dumb. Then he tried again.

You have to tell me what you think sooner or later, he explained. It's important.

If he thought I'd go over first push, he thought wrong. Head racing, I let him wait. Asking to run the test again was no go. The results of these things were scientific, which meant more or less unarguable. Dr O'Flynn's big grey face appeared in my head mouthing the word *abstain* and I swallowed him down like reflux. Mentioning that was no good either. Dr Hart might know Dr O'Flynn and engage in shoulder-to-shoulder solidarity. I needed to be calm, detached and creative. Dr Hart coughed. With time up, I stuck with the childhood pattern I knew and trusted. I unfocused my eyes, looked blank and said nothing.

Well, he said. I'll run them through for you, shall I? As I see it, you can have the baby and look after it. Or have the baby and give it away. That's what most women in your situation would do.

I noted the expression *most women*. I noted the phrase *in your situation* and gained strength. Dr Hart had not the remotest idea what *my situation* might be beyond the purely physical. Worse was his choice of the word *baby*. There was no baby. Here, he was just wrong. I needed to remember there was no baby. This was an *embryo*. Dr Hart crossed his arms to look matter-of-fact but there was no steel in him. I sniffed indecision. This was a contest now. I was in with a shout.

There will be no baby, I said. Not now, not ever. Babies ruin your life.

Don't be silly, he said. His body language softened. You're too grown-up now for that kind of nonsense. You can't make something go away by sheer denial.

I'm not being silly, I asserted. I'm trying to be clear. My mother says children ruin your life and my mother's opinion is something I take seriously. She should know.

I'm sure she doesn't mean it the way you're making it sound.

I'm sure she does. Silence. He breathed in and I played my ace. I can't have a baby. That is my situation. That's my choice.

Oh for goodness sake, he said. Surprised or not, you need to look at this rationally.

Surprise, I thought. He thinks my mood is one of *surprise*.

This kind of thing happens to young women all the time. They cope.

I imagine they all do, I said. My voice was cold. One way or another.

We were down to it now. Even Dr Hart knew what I meant. For as long as I remembered, playing in the corner while my mother and Aunty Kitty discussed their lives, I had heard allusions to gin, hot baths and falling down the stairs. Knitting needles came into the picture even if I wasn't sure how. I had heard women talking about *getting rid* as far back as I could remember and now, when I needed them, their words came back. If you remembered enough, held on to enough, all knowledge was useful eventually. It was important not to plead.

There are things people do, I said. Other things.

He looked at the floor and exhaled through his nose. Are you proposing a termination?

This wasn't a word I knew, but its meaning seemed clear. Yes, I said. I want to be not pregnant.

Dr Hart rubbed one eye and leaned forward in his chair. Dr O'Flynn sent a note to say you had been to see him.

I nodded. Dr Hart stood up, poured a glass of water from the sink he'd washed his hands in only a week ago and sipped. He looked out of the window. How are the exams going? he said.

This was new territory. Fine, I said, thinking hard. Bland answers were in order.

They're going well?

Fine.

How fine? What did you get last year?

Passes.

What kind?

I told him and he nodded and sipped. When he said nothing, I told him what I expected this time too. Encouraged by the sobriety of his face I took a risk. I'm good at exams, I said. I'm the studious type.

Do you expect good passes?

Yes, I said. I didn't care if it was immodest: passing was what I did. That was my job and always had been. My duty to my mother was to pass exams and not have babies. She'd made it more than plain.

And after?

Blindfold, I picked my answers wearing high heels in a rock pool, trying not to slip. My mother wants me to go to university.

I had no idea what *university* meant or what happened there. I wasn't even sure where the nearest one was, but I knew that *university*, a concept wearing a gown and trimmed with golden tickets, was what mum had talked about as far back as she worked out my stammer wasn't mental impairment. *University* was what she intoned to Kitty when Kitty pointed out my shortcomings as a future beautician or social hostess, a word she trotted out as a trump. *She'll go to university one day. Wait and see.* Even if I was the only one who took it seriously – her workmates in the school kitchens must have looked at her sideways from time to time – that was her ideal. I had enough nous not to say *musician*. People never understood music as work. I could not say I hoped to be a conductor because he'd think I meant on the buses. He'd be suspicious if I opted for *doctor* or *lawyer*, the commonest selections beyond reproach. So I said the obvious thing. I wanted to be a teacher. I looked him in the eye and said I wanted to be a secondary school teacher, as if it was something I had wanted for years. Only then did I wonder if my suspicions were wrong as to his reasons for asking.

If I phone the school, they can verify this? He cocked his head.

Oh yes, I said, confident. Just ask Miss Lyons. Or Mr Hetherington. He'll speak for me.

Ardrossan Academy? He picked up the folder, a pen, the boxy bit of paper with my test results on it. Just wait. Wait.

Whatever he was doing didn't take long. When he came back he examined my tummy again and slipped me an appointment card with a pink prescription. Back in two days, take the tablets if anxious. And go, right now, this minute.

I knew my own way out.

I cashed the prescription for two pills and swallowed both next morning on the way to my French exam. By the time I reached for Paper 1, my vision was spangly, my head light. The more I stared at the text, the spanglier it got. The unseen text in the afternoon seemed to have something to do with the smell of goats, a wood, mushrooms and a brush. What the hell: I wrote it all down. During Paper 2, after no lunch-break with no lunch, I fell off my chair swinging on the back two legs during the interpretation and laughed. I did get back on, but trying to concentrate was an effort. Around me, the swotty and downright desperate remnants of the fifth year were still writing as if it mattered. As if anything did. And I laughed again. Everything was funny when you put your mind to it, and wherever mine had gone, it showed. Someone helped me remember my blazer and I walked out. Neither Phillip nor Jacob were there to chat to because they didn't do French and anyway, they were leaving. Despite his love of fish, Jacob was going to have a go at catering in a Largs hotel and Phillip fancied Art College. His dad wanted him to be a draughtsman but Phillip said he'd stick out for a non-corporate life. I had no doubt he meant it. We were made of the same stuff, I thought: Phillip wouldn't want an office. He was supposed to be home working on his portfolio and I was pleased. He didn't know anything was wrong yet and not having to mind my *p*s and *q*s would be a relief. Once I'd sorted out the mess, *then* he could know, not before. I wanted no one to feel responsible, no one to find solutions they didn't owe. There was no one to lie to, no one to worry. School was empty, the last of the paper-huggers straggling home. I didn't remember hearing the bell, but the evidence it had rung was unassailable. Just me and a mongrel, looking keen. I leaned on the railings and was grateful, bone-tired: my feet, even in sling-backs, felt heavy. As I crossed Sorbie Bridge, my spine rippled with recognition and I looked over the edge, making sure nothing was staring up with dead, marble eyes. If the horses had ever been there, and I was sure they had, someone had moved them. Covering their tracks. There was not so much as a shoe nail, a single strand of long, golden hair. Only grass, rust, sleepers. One limbless doll. I almost threw up with relief.

The termination was arranged for Irvine Central less than a week away. Dr Hart asked if I was sure. He had the papers all ready but I had to be sure. It was escape from certain ruin, a guarantee of my mother's dreams and peace of mind, a way to keep the whole thing to myself and save everyone around me from disruption. Nobody needed to know what they had so nearly lost, I thought.

The ammonites with hooded eyes I had seen in the *Home Medical Encyclopaedia* did not make me flinch. I even asked Dr Hart how the procedure was done but he hedged. It was common enough, he said, akin to a D and C. A scrape to clean things out. No second thoughts? he asked. No, I said. None. He had one more thing to say.

Well, he blew his nose, all we need is your mother's signature and we can move on. I looked at him. She needs to know, he said. Whatever else you may have been thinking, she needs to know.

I felt my face sliding around while Dr Hart elaborated. At seventeen, I could not authorise my own anaesthesia. Only next of kin could do that and my mother had to be asked. To save delay, he'd ask her today. The termination taking place was in my mother's gift.

I am sure she will have strong feelings, he said. But she will have to know. And I will be happy to tell her.

My sister, I said. He looked attentive. My sister will kill me.

No, she won't, he said, weary. He had clearly heard versions of this before. People are surprising. Pull yourself together. Take a walk. Be back at five.

I closed my eyes and found a snapshot of the room waiting behind my lids, inescapable. I heard him stand, sure of our conclusion. He was not pleased but not unhappy. Dispassionate, that was the word. He was, commendably, completely in control.

We told her that same afternoon after the Art exam was

finished. I suspected I'd not done well but simply turning up had seemed an achievement. She saw a strange man's car pull up with me inside and was unsettled by the time she got to the door. Dr Hart told her to sit down as though he lived here, not her. She didn't ask why. She sat. He said what he had come to say and she took it like a tree struck by lightning. *O my God*, she chanted, rocking, holding herself tight. *Jesus dear Jesus sweet God.* Dr Hart suggested brandy. We didn't have any. I thought about fetching the sherry, then didn't. She didn't want tea or water. When the doctor reached the word *termination*, her colour came back. Her face did not return to rights completely, but the lights went back on. He let his words sink, then presented the papers. She looked at them, the doctor, then me. The doctor pointed with one long, insertionary finger. He clicked his pen. She signed.

Things were and were not the same. I told Phillip and put on a helpful face so he was not upset. He was anyway. I hadn't seen that coming. I thought he'd be pleased. My mother, as we were alone one afternoon, asked me to play *Für Elise*. I played it twice. Then she sat on the sofa and told me she had been pregnant when she got married.

It happens, she said. I was pregnant and the baby died.

It wasn't the first I had heard of Robert, my missing brother, but it was the first I'd heard of it from her. That she'd been pregnant before she married struck me as nothing at all. She was shaken, however. She looked apologetic and fearful as if she had revealed she was Bonnie Parker. She hoped it did not make me think less of her, but now was maybe the time to say. So you know now, she said. That's my secret. And now you know. That this had troubled her for years was dizzying. We sat for a while, looking out at nothing.

The bigger surprise was Cora. She did sardonic to begin with, hedging her bets but her heart wasn't in it. The evening before I was due to go in, Cora came through while I was packing a toilet bag. She never came in our room so I knew something was afoot. What it was was a present. She held out a nightie I'd never seen before, a nylon confection with roses on the bodice and a drawstring neck. Somebody gave her it, but she'd never liked it. Too frilly and she liked plain. So – she held it out in one rigid arm, her face expressionless – I might as well have it. She'd never wear it so why not.

Consultants and everything, she said. Big shots. You should look nice for your own self-respect. Some of these folk look at you like you're shit on their shoes. Here. She held it out. Bloody hospitals, she said. I hope I don't die in one.

I took the gift, its full weight no more than ectoplasm, and she strolled off to the living room, apparently satisfied. Consultants. Doctors. Real things. My mother found some fancy soap in a box and gave me a towel, smelling of fresh air and starch. She'd ironed it so all the pile moved in one direction, white straw in a gale.

Don't use hospital towels, she said. They're not clean. Use nothing you don't have to.

What to take had become a consultation, a chauffeur arranged.

Phillip's dad, in the Jag he'd restored till it looked like a car in a film, brought Phillip to our front door and carried the holdall as if I was fragile.

It's a D and C, I said, just routine procedure.

If I sounded medical and female, nobody would ask me to say any more. Phillip stayed silent. We had the feeling his dad had worked out what was really going on, but he did us proud. He was a man of few words, Mr English.

The stay was nothing much. I did not sleep or eat the hospital food and a radio played police messages all night in what I assumed was the nurses' room. Donny Osmond singing *Paper Roses*. Once, a doctor with a jet black pigtail and a henna mark on her forehead examined me as if she was stuffing a turkey and scowled when I winced.

This is nothing, she said. This is not pain. She was right.

The consultant in the operating theatre wore a three-piece suit with a carnation. I am very sure indeed about the flower and the colour. It was pink. I must have stared. Was this what I wanted? he asked, holding a needle up to the light. Could I count backwards from ten? I recollect the number eight. The rest was out of my hands.

Mum looked tired when I got back. Phillip had held my hand on the way back in his dad's car but broke when we reached the door. It was something the house did to people. Mum was in one of her knitted suits instead of a pinny and there were cakes with real cream for Phillip to take first pick.

You could just have effed off, son, Cora said. She's lucky in you.

After he went back home, refusing to kiss me at the door for reasons of his own, mum said her piece. I was too big a girl to be in with her these days, she said. It was time I had some privacy and a bit of space. Everybody needed a bit of space.

Cora tutted. What about me and Francis? We need space.

Just shut up for a minute, mum sighed. You've always got something to say. You're the only one round here with your own room. I'm saying it's time she had one of her own as well.

Cora sniffed, but she piped down. After the eggshell-treading of the last few days, the house was twitching, reclaiming the tensions that kept us on our toes.

I'll shift some sheets into the living room tonight and fold them inside in the morning. This is my bed now. I'm keeping my clothes through where you are, but I can sleep here on the divan. It's no bother and you need a bit of peace.

I looked at my hands, not sure what there was to say. It didn't seem the right thing, but it was the easy thing. The easy thing for me.

You have the back bedroom. You can put your books in. You've got your own room now just like she's got. I'm not treating you different. She got every damn thing going. You need your own room.

More fool you then. Cora's voice suggested a ceremonial

washing of hands. Teach her how to be selfish and you make a rod for your own back. You get nothing being soft but sat on. Don't say I didn't warn you.

Mum did not look crestfallen. She looked unsinkable. Firm. For a moment, with no ambiguity or mitigation, I hated Cora and wished her ill. Good things given openly made her murderous. If they were not hers, gifts filled her with the wish to seize and crush to powder. Causing physical injury was one thing: spite against generosity, against kindness itself, attacked something far deeper. For whole seconds I wished she was dead for the release of checking there was no mistake, the prospect of her consumption by flames to smoke and ash. It didn't help. So I turned to my mother and watched what she did. We blocked her out. Bookends, eye to eye knowing what we were doing, we pretended she wasn't there.

I'd like that, I said. It was tentative but audible. Thank you. That's kind.

Refusing might have been more noble, but at least for a few nights, I wanted to take. We did not touch each other or smile, but she nodded. Even if Cora hadn't been there, much more was beyond us for now. I focused on the good thing being given and not the destruction we'd been promised it would bring down on both our heads. I would give the room back, of course. Once I'd worked out where else to go. Of course. But for now, I had my own place to be, legitimate privacy.

Cora snorted. You're a bloody doormat. Always have been, always will be.

We went out together to fetch the sheets and make up the divan leaving Cora behind like Madame Defarge. We corner-to-cornered in silence, making squares of white brushed cotton, flattening candy-stripe pillow slips with the palms of our hands to make them smooth. Cora switched on the TV, unleashing *Songs of Praise.* She was in such a bad mood, she left it on. *Count your blessings, name them one by one.* We looked out of the window together when the folding stopped. And eventually, through the sermon elsewhere, the question surfaced.

What's wrong with her?

It was a question I'd been asking for years without knowing till I heard in out loud, forming and falling from my own mouth.

I mean why is she the way she is?

Don't ask me, my mother said. One of Mr Gregg's pigeons landed on the sill to watch us through the glass. It's just what she's like.

She did not look up and her mouth was tight. Whatever she thought, if she thought anything at all on the subject of her elder daughter, was not for me to know. *Lead us, heavenly Father, lead us o'er the world's tempestuous sea.* The pigeon tapped the glass wondering if we had anything to give. Mum tapped back. Feeling nothing in my head, nothing in my heart, I went to fetch bread and scattered it outside. I liked watching the birds come down, chasing after the biggest scraps. They were open-hearted things, birds, transparent. Blood was moving inside me, filtering through the assaulted muscles of the cervix as I walked, draining and clearing, leaving no visible scars behind.

At school on Monday Ken said I looked peaky. Was I all right? Of course I was all right.

You're the colour of Wensleydale, he said. Are you ill?

My exams were out of the way and classes were back to something like normal. There was a rehearsal that afternoon. I was right as rain.

Sylvia Sagan, he said. The Polish girl. She's in hospital. That disease she's got?

I nodded.

It's worse. Transfusions, the lot. He sucked through his teeth and sighed. We don't know we're lucky. Should be grateful we're healthy every day.

Sylvia, whose skin was thin and white as lint, wouldn't be at rehearsal. She was off increasingly, taking pills that didn't help. The rumour ran it would kill her one of these days. I went to the sound-proof whiteness of the practise rooms and rested with my forehead on the keys for a while because they were friendly and they were cool. I handed some finished pieces in to the Art department and tested out my casual banter. I defied the ugly gang to wash my face in the toilets then bite my lips till they were red. I looked the same as always. Absolutely fine. Susan was playing warm-ups in the main hall and stopped to wave. I told myself I was coming down with a cold and set my music on the stand. Handel *concerto grosso*, two sharps, alto clef: serious fun. We bandied an A from section to section before Ken raised the stick. Bows held high, we waited with our backs straight in that silence that is not a silence but the tension before something new begins. This, I realised, poised for the down-beat, was the best split-second of my life. I was not in hospital. I was home.

The end of term treat was Howat, the boy-wonder of my junior years, returned to play a concert for the assembled fifth year. Ken introduced him as a distinguished guest and touched him on the shoulder, flexing the arm of his jacket and smiling with what looked like pride. A former pupil was not only an example, but a privilege. He was a reminder of what we could do if we tried.

The great wooden behemoth of the school piano sat centre-stage with its teeth bared. Adjusting the lid, Howat looked fourteen: unfashionably cropped, small-boned and skinny. We rustled like birds while he sat, tested the height of the stool. And the music started from nowhere. There was no finger-flexing, grimacing or flicking of hair; no music requiring to be pulled to order on the stand. All he did was play. I don't remember the names of the pieces but I do remember listening, the feeling of being lightened and lifted by the sound that came from inside the workaday box of ivories every one of us at some time had plonked *Chopsticks* on during rehearsal breaks. We knew it had no hidden compartments, no extras in the depth of its workings: just three strings to each note, a range of dusty pegs and hammers like every other rattle box in the school. What we heard, then, was *him*: every inflection of his wrists, every movement of his fingers, all the learning and practice he had put into understanding how to make the music fine. If there had not been such distance between us, I might, like Doubting Thomas, have lifted his hands from the keyboard to see if the sound came from ten fingers alone. This was not a recording; this was one boy, two hands, three pedals and eighty-eight keys. And, of course, the thing he'd been preparing for all his life. Roy was not what I remembered. He was better than I remembered, so good the room disappeared. It took till he was done and the applause began for it to come back, and I joined in knowing what I had suspected for some time. Very few people got good. Even fewer got anywhere near *that* good. And those who did, did it alone. I'd be something if I worked hard, maybe an entertainer, an arranger, a backing singer if I got a break. Musicologists wrote books full of dates and opus numbers like scientists and even though the thought of writing a book made me wither inside, I'd do it if I had to. I wasn't reaching for the stars. I was reaching for something graspable. I'd never be Howat, he was being that already. But I'd make something, sounds or signals where nothing existed before. And that was worth remembering.

Howat took a bow looking modest because he was. For an encore he played a neat little Chopin waltz I recognised, one Ken had walked me through in lessons so I could play it too. The very idea made my heart contract. My teacher saw us at the back of the hall and waved.

O for Godsake. Susan, almond-eyed with chocolate-coloured

hair, dunted me with her elbow. Your mascara will run. Soppy doesn't suit you. Behave.

It's a cold, I said, eyes brimming. Either that or hormones.

Periods, she said. Don't start me.

The room was clapping like firecrackers. We thundered with our feet. We cheered.

13

Phillip didn't go for his Art college interview. I found out because he was a rotten liar. Whether it was failure of nerve or laziness, he didn't say and it didn't matter. It was done. We got engaged in any case and spent a day poking our noses around Argyll Arcade to settle on a fat amethyst cluster as our token of espousal. Amethyst, a stone that according to the Romans protected the bearer against drunkenness, pain and mental disorder, seemed nicer than diamonds which merged in my mind with gold-diggery more than down-to-earth romance. So purple it was black, the amethyst was more beautiful anyway. At night, in what was now my bed, I had a shot at writing a diary to record my thoughts but I didn't have any. Recording anything resembling a thought, especially if it involved what Mills and Boon called *the secrets of the heart*, was asking for discovery and ridicule. Drawings of hearts with arrows – that's how young I was – were overtaken first by recipes then shopping lists, then notes of the *washed hair, went to pictures* variety, then blank space. When Phillip took up an apprenticeship with a monster pharmaceuticals company, he got a haircut with a neat fringe and matching V-neck jumper. In a matter of weeks, his voice acquired can-do breeziness, the slow release of the word *nice* in relation to cars and the word *mate* as a general address for car mechanics, plumbers and the men on the plant involved in manual labour. He bought an ancient Lotus at a car market which we painted acid-yellow (the pot said *chartreuse*) in the driveway of his parents' smart new-build on the edge of Ardrossan near fields and trees. Out with newly acquired friends, he stood at the bar with the men while I paddled the shallows of the girlfriend pool. *Perhaps you ladies would prefer a seat* meant stay over there. I didn't like yelling at other women while Status Quo outgunned us on the juke-box. It was dull as a knitting bee with no knitting. When Phillip began to note *other couples we should meet up with now we're engaged,* I suspected our days were numbered. Once, we had sheltered in beach pagodas cuddling for warmth and wrapped in the aromas of piss and chip vinegar. We had gone to the zoo and plotted to free the animals and had drawn flowers round each other's navels with eyeliner pencil. If all before us was dinner dances, I missed how we'd been. Thinking of people as halves of a pair was boring. Pubs were boring. Devoid of marine life, smoke-filled and sex-segregated, they were a one-way route to a *her indoors and him out with his mates* future. Phillip disagreed. If Cora liked pubs for the glitter, the men and the active rebuttal of being second-rate and stay-at-home (a woman, in short), I disliked them for exactly the same reasons. If Cora was one of the boys, I wasn't. I'd read enough *Jackie*s by now to know sharing his interests was the way to foster lasting bliss but didn't see how my sitting apart, drinking vodka with women I didn't know and making rejoinders about matching towels counted as sharing anything. Reluctant to admit defeat and let him down, I gave it my best shot. I thought I'd get the hang. I was wrong.

Jacob found a flat share in Camden and broke the news that summer. Abandoning catering and Scotland in one go, he topiarised his Afro, changed his wardrobe to desert boots, jeans and close-fitting polo shirts, and took up body-building. The gym, alfalfa sprouts and protein powder were his new *affaires de cœur.* Something that wasn't Saltcoats was next on his list. His sister was going to look after the fish and the cats, he said. He didn't want me to worry. I wasn't worried. I felt a lot of things about Jacob but worry was never one of them.

Acclimatising to the idea of separation, we strolled together to the new supermarket they'd built on the space where the church used to be and went in to browse their selection of outlandish foods. Pak-choi, fresh ginger and hazelnut yoghurt were bypassed in favour of soya milk – Jacob's new drink of choice – and we walked back to the beach. The war memorial this near wire trolleys seemed insulted and the roundabout's display of geraniums had been ousted in favour of concrete. Things looked more like themselves at the sea wall so we sat and looked out to Arran. It was misty, the sky and horizon one and the same, and nothing defined from this distance. At least he wasn't going to America.

Jacob was too restless simply to admire the view. He had something to say. He was 90 per cent sure, he said. I waited. He'd been thinking about it a lot and was almost certain. In fact, he'd go as far as definite. I waited. More or less.

If you don't tell me, I'm going home, I said. Hurry up.

OK, he said. He breathed deep, opened the soya milk and took a slug. I'm homosexual.

What? I wasn't sure I'd heard right.

Homosexual, he said. Queer.

I punched his arm so I didn't look like a sap and got ready to smile.

I'm serious, he said. There was milk on his upper lip.

How do you find out something like that? I said.

How do you think? I honestly had no idea. Godsake, he said. I fancy men. I got an offer.

What about Muriel? I squeaked. Muriel was Jacob's girlfriend. She hadn't been around that long and I didn't know much about this kind of thing, but a girlfriend didn't seem to fit the picture. You were getting engaged to Muriel not that long ago. What happened there?

Stuff. He drank some more milk and wiped his mouth. Actually, a lot of stuff. The upshot was he'd told Muriel he was sorry and she was out of the picture till he was sure. Otherwise it wasn't fair. He had to be fair and he had to be sure.

I was baffled more than surprised. You're the one that always says nobody knows anything for sure. You always say keep an open mind.

I'm trying, he said. But other people want definites and maybe they're right. My brother was sure. He told me I was a fucking annoyance when I told him and he was pretty sure about that. Actually, he said I was just trying to get attention and I'd grow up.

I smiled. That was exactly the kind of thing Carl would say. He'd been saying things like it for years. Jacob didn't smile back. He was holding the carton with his nails bitten down to the quick and his jaw set. He had a steady gaze when he wanted one and he wanted one now.

So what do you think? he said. I want to know what you think.

I don't know what I think, I said. Seaweed was chasing its tail where our shadows fell, as if it was dancing. It's just – sudden.

OK, he said. Take your time. He looked at his desert boots, did the lace tighter. Then looked back up again. But if I take to wearing green eyeshadow, will you keep in touch?

You're kidding, right?

Of course I'm fucking kidding. He tried a smile that didn't work. But you won't think less of me? I'd hate you to think less of me.

That was all it took. The idea there would ever be a time I'd think less of Jacob was as far-fetched as the idea I'd think less of spring. I put my hand on his head and rubbed it like Velcro then leaned forward and, for what was probably the first time, landed a proper smacker on his cheek. He dropped the carton and spilled soya milk over the sand. The noise of it spattering blew a raspberry.

All those beans milked for nothing, he said, looking down. Now I'm a litter-lout as well.

He walked me home and asked to come in and tell my mother too. He wanted to practise telling people, he said. Not doing it felt like lies. Mum looked him up and down when he said *homosexual* and her forehead crunched.

What's that? she said.

Homosexual, he said. A jessie. A faggot.

Och son, she said. Her mouth twitched. That's all made up. Like Charles Hawtrey. Men did not fancy other men, she said soothingly. It was all just stuff on the telly and Kenneth Williams. It was kidding on.

Good-natured, he persuaded her there might be more to it than there seemed from a distance.

If it keeps you happy, she said eventually. You do what you like, son. They held on to each other, laughing at the door. Her amusement at the craziness of men liking men was infectious. It's none of my business.

He shook his head and embraced her in a way he'd never embraced me. Godsake, he said, wiping his eyes. He stroked her arm. You're priceless.

It was something I never heard anyone else tell her and made me glow. She liked boys, my mother. They brought out another side. Sons might have made her a different woman. She liked every boyfriend I ever brought to her door, every male companion and co-conspirator. When they left, disappeared or faded, she missed them and said so. When he was gone, she missed Jacob almost as much as I did, and missed him to the end of her life which wasn't that long in coming, now I think of it. Phillip told

Jacob he wasn't as queer as he thought. I told Mr Hetherington myself. Why not? he said. It's all the same thing, I suppose. He sent his best wishes, and the advice that Jacob join an all-male choir. Plenty in London, he said. Barbershop. Never enough tenors. They'll snap him up.

When I told him, Jacob shook his head in mock disappointment. Being queer used to be such a big deal, he said. Now it's ordinary. Like everything else.

Not long off the overnight bus from Glasgow and blinking in the cold dawn at Victoria, maybe it would seem that way, but I didn't fall for it. This was the boy who had shown me whole worlds in a jar of water, universes in rock pools teeming with alien life. Nothing was ordinary. He'd remember when he stopped being blasé. If you really looked, took stock of the detail, life was a constant surprise.

That last year went too fast. I don't remember in detail what music we played or everything we sang, but I remember lots of it. Warlock, Barber or Bartók with the chamber orchestra, a mixed bag of Russians and Slavs and Frenchmen with the symphony-size outfit and lots of Bach. I remember whole viola lines complete with all marked bowing and since military-precision bowing was never my *forte*, that's saying a great deal. We sawed through brand-new string quartets for local festivals and bit down on freshly composed masses with the senior girls' choir. I wrote music of my own and Ken recorded it all on thick reel-to-reel that has since been lost. I knew women did not compose – at least not according to Sir Thomas Beecham and it took years for me to find out he was wrong – but the pleasure of creating something where nothing had been before was too tempting not to try. I liked it so much I did it with words as well, but there was no one to take the words to afterwards and get them to join in. This would change.

I remember the altos press-ganged into singing the soprano line of the James Clark *Gloria* to make the opening notes harsher, Ken laughing at my outrage; I remember, note-perfect, the whole of Warlock's *Capriol Suite* that wove Elizabethan textures into something devilish and modern, and can still hear in my head Susan and pragmatic Janet Millar playing the Bach Double D so fluently I downed tools to listen rather than play.

At Christmas, we sang Britten's *Ceremony of Carols* that tumbled over its own notes like kittens from a bag and a medley of show-stoppers from *Oklahoma* and *My Fair Lady*. We belted out folk song arrangements and plainchant, war-horse opera choruses and thick German chorales. All year, and for as long as it lasted, I memorised lessons and arrangements of the furniture, the feel of the floorboards that made the stage beneath my feet. I felt the walls of the building to record their textures under my fingertips and sucked in the cast of light on the half-landing stairs that led to the music rooms and the posters of composers, all of them men, and men with beards at that. I learned without trying the words to every song, where best to breathe to cope with long or high-altitude phrases, when softness worked to better effect than hammer and tongs as if this was my last chance to understand how the thing was done. And I'm glad I did because I understand it still. At least some of it. Enough.

University as an idea had always been mum's idea. University for real was Mr Hetherington's, not mine. I had assumed a college of Music: he pointed me elsewhere. Glasgow University had a huge proportion of first-timers, he said; people who didn't know where the ropes were let alone how to pull them. The institution ought to have some kind of strategy to help people in that situation, so that had to be my best bet. They didn't, but the assumption seemed sound at the time. As a leaving gift, he handed me a paperback copy of Muriel Spark's *The Prime of Miss Jean Brodie* and a leather-bound volume of *Jacobean Love Songs*, the title in gold on the spine. Too embarrassed to ask him to pose, I took a photo of his back as he went off to his room to grade ear tests. It's lost and the copy of *Brodie* has fallen to pieces but I still have the *Songs*. Intact.

Last day, I was sent home for wearing trousers. They were 22-inch flares in black crepe from C&A so at least they were trousers of distinction. It was not my school any more and its teachers were passing to other people, but I obeyed the rules. It would have been churlish not to. Heading back home over the railway bridge I checked for dead horses, just in case; beautiful things come to mysterious grief that still, occasionally, appeared in dreams. Someone's cast-off bra, newspapers, a piece of rusty bike frame. Rosebay willowherb for miles.

That everything turned goes, almost, without saying. What you think you know is more open to treachery, upheaval, love and loss, drugs and drink, natural selection and common or garden rotten memory than you can begin to imagine at eighteen and it's just as well. My memory, my mother said, was sharp as a packet of razor blades and to some extent still is, but it will change too. Change and decay are proof of life. They are good things. They are something to trust.

The first big shift was music. Missing the madrigal group, the girls' choir, the chamber orchestra and the string quartet, I missed my champion even more. There were no practice rooms, sound-proofed or otherwise at Glasgow which meant nowhere much to hide and the B.Mus students kept away from the MAs as though we were a separate species. I could not join the choir because the orchestra needed violas. The orchestra played Late Romantics like Mahler and Brückner that some of us didn't like and couldn't play and they drafted in professionals to make good the over-reach. So much for belonging and unified effort. We were not all in this together. University's priorities confused me. I hadn't grasped that medical students were assumed, by definition, to be dirty-minded, that engineers were louts, Arts students were looking for easy options, Sociology was a joke and the only women allowed in the men's union were paid strippers. We were all supposed to love booze. I didn't know what *honours* were, that one did not complain about the foibles of some staff (*Professor So-and-so touches everybody up, it's nothing personal*) or expect your tutor to turn up (*he's at a Labour Party meeting, sweetheart)* if you'd drawn a short straw. Salts of the earth populated these hallowed halls as they populate all walks of life, but I'd been spoiled. Adrift, I hid in the library more often than not reading the starts of books to find which ones spoke back, developing a trust in the friendship of the well-ordered word I've never lost. I finished my course only because I wasn't giving Cora the satisfaction of failing. And I owed it. I owed it to a full grant and mum. I had made promises. That I was lucky was in no doubt. Luck was not to be sneezed at. I embraced as much as I could and read books. That was the luckiest bit. Books. The place was stuffed with books.

Phillip and I, *the couple*, faded by degrees. We stayed together, but still with no date and no plans to fix one, began to wonder what kind of future we had in mind. He suggested teaching and so did my mother. Teaching, I riposted, with no ideas to the contrary, was more of an *over-my-dead-body* option than they assumed. I did not want children and that included other people's. Children were for doormats. They ruined your life. Phillip's married friends were having babies. The idea brought me out in a rash. Increasingly, I understood the Phillip I loved was not the one I lived with. In my head we were stuck at New Year's Day 1973, the last before school was over. In cahoots, we'd dodged the peanuts and thick-sliced Dundee cake, the shortbread, Quality Street and Turkish delight, the dates and walnuts, cocktail onions, cheese on sticks and deep-dyed tangerines his mother had strewn around her home as a bulwark against want and went first-footing to the hinterlands of Ardrossan, in search of something wild. It was a good night for walking and the stars were out. By accident, we found Dorabella Ricci's house. It was full of Chinese waiters from the Loon Fung she'd taught to sing *Auld Lang Syne*. You had to invite them, she said. These boys, they worked hard. They were a long way from home. Phillip found a chocolate brazil in his turn-ups and a man walking a Jack Russell not far from the edge of Montfode Farm wished us Happy New Year as we staggered home. *Love's young dream*, he said, catching us kissing under a streetlamp. *Enjoy it while you can!* The fields rose with steam from cow-breath and I had opened his greatcoat, slipped my hands inside, and found the four-ply V-neck I'd knitted him for Christmas. Phillip wore everything I made him because he was that kind of boy. He knew I passed every stitch between and over my fingers with him in mind, hoping to smother him with tiny pinpoints of authentic love. Blood-warm wool, Phillip inside, the sounds of beasts. If time had stopped at that moment, I'd have welcomed the meteorite as it hurtled towards us, blazing, the size of Wales. But nothing fell on us, not then or ever. Time did the thing it always does, the thing that unravels and remakes because it must. It just ticked on.

Exactly a year later, my sister had one of her turns, showy enough to make me give up for ever the idea we'd have anything in common. A skinny friend had loaned me an evening gown in sea-green lurex that not only made me look like a mermaid, it fit. Just. Dazzled by my borrowed glamour, I headed to the living room to let mum see. I showed off silver high-heeled sandals, an array of coral-pink toes. Dazzled in her turn, my mother reached for the Instamatic on the top of the piano. If she had not been afraid she'd press the wrong button, if we had not laughed so much or our hands touched as I showed her, it might not have happened. But she did. We did. The whole thing did. Cora was minding her own business in the armchair opposite with a plate of stew on her lap. Her stare flicked up at the sound of the shutter. In stocking soles, make-up free for a night at home, her hair recently dyed so it showed shockingly black, my sister looked vulnerable. Peeled. As my mother insisted on one more shot, she looked across and stared. The stare was a little too focused. If I saw what was coming, I did not duck. In one fluid movement, she lifted the plate in one hand, wrist rising as she threw. Then, like a stone skimming water, the plate arced, struck my temple, my chest, my hip and floor, where it landed flat and whole. I felt the blow, not so much hard as surprising, close to one eye. The slither of something warmer than me making a trail through my hair behind my ear, the line of my cheek, the smell of meat. One eyelid instinctively closing over the salt-stung eyeball beneath. Cora came suddenly closer, almost crawling towards my feet and lifted the plate to tip what was left on my shoes. My mother, the camera right in her hand, sat down on the settee.

Put that down. Her voice was thick but controlled. You hear me? Put that down.

Cora, almost meek, dropped the plate and stood.

It's not me, she said. It's her.

But she did as she was told. Padding deftly through a trail of spilled carrot, she headed like a beast to its basket and sat.

What's wrong with you? My mother's voice was rising. What did you do that for? That's stewing steak. Her voice broke. That's best stuff. Look what you've done to that dress. It's not even hers.

I shifted to fetch a towel, stop the trail of gravy already dropping down my neck.

You're jealous, that's what you are, my mother said, the voice getting smaller as I went up the hallway to the bathroom. Somebody else has to get their shot at life, not just you. I don't know what I've done to deserve this. I don't.

She asks for it, Cora said. She brings it out.

The rest was lost under the sound of running water. I took the dress off to rinse and soak, washed my face and the gunky side of my hair at the sink, then brushed ready to dry. The eye, opened slowly, was not cut, just slightly swollen. It would cover. A lucky break. Over the sound of the hairdryer, I heard the conversation was done and mum had turned, as she always did in a crisis, to housework: a bucket filling, a cloth being wrung. The dress dried in minutes with the dryer up full – thank God for nylon – so I doused it in cologne and shimmied it back on, hoping for the best. Already, Phillip was being greeted at the door, mum's happier voice refound. The eye watered when poked with an eyeshadow brush, but needs must. Concealer and powder, waterproof mascara as insurance, pale lipstick to tone down the flush of my cheeks and I was back to rights. Slightly meat-scented, perhaps. There would be no dogs where we were going. I was good enough. I'd do.

Phillip was chatting to Cora in the living room. I heard them laugh as I came down the hall. She supposed university could be quite demanding in its own way. But she and Phillip knew that in comparison to work – she was flirting, drawing him into a harmless conspiracy – it was toytown, a dream come true. I checked my nails for last-minute chips, fixed my smile and breezed on through.

Phillip took a picture, the last of the roll, while Cora looked on, benign. In it, I am raising a glass as though in celebration and my eyes are watery, but Max Factor and a steady hand win through. My smile is sincere. We are on the verge of leaving. Cora carolled from the living room as I pulled the front door closed. You're only young once, she crooned. Have a lovely, lovely time.

The last time my sister hit me was 1977. It was the only time I ever hit back and I had to be told more than once before I found the gumption to respond. I scratched, truth be told, and diffidently at that. Fighting is not something I'm good at. I scratched only to satisfy her express instruction I do something for once and stop being such a stand-offish cow. Immediately, she hauled off me and ran to check her breastbone in the clock-trim above the fireplace. Her reflection, spooned out of shape from the convex face, smiled.

Look, she said. See what that cheeky so-and-so did. She seemed delighted. Who'd have guessed the bitch had it in her?

If I'd only shown a bit of fight sooner, she explained, settling back into her chair, just shown some gumption quicker, there would have been no need. Now she was reassured. She had taught me to react, stick up for myself. It was pathetic but it was something. She had given me a gift, she beamed. So she could take a back seat now, have a rest and let me look out for myself.

I won't have to hit you again. She made a pledge. That's a promise. I won't hit you again.

I remember the tone of her voice and the odd, earnest expression. I remember the black skirt and V-neck, her freshly cut new-length hair. I remember the big score my nails left on her breastbone shifting when she swallowed, her refusal to use the Dettol my mother brought, reeking, on a cotton pad. I remember the acrid taste of bullshit in my mouth, its queasy swirling in my oesophagus, the desire to lie down and make what had happened go away. It felt like the worst thing in the world.

The sensation of skin under my fingernails stayed for weeks, worming under the keratin to the nerves beneath, but it passed. Even now, thinking about that moment has me reaching for nail scissors and a stiff brush to make myself clean. But she kept her word. She never, not flesh to flesh, tried to hit me again. When I became a teacher, she reminded me I could punish children with a belt if it took my fancy. That I never did amused her. Me and my fancy ideas, saddled with other people's children and not trying to retaliate. I can imagine her tilting her head back and laughing at the ironies, the birds home to roost, how stubborn I could be. On the last count, she was right.

Jacob emigrated to Canada in the end. He joined a gay men's choir, then disappeared some time after I found out he'd been diagnosed with some new-fangled retrovirus and was putting his faith in AZT. Though I lost him, I am hopeful he is still out in the wide world and that the soya milk paid off. Cora did not emigrate, but she traded the front room of my mother's home for a shore-side flat, giving a week's notice. She had been saving up in secret for almost two decades and could finally make the move without having to resort to the council. She was gone one evening when I came back off the last train and the house felt different, flushed with healing ions. We'd lived on top of the national grid for ages, now someone had switched off the plant for refurbishment and left the building alone. I inherited her chair at the fire and knitted there as though someone had to. It absorbed my fingers and passed the time, even if now and then the tang of nicotine from the armrest reminded me where I was. My mother sang more around the house and took Cora's left-behind bed for the pleasure of returning to a mattress. She bought new curtains and peach-coloured paint to cover the smoky-yellow walls and I decorated, one in the eye for Uncle Vince who said it was something women couldn't do because of their arms. We repainted the hall. Mum made too much food at tea-time for years, adapting to loss, but they were cracking down on dinner-ladies taking leftovers home in any case. A last sherry with colleagues after second serving one Friday made do as her retirement ceremony after fifteen years of solid service, and with one bound she was free: state pension, her own back garden for potatoes to grow in, dahlias and

Queen Elizabeth roses out the front. She ought to have been laughing.

The suggestion of tears the day I left with my suitcase for Phillip's flat was unexpected. Neither of us mentioned it had happened. Mere months later, her kitchen flooded in the wake of a thaw and clearing it up led to a severe pulmonary infection she refused to take to hospital. Delirious, furious and abject by turns as she lay in the dark back room all over again, she said she was afraid to die. It was something I had always known, but hearing it aloud was unnerving. Sitting on the bedspread we had once shared, trying to raise her enthusiasm for a cup of tea or a tune on the piano, I felt young and useless all over again. Her eyes fixed on the curtains, their pattern of falling leaves. The light, she said, hurt. Rose and Angus had moved away and there was bad feeling between them. Resentment about the time they had tried to gain custody of me when I was six had resurfaced, refusing to simmer down. There's only so long you can keep a lid on things, she said. Only so long you can last. I was not to tell Rose she was sick. When I opened the curtains, she shrank. She did not want to see the pigeons or the drying green. She wanted the half-light at most. Ideally, the dark. Eventually she was persuaded to listen to one Mario Lanza song – *On with the motley* from *Pagliacci*. After that, she wanted peace. As I had done when I was four on the walk home from Granny McBride's in Guthrie Brae, all I had to do was listen. I saw myself in the dresser mirror, wearing the wrong clothes, the wrong height, the wrong hair, but me all the same, only now I wasn't holding her hand. She was too restless to touch and threw the sheets on the floor, twisting and untwisting a corner of the spread. She took her wedding ring off and put it back on till her knuckle was raw. Eventually, the thing to listen to arrived. It was the babies, she said. The babies showed up in her dreams. They wouldn't leave her alone.

Something was coming. I sat on the edge of the bed and waited to let what would emerge in pieces. My father, it seemed, was older than I thought. He burned down the shop with no insurance and the bugger died. Rose had tried to steal me. There was some business about bad blood and conspiracies and fighting for every damn thing you got. And then there was Cora. Thank God for the Salvation Army. Thank God for the tambourines.

I knew bits of this already, or had read between the lines – some stuff you worked out without even being aware you had done it – but the Salvation Army seemed her own invention, not just unexpected but bizarre. Maybe she was delirious. Maybe they were part of the dreams. I tried not to look like a priest. I tried to look like nobody and touched her forehead. She pulled away.

What did the Salvation Army do? I asked, not sure there would be a rational answer. What happened and what did they do?

In stages and disconnected degrees, she told me. It was rational if discontinuous. Cora, who had left her baby son and husband behind in Glasgow and come back with a suitcase to our front door, Cora who would never sit at peace or do what she was told, had other babies. No one was supposed to know. She went away in secret – there were two or maybe three, it was hard to be sure –

and the Salvation Army in those days used to take the girls in. There was a hostel in Glasgow where girls could live out their time so no one would find out or see them, a place with dormitories and a locker. She was very specific about the locker, its neat and private little key. And when all was said and done, they took the babies away. The Salvation Army had taken the babies somewhere safe.

I tried to imagine a Cora not much older than I was now, Cora reduced to being in a dormitory of women, all swollen as pea pods, resistant to belonging and counting days. I tried to imagine the Salvation Army staff in uniforms and red-lined bonnets, their tambourines set aside for once to rock the babies where they lay in borrowed shawls before they passed them on to others. I imagined a small queue, two couples at most, waiting in line to receive. One hand to another, the babies had slipped away and disappeared, minnows lost to a vast, dark ocean.

Some people want them, my mother said. They take them in. She did not use the word *adoption* but it was what she meant. All those babies, she said. Such a big room. All those girls.

Neither of us spoke for a while. How much she was aware I was even there was uncertain. When it came again, her voice was calmer. The babies had dark hair, just like Cora. All boys. Maybe one day they would come to the door in the course of seeking their mother and she'd have to see them too. They'd find Cora and they would be entitled to judge. She had helped, so they'd judge her too. There were other people than Cora. She knew that now. And they would surely judge.

In the sound of breath, I thought about Cora's disappearances when I was small: that Cora might vanish but always come back, suitcase in hand, was part of how we lived. I thought about her in the Melbourne and the West End café reeling in men then chucking them back overboard and laughing. *Everything's a joke to you, it's time you grew up.* I thought about good-looking man-mountain Big Davie Stewart who carried me on his shoulders when Cora wasn't in and bought me lollipops; Daft Sandy with his cowboy ties and Pringle cardigans; American sailors stooping to get in our attic door. She appeared in my head in a dancing dress and dead-straight seams, revolving neon lights behind her at the fair. *It's just a fish,* she said. *We could chuck it down the drain and have a good time. You don't need to keep it.* And a man followed us, but we went home. Her neat French roll, her painted, typing fingers, the Glasgow train every day without fail. Cora who was never ill and who was never still, who spent her time with crossword puzzles and card tricks and complicated patterns made of single strands; my sister who gave nothing away if she could help it yet who had given me a nightdress, had given away her children. Jesus. Jesus Christ.

Mum, still weighed in the balance and found wanting if this was the moment of death, stopped shivering eventually and fell to sleep. Whether she remembered the incident or the detail of what she told me I have no idea. Whether she did or not, she recovered, not fully but towards better health, and we did not return to the subject. I hadn't the nerve. The recovery lasted six months. Then, with no kitchens or children to feed, she died following a series of heart attacks brought on by walking into the sea in the dark. Her wrists were see-through when I saw her and she looked withered, light enough to lift without effort. The phone I'd had installed for emergencies was off the hook, untouched.

We had three days to empty the flat and found the space under the sink filled with sugar sachets and tiny oblongs of ketchup hoarded from cafés, shoeboxes full she had saved for a rainy day.

You think you know somebody, Cora said. Eh? Then you find you know nothing. You know damn all.

The squabble about the funeral could have been predicted, but Cora held her own.

This was what she wanted, she blustered, still at the crematorium gates. Burned and scattered. Like it or lump it, but don't complain to me.

That we complied with our mother's wishes with regard to refusing flowers was bad enough: the lack of get-together with no scones threatened to snap the camel's back.

You don't have a funeral without a do, Uncle Jack insisted in his mayoral voice. It's mean-minded.

Well, you do now, Cora said. It's not mean, it's what she wanted. You'll just have to fork out for your own bloody dinner and sit in the pub. It'll do you no harm.

We left side by side in what probably looked like a gesture of solidarity. It wasn't. There was just nothing more to say. Mum had been very clear. We were versed in her preferences and this was delivery in full: a grand non-gesture that seemed to let them know she'd been fine without them before and she'd be fine now. They'd shown up and now they could go home. Cora asked how the teaching was going. She bet I was good at it.

Mind you used to batter those dolls eh? You were always a smart cookie.

She planned to keep in touch with me and make sure I was all right. I hoped she was lying.

Phillip not leaving with me to go back to work didn't help and we split for good not long after. No hard feelings. We did not get married. Of course not. I kept the amethyst ring and went down to see his parents on a whim-purchased Suzuki with my hair cut down to the bone to let them know. They were damned decent about the whole thing considering what I said was probably garbled. I gave them my mother's crystal fruit-bowl as a parting gift then headed east. The ring was stolen in a break-in three years later along with my mother's and my grandmother's paper-thin wedding bands, a handful of rock CDs and a reel-to-reel tape of mum and Aunty Rose singing at New Year. The thieves, showing very specific taste, left all the classical LPs, every last one sifted out of the haul as though they weren't worth carrying. They stole the tape Ken made for me without knowing what it was and I enjoyed the thought of them putting it on, finding only the singing voices of teenage girls crooning the words of W. B. Yeats poems. They didn't trash the place. Lucky. I've always been lucky.

Cora kept hold of the Married Man for a while. Then came someone else I forget, then someone else or maybe several, and finally Sandy, Daft Sandy, the rebounding beau from decades before, resurfaced with his quiff intact to reclaim the Love of his Life. I heard that over time my sister left the Glasgow broker to become a school secretary, defying the dress codes at work and bossing the teachers around without compunction or fear. We avoided contact, reluctant to admit the other existed even by post, though I retained a hand-written note with her address on it, filed away again under *stuff* in an envelope that resurfaced every so often only to be put back in. I hoped, in a non-specific and unconvinced way, I might be able to talk to her one day without feeling my insides were being scooped out by a red-hot spoon or staying by the nearest door in case the need to get away overcame me. It is possible I thought I might use the address in an emergency, though what kind of emergency would be improved by getting in touch with my sister remained undefined. I know that at least one of her lost boys sought her out because I was there when it happened. Her son by marriage tracked me down for her funeral, a humanist affair with Sandy at the helm, still with his crooked smile, his hair just so, his slim, black patent shoes.

My mother was half-right. It was the fags, not a man driven to strangle her with her own nylons, that got Cora in the end. She had continued to smoke from a wheelchair; indecorous, rude, quite literally undimmed. Sandy, despite the implications of his name, was her rock. Daft Sandy, who had cried so often on my mother's shoulder, had had the generosity to return the favour. I hoped someone had put lipstick on her face before the send-off. Good stuff, not a casual selection from the embalmer's standard-issue box. She would not have liked to wear someone else's choice. Even full of contempt for the idea of funerals and demanding they stick her in a bin-bag when the time came, she'd have liked at least a slick of *Saharan Sands.*

I do not miss her. Of course not. I still admire her in the way I admire the tenacity of jungle carnivores – the more for their being nowhere near me – but that's a different thing. I miss my mother in a complicated way and have a picture of her smiling from before I was born, on a pin board at home. I miss my Music teacher, Mr Hetherington, who died of Parkinson's disease: a musician taken over by trembling, a singer whose voice refused to do as it was told.

I know no one who has died of so-called *natural causes.* Maybe it's the company I keep. Now fifty-five, I no longer make use of the skill Aunty Rose gave me to make my own clothes though I did for years. Instead, I knit. I knit a lot and the needles go with me if I travel. I apply at least lipstick before leaving the house in what seems to be the belief I may meet my mother unexpectedly and be told off for *not trying*. *Not trying* is something our lot do not do. I no longer sing and reticence merely lessens ability, but I married a singer so I don't have to. One long-denied cat, then several others, share the house. Animals count. One day I'd like a goat like the one in the French exam but that's a way off. I still walk in graveyards and am fond of Highgate and the Glasgow Necropolis, though small gems, like the tiny graveyard on Jura where the headstones face the sea, are my favourites. I do not look for dad. I miss music so much there is some I dare not listen to alone, but reading is unalloyed. Books are company, education, incontestable *terra firma*. My Latin is grown rusty, but it services. On the odd trip to Roman ruins, I have been known to stand in broken theatres and recite Virgil. Dr Nisbet would be proud.

Best of all, I am good with everyday peace and everyday wonders: soap bubbles, cloud formations, birds. And I have a son. My mother would be astounded. After all her warnings, those careful, misguided words. Me. I am astounded. I have a son.

14

Let's save time and agree. Having children changes everything. Admit or deny them, love them or run, they're where everything turns.

That my adolescence coincided with the advent of mass-produced, reliable contraception was an all-round bonus. For that alone, my sister called me spoiled and my mother, repeatedly, assured me I didn't know I'd been born. Sugar-coated, popped fresh from a foil-sealed pack every day and no need, even, for water, the Pill altered the meanings and directions of lives. Swollen breasts, mood swings and increased tendency to cry for no reason was nothing, *nothing*, compared to the upside and that upside was the illusion, at least, of control. Anything, my mother told me, was better than *paying the price* and the price for children, as everyone knew, was the ruination of a future, the end of your life. Being *caught out* was for other, less canny people. I was, or so I imagined, in the clear.

As it turned out, my progress was not as hiccup-free as it might have been, but back-street abortion was something I never had to resort to *in extremis* as my mother had. She made no secret of the fact I slipped under the radar as potential brothers and sisters had not. She'd have been an opera singer if it hadn't been for me, a business woman, a factory owner with a car. Who knew? For years, I was nothing but grateful I existed at all, grateful I was childless by choice. My sister had run away from her baby and never looked back. My bodily integrity, allegedly, was all my own.

When I finally fell, what struck me, after the initial ripple of stunned affront, was how little I knew, or had cared to find out, about birth at all. Up till then – my mid-thirties – all efforts had gone into avoidance as a matter of course. Behind a shield of drugs, rubber and glow-in-the-dark creams, I hadn't once stopped to wonder about what the nine-month wait was doing under cover of darkness, never mind what a resulting baby might mean. A real baby, not a bogey-man. Something grew inside you. It was science fiction, an invasion by a body-snatcher. And it was real. Lucky down to the marrow, I wondered what happened if I resolved to grasp this as lucky too. Keen to at least use the opportunity to expand my education, I did what I always do and bought books. I read anatomies and antenatal tomes and nursing manuals and children's picture books with cartoon fallopian tubes, midwifery texts and historical accounts of caesarian procedures, forceps and dilators. I grasped what it was contractions were for. I leafed through herbals and natural childbirth manuals, read fanciful accounts of cravings and the growing of overnight moustaches and tried to filter the facts. Stuff happened, however. Stuff the books and certainly no one I knew said anything about.

The mother that otherwise might have been a source of information had been dead ten years, my aunts were lost and cousins had never much been part of the picture anyway. My sister was best kept at bay. The only thing to do was watch. Wait and see what was to be learned. That habit had never let me down.

By the time those little shark's fin elbows were zipping past my navel at night, I was thrilled. More, I found that in among the other beached bellies in antenatal, there was something unsuspected. Company. Even if we hardly spoke, we had something remarkable in common, these women and me. Subject to the same forces, we were getting bigger, more to be reckoned with. We were houses for something – someone – more than ourselves. Down to the muscle and bone, I felt *found*.

After the shouting and cutting was over, when a doctor whose name I do not remember landed something on my stomach that felt like eight pounds of steaming pork-links, I had almost forgotten what the upheaval had been about. Till some instinct made me reach, find one slithery, fresh-made limb. Touched, it moved. This was my baby. The realisation made me laugh out loud. This, after years of not having a clue, this very moment and all thereafter was what I was for.

Rattling in the stirrups like Marley's ghost, I was sewn together enough to bathe. The baby stayed with a nurse who looked far more trustworthy than I felt and I climbed into the enamel tub alone. My legs seemed not to belong to me and blood, a scarlet stream that refused dilution, snaked out of me and into the water like bright seaweed. I must have looked surprised.

Everybody bleeds, a nurse said, clattering through with a towel. There's always blood.

She wrapped me in a sandpapery NHS rag with holes big enough for fish to swim through and despite my wariness of strangers, I let her. I watched as she brushed my arms dry and warm again under the garish light and lifted my head. It was still there; a noise like a querulous cat, not far off. Getting louder.

That's him, the nurse said. There was a smile on her face, one eyebrow raised. You've forgotten already. That's your son making that noise. You'll find out what *no rest for the wicked* means now, all right. Best of luck.

He was settled on blankets in a perspex box beside what was to be my bed and made rootling, sucking noises all night with his mouth in a kiss shape. Eventually I wanted to do something, even if I wasn't sure what. Carefully, I worked my hands like hooks under each tiny eggcup of his armpits the way a child might tackle an unfamiliar doll, then held him at arms' length, peering at his face in the hope there might be instructions written on his forehead. There weren't. He had watery eyes, a wide, bird mouth. And he was quivering, shaking from head to foot with the force of the noise he felt driven to make. I was terrified. And in love. You were supposed to tell your family. That was what other people did. Birth announcements, that kind of thing. Somebody, surely, should know.

After six months, I sent my sister a photograph through the post. I had no idea whether she had moved or died, whether it was stupid or hopeful, but I thought it was worth a shot.

Somebody ought to know he existed. Somebody who attached to the word *family.* I had no grandmother or grandfather to offer, no cousins I'd have recognised, so she was my best bet. The baby did not look like me, I reassured myself, walking away from the post box. With luck he did not look like any of the babies she had cradled briefly then offered to the Marching Band. He would look like nothing to her. Nothing bad would happen. I told myself this stuff again, again. Things had a fighting chance of being fine.

Two weeks later, my sister turned up at my front door in a hand-knit cable cardi, still-thick hair permed in fat, grey curls. The jumper was green four-ply, its design intricate enough to cause optical distress and she wore a feather, a curled grey grouse sprig, on her breast. She caught my gaze and smiled.

Still knitting, she said. Never stopped. You've got to do something eh?

She'd put on weight and her skin was shiny. No powder. She was not wearing mascara. I calculated that neither were good things to say. Her love life had settled down, she said, and she was retired. I asked if she missed being a school secretary, the children and the bustle. She did not ask how I knew that. It didn't occur.

Nah, she said. No point missing what's finished, is there?

No, I said. There's not.

We went out to a café because it was the only thing I could think of to pass the time. The baby had been asleep all this while, tucked in a carry-seat under a floral blanket. I didn't want to wake him up or draw attention. Now, her salad barely touched, she pushed her knife and fork aside and took things into her own hands. She waved her fingers in front of his face till he opened his eyes and looked. He seemed perfectly calm. Battling her weight, she winched over to my side of the too-small table this place thought fit for two and lifted him up in one sweep. She knew to cradle his head, not leave his neck unsupported. She turned the ashtray away from his face.

How's that? she said. She wiggled him from side to side, holding his face up to hers. OK? He hung there like washing, looking back. Yoo hoo, she said. Who are you, eh? Her eyebrows, unpencilled, made her look vulnerable, unfinished. Is he quiet? she said, turning to me. She bounced him while I fished for what to say. I mean does he sleep good? Give you peace? No, I said. He hardly sleeps at all. He's lively.

Disny look it the now, she said. Do you? Eh? He grizzled and her eyes softened as she lowered him to lap level. Not if you belong to Dopey Dinah here? She grinned. Never thought I'd see you with a wean, she said. She shook her head in disbelief. Just shows you. You never know what's coming eh?

He looked up at her, and for one awful moment I thought she was going to weep. Then it seemed more likely and somehow worse that she might, dear God, sing. She did neither of these things. Just wrinkled her nose and made a clucking noise, hovering above him with a look of mock astonishment.

It's your Aunty Cora, she said. Look! Mummy's big sister. Your Aunty Cora!

My eyes filled up so I headed for the till to settle. She was due at the station at four in any case and I did not want to allow enough time for things to turn on a sixpence or to ask what I knew about her past, though I doubted she cared. When I came back to the table, my boy was back in his carry-cot again and her seat was empty. I thought for a moment she had just upped and gone, then I saw the napkin. AWAY FOR A FAG in blue biro. After a few minutes she was back, breezy, ready to go. I offered a lift and she hesitated only briefly. You've a car I suppose, she said. I think it was a joke.

At the station, she preferred to go in alone. I did not argue. Then, unexpectedly, she offered to pose for a photo. I'm the kind that keeps a camera in the glove compartment, and somehow, she knew. Cmon, she said. I'm in a hurry. I took a single snap of her holding her nephew and smiling her photograph smile. The catch of her brooch fell open as she handed him back to me, swinging on its hinge. She unhooked it and pressed it into my hand. Chuck it away for me, hen. I'm away. Tata.

We exchanged no gifts. We exchanged no embraces or old-times stories or photos, no details of pets or friends. All we had done was sit side by side for the first time in a decade, avoiding the bleeding obvious. Maybe this was how all sisters behaved. Maybe it didn't matter. She had not asked how I was or what I did for a living these days, had not asked about my financial health, my marital status or my son's paternity, and I had not asked about the same in return. What I knew of her life or she of mine remained as little as either of us could make it. What pleased me most was that she was managing. She was oblivious and impervious, still Cora, impervious as granite. She walked off, faltered at the open gates of Central Station, and turned to wave. I can still see her doing it. The briefest, most fleeting of gestures as if it didn't matter now. The meeting was over.

It was when she turned away again I felt it, a surge in the chest that threatened to drag me down some awful drowning well of rage and grief. We had not mentioned my mother. Our mother. We had said nothing of who or how she had been in our lives, nothing of our most important connection as though she didn't matter. Nothing about our children, the understandings we had been reaching, quite separately, of life. Nothing, in effect, that meant anything at all. This would be the last time I saw her. I knew it as I watched her fade into the crowd. The baby was watching too. He squirmed, eager to get on with what remained of our day.

That was your Aunty Cora, I said. See? Bye bye. Bye Aunty Cora.

He was too small to respond so I lifted his hand and flapped it for him. Knowing she wasn't watching, I waved too. We were done.

I dropped the brooch into a grit bin at Central Station and the two of us swung into Glasgow traffic, seat-belts buckled. His face showed in the rear-view mirror, eager. He knew where we were going. Home.

Acknowledgements

A roster of kindnesses.

Parts of this book were written during a residency in Villa Hellebosch under the Writers in Residence scheme of *Het beschrijf* and the Flemish Department of Culture; other parts at Jura Lodge under the Writers in Residence award endowed by Jura Malt Whisky. I am grateful for their support, generosity and will to endow money to the Arts.

Thank you also to the former Scottish Arts Council and the Scottish Book Trust for their steadfast encouragement in lean times; to Ilke Froyen, Alexandra Cool and Catriona Mack for looking after me far from home; to Jenny Diski and Barbara Gowdie for being a shot in the arm by writing.

More broadly, thank you to the Music teacher who taught as though it mattered (and to all teachers who do the same); to the political foresight that created the grants that gave me access to it; to the NHS, the fire service, the General Register for Scotland and small Italian cafés. God bless and shelter the BBC and the Salvation Army – thank God for the tambourines.

I am beholden to Bella Lacey, Pru Rowlandson, Henry Jeffreys,

Phillip Gwyn Jones and the fine people at Granta; to my loyal Man in London, Derek Johns; to AP Watt's Yasmin and Juliet; to Dr Grant Wilkie (the NHS again) and to the people who buy the books.

And home. And Jonathan. Of course.